The Reading of Imagery in
the Chinese Poetic Tradition

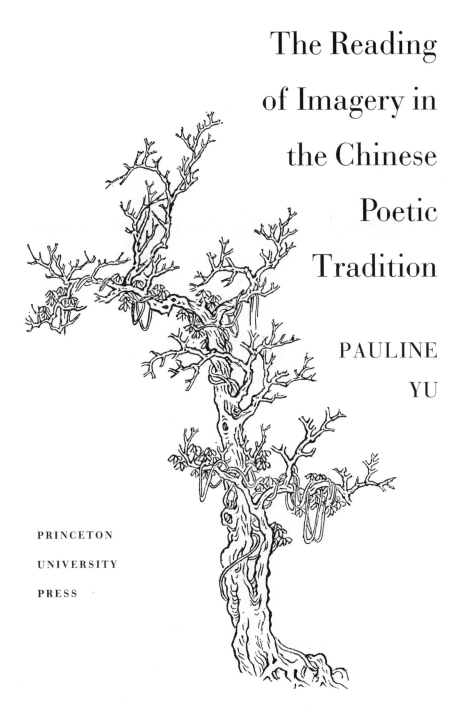

The Reading of Imagery in the Chinese Poetic Tradition

PAULINE YU

PRINCETON

UNIVERSITY

PRESS

Copyright © 1987 by Princeton University Press
Published by Princeton University Press, 41 William Street, Princeton, New Jersey 08540
In the United Kingdom: Princeton University Press, Guildford, Surrey

Library of Congress Cataloging in Publication Data will be found on the last printed page of
this book

ISBN-0-691-06682-5

Publication of this book has been aided by a grant from the Lacy Lockert Fund of Princeton
University Press

This book has been composed in Bauer Bodoni by Asco Trade Typesetting Ltd., Hong Kong

Clothbound editions of Princeton University Press books are printed on acid-free paper, and
binding materials are chosen for strength and durability

Printed in the United States of America by Princeton University Press
Princeton, New Jersey

OVERLEAF: Wang Wei's style of painting trees from *The Mustard Seed Garden Manual of
Painting* (Bollingen Series, Princeton University Press, 1977)

DESIGNED BY LAURY A EGAN

TO MY PARENTS

Contents

Preface

THIS STUDY has experienced a number of metamorphoses since its original inception. It began as an outgrowth of my work on the Tang dynasty poet Wang Wei, of whose rich and varied corpus the limpid depictions of natural scenes have been most appreciated by countless generations of readers. In this next book I first intended to place him within the tradition of nature poetry in China, with an interest in tracing its philosophical and religious, as well as literary, sources. I soon decided, however, that such a comprehensive study might be less fruitful and cogent than one with a more concentrated focus and consequently narrowed my topic down to a consideration of nature imagery alone. Again, it was not long before yet another reformulation occurred, as it became evident that a study of nature imagery, which comprises the bulk of the traditional poet's materials, necessarily implied an examination of Chinese poetic imagery in general.

Thus whereas from one point of view my topic has been narrowed significantly, from another its scope has become immeasurably broader. I have been concerned with the theory, practice, and interpretation of poetic imagery, and with placing literary developments within an historical perspective as well. In particular, I have tried to delineate the cultural presuppositions that I believe distinguish attitudes toward poetic imagery in classical China from those commonly taken for granted in the West. These dissimilarities argue against the all-too-frequent unqualified adoption of Western rhetorical terms to apply to a body of writing rooted in a very different set of assumptions—hence my starting point in a chapter that attempts to draw those lines more clearly. The continuing oscillation between conventional and empirical readings of Chinese poetic imagery, for example, both of which assume the existence of correspondences—whether within categories of images or between image and external content—finds no real counterpart in Western literature, with its presumptions of mimesis and fictionality. And because imagery constitutes the very core of Chinese poetic practice, I have found that my examination has led unavoidably to questions about the nature and function of the poetry as a whole.

Needless to say, I have not been able to do justice to all the issues I may have raised; my aim has been rather to trace the broad outlines of trends with the help of a few isolated examples. I have been especially interested in the commentary legacy of the two earliest poetic anthologies, the *Classic of Poetry* and the *Songs of Chu*, whose true influence has in my view been too often dismissed because of readings that seem too far-fetched to critics to allow them to take their underlying assumptions seriously. And while critical interpretations cannot be proven to have coincided with authorial intentions, the dogged persistence of certain principles governing the former should alert us to the likely existence of certain broadly cultural presuppositions that would shape the latter as well. The Chinese poetic tradition is by no means a monolithic one, of course, but it is my conviction that the assumptions I shall be discussing in the chapters to follow are the most powerful and pervasive ones within it. I have chosen to focus in particular on the rhetorical vocabulary deriving from the commentary literature on the *Classic of Poetry*, the terms *fu*, *bi*, and *xing* ("exposition," "comparison," and "stimulus"), that, as the Yuan dynasty critic Yang Zai 楊載 put it, can justifiably be called "the proper source of poetics and the standard of all rules." The many transformations that their definitions undergo over the centuries can, I believe, be shown to chart the course of significant developments in Chinese poetic theory in general.

My own interest in the problem of imagery has been stimulated by a veritable burgeoning of literature on the topic in both China and the West. The past ten years have seen the proliferation of articles, monographs, and special issues of journals devoted to the subjects of imagery, metaphor, and allegory in the West. In China the republication in 1978 of a letter of 21 July 1965 written by Mao Zedong to Chen Yi praising the use of imagery in classical poetry prompted a spate of articles on *fu*, *bi*, *xing* and "imagistic thinking" in general. Much of this work has been very helpful to me, as my footnotes will demonstrate, and among Western scholars of Chinese poetry I have also found the work of James J. Y. Liu, Yu-kung Kao, Tsu-lin Mei, and Stephen Owen, whose interests in broader issues in Chinese poetic theory are so congenial to my own, especially thought-provoking. In particular, Professor Owen's concerns in his recent book, *Traditional Chinese Poetry and Poetics: Omen of the World* (Madison: University of Wisconsin Press, 1985) overlap with mine to a remarkable degree, but the book unfortunately did not reach me in time for me to benefit from his discussions here.

Some of the groundwork for this book was laid in two previously published articles: "Metaphor and Chinese Poetry," *Chinese Literature: Essays, Articles, Reviews*, 3.2 (July 1981), 205–24, and "Allegory, Allegoresis, and the *Classic of Poetry*," *Harvard Journal of Asiatic Studies*, 43.2 (Dec. 1983), 377–412. I am grateful to the editors of the journals in which they appeared for permission to reprint some of my earlier discussions in considerably revised form. Earlier versions of translations of poems by Wang Wei appeared in my book, *The Poetry of Wang Wei: New Translations and Commentary* (Bloomington: Indiana University Press, 1980), and a portion of my discussion of the *Classic of Poetry* was also included in a paper I presented at the first Symposium on Comparative Literature in the People's Republic of China, sponsored by the Committee on Scholarly Communication with the PRC and the Chinese Academy of Social Sciences.

I would also like to acknowledge the financial support of a number of organizations over the past several years. A Summer Stipend from the National Endowment for the Humanities in 1981 and a Faculty Summer Research Grant from the University of Minnesota Graduate School in 1982 enabled me to complete my discussion of imagery in the *Classic of Poetry*. Grants from the University of Minnesota Graduate School also supplied me with the able research assistance of two students, April Lü and Zhang Wenying, and a travel stipend from the Bush Foundation Sabbatical Fund allowed me to make fruitful trips to East Asian libraries on the East and West coasts. Most important, the generous funding of a John Simon Guggenheim Memorial Foundation Fellowship permitted me the luxury of a sabbatical leave in 1983–1984 to complete the manuscript. For support from all of these quarters I am extremely thankful. I would also like to thank the scholars who reviewed this manuscript for Princeton University Press; their comments and criticisms were extremely helpful, although any remaining errors or oversights are, of course, my own responsibility. And, finally, I am grateful as always to my husband, Ted Huters, for his continued encouragement, wisdom, and critical insight, and to our children, Emily, Matthew, and Alex, for timing their arrivals so considerately to coincide with the completion of various stages of the study, and for providing me with constant sources of joy ever since.

The Reading of Imagery in
the Chinese Poetic Tradition

CHAPTER ONE

Setting the Terms

I.

IMAGERY has been a central concern of Chinese poetics from its very beginnings, but interest in the topic in Western literary theory is a relatively recent phenomenon. C. Day Lewis may claim that "the image is the constant in all poetry, and every poem is itself an image,"[1] yet his study makes equally clear that this is at the same time a modern point of view. Controversies over the very meaning of the term are similarly of recent provenance. One standard reference work, after defining "imagery" as "images produced in the mind by language, whose words and statements may refer either to experiences which could produce physical perceptions were the reader actually to have those experiences, or to the sense-impressions themselves," goes on to describe the confusion that has arisen from the application of imagery to literary study, "for it is used variously to refer to the meaning of a statement involving images, to the images themselves, or to the combination of meaning and images."[2]

Up through the Renaissance, however, the meaning of the term, if part of one's critical vocabulary at all, was not generally subject to dispute. "Image," *eikon,* or *imago* "originally meant no more than picture, imitation, or copy," a device useful for the purposes of *enargia,* "the process of making the reader seem to see something."[3] There are two important concepts here. The first is the fluidity with which definitions of imagery can shift their focus from perception to imagination—from an image as something external to or independent of any viewer, a picture, to something

[1] C. Day Lewis, *The Poetic Image* (New York: Oxford University Press, 1947), p. 17.

[2] Norman Friedman, "Imagery," *Princeton Encyclopedia of Poetry and Poetics,* ed. Alex Preminger et al.; enl. ed. (Princeton: Princeton University Press, 1974), p. 363. For a discussion of conflicting usages of the term "imagery" across disciplines, see W. J. T. Mitchell, "What Is an Image?" *New Literary History,* 15.3 (Spring 1984), pp. 503–37.

[3] Ray Frazer, "The Origin of the Term 'Image,'" *ELH,* 27 (1960), p. 149. I have found Frazer's brief account of the history of the term quite helpful and shall be relying on it heavily in my own discussion.

visualized or imagined by a reader. The second key word here is imitation, for it recalls the literary theory dominant in the West through the eighteenth century—mimesis, usually translated as "imitation" or "representation." Because it is crucial to an understanding of conceptions of imagery, a brief albeit necessarily oversimplified discussion of the notion seems warranted.

As is well known, the theory of mimesis traces its roots to Plato's *Republic*, which lays the groundwork for Western discussions of the lyric in Book III when Socrates differentiates between the two ways in which "any story or poem deals with things past, present or future": "it employs either simple narrative [diegesis] or representation [mimesis]."[4] This leads to the observation "that poetry and fiction fall into three classes. First, that which employs representation only, tragedy and comedy.... Secondly, that in which the poet speaks in his own person; the best example is lyric poetry. Thirdly, that which employs both methods, epic and various other kinds of poetry."[5] Although Plato distinguishes between diegesis and mimesis in this passage, in the tenth book, where he is concerned more directly with questions of art, he suggests that the latter is in fact the function of all poetry—whether dramatic or narrative,[6] and in fact of all artistic creation. It is here, of course, that he condemns art for necessarily being twice removed from true reality.[7]

Mimesis remains the primary notion of artistic production for Aristotle in his *Poetics*; epic, tragedy, comedy, and poetry differ only in the means,

[4] Plato, *The Republic*, trans. H. D. P. Lee (Baltimore: Penguin, 1955), p. 131.

[5] *Ibid.*, p. 133.

[6] Indeed, Gérard Genette has argued that Plato's distinction between mimesis and diegesis, drama and narrative, is erroneous because dramatic dialogue is not truly mimetic after all. It is a "repetition" (if literally true) or "constitution" (if fictional) of speech and not a true "representation," for it "tells itself": "If we call poetic imitation the fact of representing by verbal means a non-verbal reality and, in exceptional circumstances, a verbal reality (as one calls pictorial imitation the fact of representing in pictorial means non-pictorial reality and, in exceptional circumstances, a pictorial reality), it must be admitted that imitation is to be found in the five narrative lines [quoted earlier from *The Iliad*] and not at all in the five dramatic lines, which consist simply in the interpolation, in the middle of a text representing events, of another text directly taken from those events: as if a seventeenth-century Dutch painter, anticipating certain modern methods, had placed in the middle of a still life, not the painting of an oyster shell, but a real oyster shell.... Literary representation, the *mimesis* of the ancients, is not, therefore, narrative plus "speeches": it is narrative, and only narrative. Plato opposed *mimesis* to *diegesis* as a perfect imitation to an imperfect imitation; but (as Plato himself showed in the *Cratylus*), perfect imitation is no longer an imitation, it is the thing itself, and, in the end, the only imitation is an imperfect one. *Mimesis* is *diegesis*." From "Frontiers of Narrative," in *Figures of Literary Discourse*, trans. Alan Sheridan (New York: Columbia University Press, 1982), pp. 131–33.

[7] "So the tragic poet, whose art is representation, is third in succession to the throne of truth; and the same is true of all other artists." *The Republic*, p. 334.

object, or manner of imitation or representation. As for manner, for example, "one may either: (1) speak at one moment in narrative and at another in an assumed character, as Homer does; or (2) one may remain the same throughout, without any such change; or (3) the imitators may represent the whole story dramatically as though they were actually doing the things described."[8] But whereas Plato had banned dramatic poetry from his Republic because it was most strongly and deceitfully mimetic, for Aristotle this only redounds to drama's favor. Aristotle accepts imitation as a fundamental human instinct and turns his teacher's disesteem for mimesis on its head. Plato had criticized poetry for lying at one remove from concrete reality, already but a pale imitation of the timeless Forms, but Aristotle redefines and re-evaluates the nature of this distance. Poetry is indeed removed from sensible reality, but that is not in fact its true object of imitation anyway. It does not present what is or has happened, in a literal attempt to copy reality, but rather what might happen, what is possible by virtue of the laws of probability or necessity, and universal human modes of thought, feeling, and action. "Hence poetry is something more philosophic and of graver import than history, since its statements are of the nature rather of universals, whereas those of history are singulars."[9] Moreover, the poet represents these universals through human action, and it is in the devising and constructing of plot (*mythos*) that the poet proves to be a "maker."

Despite the differing evaluations of Plato and Aristotle, mimesis lies undeniably at the core of Greek poetics and of its legacy. Earl Miner has noted that the concept owed its importance to the position of drama within Greek culture at the time;[10] philosophical presuppositions must also have motivated the development and persistence of the notion. Mimesis is, after all, predicated on a fundamental ontological dualism—the assumption that there is a truer reality transcendent to the concrete, historical realm in which we live, and that the relationship between the two is replicated in the creative act and artifact.

These same assumptions were confirmed by Christian doctrine as well. It has been argued that the Christian world-view is less disjunctive than the Platonic, as in the following passage:

> In the Platonic conception the spiritual truths are shadowed by the unreal visible world. But to Christianity the unbridgeable gap between

---

[8] Aristotle, *Poetics*, trans. Ingram Bywater (New York: Modern Library, 1954), 1448a/p.226.

[9] *Ibid.*, 1451b/p.235.

[10] Earl Miner, "On the Genesis and Development of Literary Systems," Part I, *Critical Inquiry*, 5.2 (Winter 1978), p. 350.

Creator and creation has been bridged by the Word made flesh. Creation itself becomes part of God's truth, because God has become part of concrete experience. The visible world does more than represent truth, it partakes of truth....[11]

Yet the assumption of some dichotomy remains fundamental, and whether "bridged" or not, the "gaps" are there—between flesh and spirit, or between this world and the next. Similarly, the Aristotelian notion of the poet as maker or fabricator engaging in poeisis could find a congenial divine model in the Biblical account of creation. Sir Philip Sidney synthesizes these views when he writes, echoing Julius Caesar Scaliger, that "the poet ..., lifted up with the vigour of his own invention, doth grow in effect another nature, in making things either better than Nature bringeth forth, or quite anew, forms such as never were in Nature," a privilege granted to and exemplified for the poet by "the heavenly Maker of that maker, who, having made man to His own likeness, set him beyond and over all the works of that second nature: which in nothing he showeth so much as in Poetry, when with the force of a divine breath he bringeth things forth far surpassing her doings."[12]

An understanding of the notion of mimesis and in particular of its links with poiesis can help to elucidate the general lack of interest in the image prior to the seventeenth century. This disregard is paradoxical only if one misconstrues mimesis as aiming for the proto-photographic representation of sensible reality. For the Renaissance poet, on the contrary, imitation involved not a literal replication but rather the artful embellishment and ordering of nature, whether based on Platonic ideal Forms or Aristotelian universals. As demonstrated by Rosamond Tuve, Elizabethan and Metaphysical poetry is rich in sensuous language, but not for the purposes of offering a natural or truthful report of experience or creating a unity of impression and mood, and not to be judged by standards of vividness or accuracy. Instead, these figures were but one of several rhetorical and logical tools that enabled the poet to convey his argument in a pleasing, decorous, and therefore effective way, and thereby to display his technical virtuosity as a maker or fashioner. The figures were more likely devised than perceived, and in any case the interest was in the interpretation, and not the act, of perception: the poet's "subject was still 'his meaning,' not 'himself seeing it.'"[13]

[11] Holly Wallace Boucher, "Metonymy in Typology and Allegory, with a Consideration of Dante's *Comedy*," in Morton W. Bloomfield, ed., *Allegory, Myth, Symbol*, Harvard English Studies 9 (Cambridge, Ma.: Harvard University Press, 1981), p. 135.

[12] *An Apology for Poetry* (published 1595), included in Walter Jackson Bate, ed., *Criticism: The Major Texts*, enl. ed. (New York: Harcourt Brace Jovanovich, 1970), pp. 85, 86.

[13] Rosamond Tuve, *Elizabethan and Metaphysical Imagery: Renaissance Poetic and Twentieth-Century Critics* (Chicago: University of Chicago Press, 1947), p. 43.

Figures, however, and metaphor in particular, came under heavy attack during the seventeenth century by advocates of the "plain style," who preferred "perspicuity" and "naturalness" to the self-conscious artifice of rhetoric.[14] "The proscription of rhetoric proscribed the chief critical vocabulary of the past. Image was one of the terms to fill the vacuum."[15] Thomas Hobbes played a key role in this transformation, not only in attacking highly figurative language but in preparing the critical ground for the new conception of the term. By arguing for the sense origin of all knowledge, in the first two chapters of his *Leviathan,* he transformed the image into a fundamental link between experience and knowledge. In so doing, he also shifted the emphasis in the conception of the term itself, from that of a "picture" with an objective and independent status to that of a perception that could not be considered apart from a sentient mind. "Sensations, he said, were registered in the mind in 'images'; an object perceived caused an impression or print which could convey the idea of the subject to the mind. Hobbes also formulated the theory of the 'fancy,' or imagination, as a vast storehouse of all past sense impressions or images."[16] Although, unlike later literary critics, Hobbes felt that it was the power of judgment, and not the imagination, that enabled one to perceive similarities between things, the epistemological importance he attributed to the image helped to foster the development of a new subgenre of descriptive nature poetry, in which elements of the landscape were presented not merely as illustrations for intellectual or spiritual arguments but as important for their own sake and for the sake of the poet's response to them.

Moreover, it was not long before the word "image" came to be used to mean figurative language, and especially metaphor—the very devices that had been so roundly disparaged by seventeenth-century critics and philosophers. The word's present-day doubleness of meaning—as both sensuous content and figurative language—can thus be traced to this point. Ray Frazer argues that imagery was first employed in this way by John Dryden in 1674 to describe Abraham Cowley's metaphorical practice, and he offers the following passage from a 1711 treatise as evidence of the extent to which description and metaphor were identified and viewed as an essential element of poetry:

---

[14]The classic discussion on this subject has been provided by Morris Croll in two essays reprinted in Stanley E. Fish, ed., *Seventeenth Century Prose: Modern Essays in Criticism* (New York: Oxford University Press, 1971): "Attic Prose: Lipsius, Montaigne, Bacon," pp. 3–25, and "The Baroque Style in Prose," pp. 26–52. Ray Frazer gives some good examples of the hostility toward figures evident in a variety of writers in "Origin," pp. 150ff.

[15]Frazer, p. 150.

[16]*Ibid.,* p. 154.

Poetry consists more in Description, than is generally imagined. For, besides those longer and set Descriptions of Things, Places and Persons, there are numberless others, unobserved by common Readers, contained in one Verse, sometimes in one Word, to which the whole Beauty of Thought is owing; and which wonderfully affect us, for no other Reason but because they are Descriptions, that is, impress a lively Image of somewhat upon the Mind. To this it is that metaphorical Expressions, when selected with Judgement, owe their Beauty and their Elegance; every Metaphor being a short Description.[17]

In addition to the epistemological theories of Hobbes and Locke and the associationist psychology which grew out of them, two literary events in the seventeenth century also contributed to the elevation of the image as newly defined. One was the publication by Cowley in 1656 of his *Pindarique Odes*, and the other the translation of Longinus' *On the Sublime*, published in 1652 although not widely influential until some twenty years later.[18] Both volumes proved to be contemporary literary sensations and were important together in popularizing a new "sublime" mode in English poetry:

a form attempting to give embodiment to a "lofty" and "inspired" soul in a state of transport; a form, therefore, admitting only the most elevated of subjects, the divine and the heroic; a form comparatively short in length, irregular in its verse form, abrupt and sudden in its transitions, and, in figurative language, *"Bold, even to Temeritie,* and such as I [Cowley] durst not have to do withal in any other kind of *Poetry....*"[19]

Cowley's works were regarded as the prime embodiment of Longinian sublimity and were in fact linked by Dryden when he first used the term imagery to mean figurative language and argued for the necessity in particular of bold imagery in poetry, in the essay cited above.[20] Not only did this new notion of the sublime significantly shake up the traditional

---

[17]Joseph Trapp, *Lectures on Poetry*, trans. E. Bowyer (London, 1742), p. 103. Dryden's use of image to mean metaphoric language appears in his "Apology for Heroic Poetry and Poetic License," *Works*, ed. Sir Walter Scott and rev. George Saintsbury (Edinburgh, 1882–1892), V, 1,119. For both references see Frazer, p. 158.

[18]Norman Maclean, "From Action to Image: Theories of the Lyric in the Eighteenth Century," in R. S. Crane et al., *Critics and Criticism Ancient and Modern* (Chicago: University of Chicago Press, 1952), pp. 412ff.

[19]*Ibid.*, p. 420. The citation is from Cowley's *Poems*, ed. A. R. Walker (Cambridge, 1905), p. 11.

[20]I.e., "The Author's Apology for Heroic Poetry and Poetic License." Maclean dates this essay to 1677, Frazer to 1674.

hierarchy of poetic forms, arranged purely according to subject matter, it also played an important role in the shift of critical attention to the poet as individual creator and helped to redefine that poet—from a maker of plots to a maker of images.

Nineteenth-century Romantic poets and critics were of course to reverse the conception of the imagination from Hobbes' passive receptor and storehouse of images to the primary active source of them. The increasing disfavor with which the mimetic theory of literature was regarded and consequent focus, first on perception and then on creation, also shifted critical attention from the intellectual or didactic argument of the poem to its description, and finally to the personal emotions expressed.[21] The role of imagery changed as well.

In its original meaning of picture or copy, well into the seventeenth century, imagery had been a rather insignificant element of poetry. The mimetic poet was not, after all, a copyist of nature but rather an artificer, someone who contrived striking figures to ornament, illuminate, and advance an intellectual or spiritual argument. Then the Hobbesian link of imagery to knowledge made new poetic room for description for its own sake. Most important, however, was Dryden's identification of imagery with figurative language in general and stress on its importance in poetry, which led, over the next two centuries, to theories claiming that imagery and imagistic language were in fact the very differentiae of poetry itself. We can see this attitude adumbrated in Anna Barbauld's Preface to *The Poetical Works of Mr. William Collins* (London, 1797), which distinguishes between two "classes" of poetry. The first includes such species as epic, dramatic, descriptive, and didactic poetry—"all in which the charms of verse are made use of, to illustrate subjects which in their own nature are affecting or interesting." As for the second, it

> consists of what may be called pure Poetry, or Poetry in the abstract. It is conversant with an imaginary world, peopled with beings of its own creation. It deals in splendid imagery, bold fiction, and allegorical personages. It is necessarily obscure to a certain degree; because, having to do chiefly with ideas generated within the mind, it cannot be at all comprehended by any whose intellect has not been exercised in similar contemplations; while the conceptions of the Poet (often highly metaphysical) are rendered still more remote from common apprehension by the figurative phrase in which they are clothed. All that is properly *Lyric Poetry* is of this kind.[22]

[21] The standard history of this transformation is M. H. Abrams' *The Mirror and the Lamp: Romantic Theory and the Tradition* (New York: Oxford University Press, 1953).

[22] Cited in Maclean, p. 440.

Although this passage anticipates many typically romantic and modern views of poetry, it retains the traditional conception of figurative imagery as the "garb"—though in this case more disguise than ornament—of a poem's ideas. This attitude never entirely disappeared, so that A. E. Housman, for example, could still write, more than a hundred years later, that metaphor and simile were mere "accessories" to poetry, employed by the poet "to be helpful, to make his sense clearer or his conception more vivid," or "for ornament," because of the image's "independent power to please."[23] Most twentieth-century notions of the image, however, were either to fuse the two—object and idea—or attempt virtually to eliminate the latter altogether. Thus T. E. Hulme tries to distinguish between the language of prose, in which concrete things are employed only as abstract, unvisualized "counters," and that of poetry, which

> is not a counter language but a visual concrete one. It is a compromise for a language of intuition which would hand over sensations bodily. It always endeavours to arrest you, and to make you continuously see a physical thing, to prevent you gliding through an abstract process. It choose fresh epithets and fresh metaphors, not so much because they are new, and we are tired of the old, but because the old cease to convey a physical thing and become abstract counters.... Images in verse are not mere decoration, but the very essence of an intuitive language.[24]

Hulme's rejection of intellectual abstraction represents an extreme position, but it also testifies to the distance traveled by the image—from being an artful embellishment to logical argument to its virtual supplanter. But since his images do include metaphors, they are not just things presented in themselves, as it were, and devoid of meaning—that meaning is simply defined as "intuitive" rather than rational. In any event, Dryden's identification of imagery with metaphor is now clearly taken for granted, and it is to an examination of the assumptions underlying the latter that we now turn.

II.

If the definition of imagery has been shown to shift in often perplexing ways, the confusion becomes even more exacerbated when one turns to

[23] A. E. Housman, *The Name and Nature of Poetry* (Cambridge: Cambridge University Press, 1933), p. 14. Cited in Cleanth Brooks, "Metaphor and the Tradition," in *Modern Poetry and the Tradition* (Chapel Hill: University of North Carolina Press, 1967), p. 4.

[24] T. E. Hulme, "Romanticism and Classicism," in *Speculations* (New York: Harcourt, Brace and Co., 1924), pp. 134–35.

metaphor. Part of the problem derives from the fact that the two terms are, as we have seen, frequently identified. Indeed, C. Day Lewis, immediately after proclaiming that "the image is the constant in all poetry, and every poem is itself an image," goes on to write that "Trends come and go, diction alters, metrical fashions change, even the elemental subject-matter may change almost out of recognition: but *metaphor* remains, the life-principle of poetry, the poet's chief test and glory."[25] Following Dryden, he glides into this substitution without so much as a comment.

I shall not be attempting to specify precisely the meaning of either of these terms or, for that matter, of allegory in the following section, for my interests lie rather in sketching out the range and implication of their usage. It seems to me that certain generally held assumptions do prevail, and I shall be taking them for granted. Imagery thus remains for me the most inclusive term of the three, encompassing both the verbal depiction of sensuously apprehensible objects and figurative language which usually involves some process of comparison and/or substitution. The former subcategory includes not only objects which function primarily as description but also those which are important for their evocative powers, emotional or intellectual associations as well.

Christine Brooke-Rose insists that this kind of suggestive imagery should be distinguished quite clearly from metaphor proper:

> To my mind, the kind of literal but symbolic noun found in Yeats and Eliot is not metaphor at all, since no other definite though unstated object is being changed into something else: the poet simply mentions something and various connotations arise in our minds, as they might if we ourselves saw the same thing in fact; or he makes them arise in our minds by mentioning it in a context of other objects. Hence the importance of juxtaposition in modern poetry. But the thing mentioned is literary, it belongs to the scene of the poem. It is not a "replacement" of an unmentioned but guessable term as is the true Simple Replacement of Metaphor.[26]

Brooke-Rose also takes issue with modern poets' treatment of these images, particularly the methods of such Imagists as Ezra Pound: "The mere putting down of one literal statement after another, even without rhetorical repetition, constitutes 'imagery'; mere juxtaposition is enough to imply a connexion, however remote, between one 'image' and another." Terming this parataxis a 'dangerously lazy method" when compared with the

---

[25] *The Poetic Image*, p. 17. Emphasis added.

[26] Christine Brooke-Rose, *A Grammar of Metaphor* (London: Secker and Warburg, 1958), p. 35.

11

grammatical transformations of metaphor as she defines it, Brooke-Rose refuses to regard, with Pound, juxtaposition, metaphor, and simile as of one piece: *"In terms of cognition or visualisation it may not matter*: in terms of syntax, it does" (pp. 91–93). Some critics have rejected such purely grammatical distinctions; Philip Wheelwright, for example, regards this kind of often vaguely suggestive imagery as in fact one of the most important types of metaphor and argues that the "test of essential metaphor is not any rule of grammar, but rather the quality of semantic transformation that is brought about."[27] Yet the majority of theoretical formulations, while perhaps not so narrowly defined as Brooke-Rose's, have supported her basic contention that there is a difference between an evocative image, which is, however, not necessarily "symbolic"—fixed, universal, recurrent, or abstract—and the often more grammatically distinctive metaphor proper. This will be especially important when we examine the Chinese poetic tradition.

What then is metaphor? "There is a code," Jacques Derrida observes, "a program, a rhetoric, if you will, in any discourse about metaphor: *in the first place*, by custom, Aristotle's definition is to be recalled, that at least of the *Poetics.*"[28] At first glance Aristotle defines the issue in an apparently straightforward manner: "Metaphor consists in giving the thing a name that belongs to something else; the transference being either from genus to species or from species to genus, or from species to species, or on grounds of analogy."[29] Of these various possibilities, he writes in the *Rhetoric*, analogy is the most sophisticated, because it involves two relations between four things: if A:B::C:D, then D can be substituted for B, and vice versa (1410b, p. 187). From this point of view, metaphor can be defined as quintessentially "poetic" language, for it offers a means of avoiding prosaic expression through a deviation from ordinary discourse (*Poetics*, 1458b, p. 253).

Yet in these same two works Aristotle also suggests that metaphor involves more than a mere transference or substitution of name, an assumption already implicit in his preference for the complexity of proportional analogy. Metaphor is not just a linguistic phenomenon, it is a mode of cognition; by naming the nameless it imparts "fresh" knowledge and thus enables us to learn (*Rhetoric*, 1410b, p. 186). The metaphor-maker looks and thinks in a fundamentally new way, and the significance of this achievement is evident in Aristotle's summary remarks on the subject in

[27] Philip Wheelwright, *Metaphor and Reality* (Bloomington: Indiana University Press, 1962), p. 71.

[28] Jacques Derrida, "White Mythology: Metaphor in the Text of Philosophy," trans. F. C. T. Moore, *New Literary History*, 6.1 (Autumn 1974), p. 30.

[29] Aristotle, *Poetics*, 1457b/p.251.

the *Poetics*: "The greatest thing by far is to be a master of metaphor. It is the one thing that cannot be learnt from others; and it is also a sign of genius, since a good metaphor implies an intuitive perception of the similarity in dissimilars" (1459a, p. 255), and the ability, therefore, to relate the apparently unrelated, to think of one thing, unnamed, *as* something else.

Aristotle's two emphases on transference and cognition laid the groundwork for what have become the two primary modes of talking about metaphor, what Jonathan Culler has christened (and, quite appropriately, with a metaphor), the *via philosophica* and the *via rhetorica*:

> The former locates metaphor in the gap between sense and reference in the process of thinking of an object *as* something. The latter situates metaphor in the space between one meaning and another, between the literal or "proper" verbal expression and its periphrastic substitute. And so whereas the former makes metaphor a necessary and pervasive feature of all language, which with its verbal detours gestures obliquely towards a world of objects, the latter makes it a special use of language which can be isolated and studied against the background of a non-metaphoric use of language.[30]

In general, it is the *via philosophica* which has yielded some of the more fruitful insights into the metaphorical process and its impulses. Rhetorical analyses such as those of Brooke-Rose are useful only to a certain extent; the classificatory schemes are usually based on too restrictive a concept— metaphor as pure substitution, for example—and too mechanically applied to be comprehensive or illuminating. Looking at metaphor as a mode of thought and means to knowledge, to be considered within a larger set of cultural and philosophical presuppositions, can go beyond this preoccupation with what are often superficial linguistic phenomena, although it may incorporate an assumption of a distinction between metaphorical and non-metaphoric language as well. This is evident in, for instance, Ricoeur's statement that metaphor "teaches something, and so it contributes to the opening up and the discovery of a field of reality other than that which ordinary language lays bare."[31]

The instructive powers of metaphor were of course stressed by Aristotle, although the Greek philosopher did not go so far as to claim explicitly for metaphor the opening up of a new "field of reality." Rather, one learned simply from the metaphorical act of drawing connections between pre-

[30] Jonathan Culler, "Commentary," *New Literary History*, 6.1 (Autumn 1974), p. 219.

[31] Paul Ricoeur, *The Rule of Metaphor: Multi-disciplinary Studies of the Creation of Meaning in Language*, trans. Robert Czerny et al. (Toronto: University of Toronto Press, 1977), p. 148.

viously unrelated things or situations, an assumption that could be granted regardless of the relative importance attributed to metaphor within the literary work as a whole. Samuel Johnson describes it, for example, as an aspect of wit, an activity of mind, to be "rigorously and philosophically considered as a kind of *discordia concors*; a combination of dissimilar images, or discovery of occult resemblances in things apparently unalike." While he believed, of course, that the Metaphysical poets carried this to an extreme ("the most hetrogeneous ideas are yoked by violence together; nature and art are ransacked for illustrations, comparisons, and allusions"), he did grant nevertheless that "their learning instructs, and their subtlety surprises."[32] And although writing from a romantic position that questioned the primacy of wit and intellect in poetry, Shelley could similarly remark on the educative value of metaphor, which "marks the before unapprehended relations of things and perpetuates their apprehension."[33]

Changes in critical attitudes toward metaphor, not surprisingly, have gone hand in hand with changes in critical conceptions of poetry. As classical mimetic theories yielded to romantic emphases on the individuality and inward state of the poet, metaphor moved from its status as illustrative ornament to the very soul of the poem. Yet a fundamental Aristotelian assumption behind mimesis was never abandoned—the notion of the poet as maker and of the poem as something made, existing in relation to reality (however defined) yet ontologically distinct from it. The poet is a maker precisely because he imitates: "*mimesis* is *poiesis*, and *poiesis* is *mimesis*."[34] Whether one condemns the fabrication for its distance from ultimate truth (Plato's legacy) or praises it for its access to universals beneath the surface of daily events (Aristotle's), the view of poetry as a representation removed from the level of concrete reality has prevailed.

This presumption of fictiveness can be found in any number of contemporary critical statements on poetry. Thus Cleanth Brooks, for example, claims that "The poem, if it be a true poem is a simulacrum of reality—in this sense, at least, it is an 'imitation'—by *being* an experience rather than any mere statement about experience or any mere abstraction from experience."[35] From a different perspective Susanne Langer writes that "The poet uses discourse to create an illusion, a pure appearance, which is a non-discursive symbolic form.... The poet's business is to create the

[32] Samuel Johnson, *Life of Cowley* (pub. 1779–1781), excerpted in Bate, p. 218.

[33] Percy Bysshe Shelley, *A Defence of Poetry* (pub. 1821), included in Bate, p. 430.

[34] Ricoeur, *The Rule of Metaphor*, p. 39.

[35] Cleanth Brooks, "The Heresy of Paraphrase," in *The Well Wrought Urn* (New York: Harcourt, Brace, and World, 1947), p. 213.

14

appearance of 'experiences,' the semblance of events lived and felt, and to organize them so they constitute a purely and completely experienced reality, a piece of *virtual life*."[36] The notion that poetry is a mimetic art has been developed most explicitly and persuasively by Barbara Hernnstein Smith, who argues that "we may conceive of a poem as the imitation or representation of an utterance. This is not to say that a poem is a false or merely 'emotive' form of speech. It is an imitation in the same sense that a play is the imitation or representation of an action."[37] Whereas she notes that by "poetry" here she is speaking of both verse and prose, in a later essay, "Poetry as Fiction," she develops the argument with specific reference to poetry alone.[38] And Samuel Levin, writing from the point of view of linguistics, proposes that poems begin implicitly with the following sentence: "I imagine (myself in) and invite you to conceive a world in which.... The assumption is that the deep structure of every poem contains [this] as its topmost sentence, and that that sentence is deleted in going from the deep to the surface structure of the poem."[39]

In apparent dissent from this view, Käte Hamburger tries to distinguish lyric poetry as a "reality-utterance" (*Wirklichkeitsaussage*) from the mimesis of reality in fiction: "Precisely this differentiates the lyrical experience from that of a novel or drama, that we do *not* experience the utterances of a lyrical poem as appearance, fiction, illusion.... For we always confront it without mediation, just as we confront the utterance of a true 'other,' a Thou speaking to Me."[40] Yet even she takes care to point out that she is talking about the way in which one apprehends a poem; while rejecting the popular distinction between a "lyrical" and an

[36] Susanne K. Langer, *Feeling and Form* (New York: Charles Scribner's Sons, 1953), pp. 211–12.

[37] Barbara Hernnstein Smith, *Poetic Closure: A Study of How Poems End* (Chicago: University of Chicago Press, 1968), p. 15.

[38] Smith, *On the Margins of Discourse: The Relation of Literature to Language* (Chicago: University of Chicago Press, 1978), pp. 14–40.

[39] Samuel R. Levin, *The Semantics of Metaphor* (Baltimore: Johns Hopkins University Press, 1977), p. 116.

[40] Käte Hamburger, *Die Logik der Dichtung*, 2d rev. ed. (Stuttgart: Ernst Klett Verlag, 1968), p. 216. Unless otherwise noted, all translations are my own.

Elsewhere Hamburger presents more directly her rejection of the idea of lyric as mimesis: "Fiction is a mimesis of reality because it is not an utterance, but rather representation, 'imitation,' whose material is language just as marble or color are those of the plastic arts. Fiction is mimesis because the reality of human life is its subject matter. The alteration that it performs on this subject matter—even if it be of surrealistic absoluteness—is thus of a categorically different sort than the transformation that the subject of the lyrical utterance effects on the object of his utterance. He transforms objective reality into subjective experiential reality, which is why it therefore remains reality." (p. 227)

"empirical" self,[41] she also notes that the "logical identity" between the subject of the poetic utterance and the actual poet does not mean "that every utterance of a poem, or even the whole poem, must coincide with a real experience of the poetizing subject," nor, furthermore, does the lyrical utterance wish to have a *"function in any connection with objects or reality."*[42]

The relations traced by metaphor have played a key role, especially since the nineteenth century, in this Western conception of poetry. The following passage from Wordsworth's *Prelude* sums up in a nutshell some of these persistent assumptions behind the metaphorical activity and bears close attention:

> ... The song would speak
> Of that interminable building reared
> By observation of affinities
> In objects where no brotherhood exists
> To passive minds.[43]

The last three lines here offer yet another reformulation of Aristotle's observation that metaphor involves the "perception of the similarity in dissimilars," an intuitive talent granted to but a select few and thus "a sign of genius." That metaphor asserts "affinities" between two previously unrelated things provokes disagreement only when critics try to specify the details of the process. One particularly influential definition has been provided by I. A. Richards: "when we use a metaphor we have two thoughts of different things active together and supported by a single word, or phrase, whose meaning is a resultant of their interaction."[44] Furthermore, what is important about these "affinities" is that they result from an active linking of objects taken from different contexts, if not

[41] As Hamburger explains it, there is no formal basis for making this distinction: "We do not have the possibility and thereby the right to claim that the poet meant the utterance of the poem—no matter whether or not it follows the first-person form—to be about his own experience, nor to claim that he did not mean 'himself.' We can no more decide this than with any other non-poetic utterance. The form of the poem is that of an utterance, and this means that we experience it as the field of experience of the subject of the utterance—which is precisely what enables us to experience it as reality-utterance." (p. 219)

[42] *Ibid.*, pp. 220, 213. Emphasis in original.

[43] From Book II: "School-Time," lines 382–86, 1850 version, in Wordsworth's *The Prelude: A Parallel Text*, ed. J. C. Maxwell (Middlesex, Eng.: Penguin, 1971), p. 94. Also cited in Lewis, p. 36, and Ricoeur, p. 341n46.

[44] This well-known formulation is given in Richards' *Philosophy of Rhetoric* (New York: Oxford University Press, 1936), p. 93. It became so widely accepted that it appears in numerous subsequent discussions as one of the most important ways of analyzing metaphor, referred to simply as the "interaction" theory.

altogether different "worlds"—the "familial" relationships are "engendered" thanks to the poet. W. M. Urban, for example, defines metaphor as "a word transference from one universe of discourse to another."[45] Other critics stress the "disparity" between the "different spheres of thought" linked by metaphor,[46] or distinguish metaphor, which joins a "plurality of worlds," from metonymy, which involves "movement within a single world of discourse."[47] As a result, then, the conjunction may be so new as to be jarring, and "we find poetic truth struck out by the collision rather than the collusion of images."[48]

The most fundamental disjunction posited and bridged by Western metaphor is more than verbal—it is that existing between two ontologically distinct realms, one concrete and the other abstract, one sensible and the other inaccessible to the senses. Once again, then, we return to the importance of the dualism at the heart of Western philosophy. Indeed, Heidegger argues that the dependence goes both ways:

> The notion of transposition and of metaphor (*Metapher* [*Übertragung*]) rests on the distinction, not to say the separation, between the sensible and the non-sensible, the physical and the non-physical, is a basic feature of what is called "metaphysics," and confers on Western thought its essential characteristics. Once the distinction between the sensible and the non-sensible is recognized to be inadequate, metaphysics loses its authoritative role as a mode of thought. Once this limitation of metaphysics has been seen, the determining conception (*massgebende Vorstellung*) "metaphor" collapses of itself.... The metaphorical exists only within the boundaries of metaphysics.[49]

The primacy of metaphysics has, of course, remained unquestioned until recent times, and metaphor has depended on the assumption of a fundamental otherness of reference: "Metaphor exists only to the extent that someone is supposed to be manifesting by an utterance such-and-such a thought which remains in itself unobvious, hidden, or latent."[50] There is an ideal world beyond the physical one for which equivalences are to be

[45] W. M. Urban, *Language and Reality* (London: Allen and Unwin, 1939), p. 433. Cited by Monroe Beardsley in *Aesthetics: Problems in the Philosophy of Criticism* (New York: Harcourt, Brace and World, 1958), p. 161.

[46] David Lodge, *The Modes of Modern Writing: Metaphor, Metonymy, and the Typology of Modern Literature* (Ithaca: Cornell University Press, 1977), p. 75.

[47] René Wellek and Austin Warren, *Theory of Literature*, new rev. ed. (New York: Harcourt, Brace and World, 1956), p. 195.

[48] Lewis, *The Poetic Image*, p. 72.

[49] Martin Heidegger, *Der Satz vom Grund*, cited in Derrida, "White Mythology," p. 26n22.

[50] Derrida, p. 50.

17

found, the "correspondences" of which Baudelaire wrote in his sonnet of that title, and it is metaphor—in J. Middleton Murry's words—that "charts the non-measurable world."[51] These two worlds, moreover, are generally of unequal importance. The ontological status of the planet to which Donne compares his soul in "Good Friday. 1613," or the "bare ruined choirs" of Shakespeare's seventy-third sonnet, or the child whom Baudelaire comforts in "Recueillement" remains secondary to the abstractions the objects make vivid.

What does the poet achieve, then, by observing these "affinities" between previously distinct entities? To return to the passage from *The Prelude*, we can see Wordsworth suggesting the virtual nature of the poem— "the song *would* speak"—provisionally, a fictive utterance. Through metaphor the poet erects an "interminable building"; from one link the poet goes on to construct an entire world, a web of endlessly resonating correspondences. Metaphors in Western poetry are therefore rarely isolated figures but are extended in some fashion as the poet develops the implications of the affinities. In other words, as Wordsworth suggests, the act of connection becomes one of construction and creation, which again affirms metaphor as more than a mere ornament or figure of speech, but rather as a way of thought. The novelty of the analogy-making emphasized since Aristotle becomes fundamental here. Max Black can write, therefore, that it would often be more illuminating "to say that the metaphor *creates* the similarity than to say that it formulates some similarity antecedently existing."[52] And in concurring with this statement, Ricoeur argues that "one must say that metaphor bears information because it 'redescribes' reality."[53] As "redescription" metaphor is an act of fiction, the edifice erected by the poet as fashioner of another world, one which is presumed to be as absolute and autotelic as the one on which it is modeled, "other" in that it is both beyond this world and imagined. In the hands of some poets this notion, finally, becomes the quintessentially poetic one: "Reality is a cliché from which we escape by *metaphor*. It is only *au pays de la métaphore qu'on est poète*,"[54] writes Wallace Stevens. It is through metaphor, he writes elsewhere, that the Western poet can be found

---

[51] J. Middleton Murry, *Countries of the Mind*, excerpted in Warren Shibles, ed., *Essays on Metaphor* (Whitewater, Wi.: The Language Press, 1972), p. 33.

[52] *Models and Metaphors: Studies in Language and Philosophy* (Ithaca: Cornell University Press, 1962), p. 37.

[53] *The Rule of Metaphor*, p. 22.

[54] Wallace Stevens, "Adagia," in *Opus Posthumous*, ed. Samuel French Morse (New York: Alfred A. Knopf, 1966), p. 179.

>   ... shrinking from
>   The weight of primary noon,
>   The ABC of being,[55]

turning away from sensory reality, whether through metaphysics or artifice.

If Stevens represents an extreme of philosophical and literary idealism,
his position is at the same time one whose roots go back to the earliest
Western theories of poetry. The mimetic assumptions at the heart of the
Western tradition, we have seen, conceive of the poet as artificer, as a
maker of fictions that represent yet are different from, other than, the
phenomena of the concrete, sensible world. Metaphor, as the recognition
or even creation of similarity in difference, and as a process that functions
by virtue of otherness in reference, encapsulates these same presuppositions. The assumption of a fundamental dualism between the physical
and the metaphysical is crucial here, and one that should be borne in
mind when we turn to an examination of the Chinese poetic tradition.

III.

Most of the generalizations I have just made about metaphor could be
applied *a fortiori* to allegory, since early definitions viewed the latter as
simply an extended use of the former. Quintilian in his *Institutes*, for example, writes that *"Allegory*, which is translated in Latin by *inversio*,
either presents one thing in words and another in meaning, or else something absolutely opposed to the meaning of the words. The first type is
generally produced by a series of metaphors."[56] He viewed the temptation
to indulge in an excess of metaphor as a real and dangerous one, likely to
produce nothing but enigmas, defined as obscure allegory, but his definition held sway for centuries. A sixteenth-century rhetorician thus declares

[55] Stevens, "The Motive for Metaphor," in *Poems*, ed. Samuel French Morse (New York:
Vintage, 1959), p. 109.

[56] *The Institutio Oratoria of Quintilian*, trans. H. E. Butler (Cambridge, Ma.: Harvard
University Press, 1959; 4 vols.), III, 327.
Cicero also disputes the logical validity of any distinction between metaphor and allegory:
"When there is a series of metaphors (*tralationes*), the meaning becomes completely different; in this case, too, the Greeks call it ἀλληγορια; etymologically, that is fine; logically, it
would be better, with Aristotle, to classify all of these figures under the name of metaphor."
From *The Orator*, XXVII; cited in Jean Pépin, *Mythe et allégorie: les origines grecques et les
contestations judéo-chrétiennes*, new rev. and enl. ed. (Paris: Etudes augustiniennes, 1976),
p. 89.

that "An Allegorie is none other thing, but a metaphor used throughout a whole sentence or oration,"[57] and Rosamond Tuve confirms the widespread acceptance of this assumption: "*allegoria* doesn't use metaphor; it is one. By definition a continued metaphor, *allegoria* exhibits the normal relation of concretion to abstraction found in metaphor, in the shape of a series of particulars with further meaning."[58]

Various theoretical refinements of this definition have, of course, been offered. Ricoeur explains, for instance, that, on the one hand, a metaphorical statement incorporates non-metaphorical terms with which the metaphorical term interacts; one could cite "the ship plows the sea" as a classic example of such a complex of words in which one term is taken literally ("ship") and one figuratively ("plows"). Allegory, on the other hand, is made up exclusively of metaphorical terms, all of which are taken figuratively, hence producing a tension not so much in their proposition as in their context. It produces two parallel interpretations, each equally coherent if not of the same ultimate importance.[59] It is evident, nonetheless, that Ricoeur is still working within the guidelines laid down by Quintilian.

There are a number of assumptions that follow from regarding allegory as extended metaphor and with which few writers in the Western tradition have disagreed. In the first place, since metaphor presupposes fictiveness, it is not surprising to find allegory defined as a "fictional mode" relying on "structured narrative."[60] The importance of sequential continuity in allegory has not generally been subject to question, although Michael Murrin argues that it did not develop until medieval writers began expanding upon what were but tendencies in that direction—Virgil's consistently allegorical treatment of the gods in the *Aeneid*.[61] Even more important, in any case, is its fictive, fabricated, artificial status. In other words, a Western allegory cannot be taken at face value as a literal record of actual events; rather, it is a system of signs whose very meaning consists in asserting their fictiveness and their function as signifiers for something

[57]Thomas Wilson, *The Arte of Rhetorique* (1553; rpt. Gainesville, Fla.: Scholars' Facsimiles and Reprints, 1962), p. 198. Cited in Joel Fineman, "The Structure of Allegorical Desire," in Stephen J. Greenblatt, ed., *Allegory and Representation*, Selected Papers from the English Institute, 1979–1980, New Series, No. 5 (Baltimore: Johns Hopkins University Press, 1981), p. 54n14.

[58]Tuve, *Elizabethan and Metaphysical Imagery*, pp. 105–06.

[59]Ricoeur, *The Rule of Metaphor*, pp. 171, 190.

[60]Gay Clifford, *The Transformation of Allegory* (London: Routledge and Kegan Paul, 1974), pp. 5, 14. Cf. also Northrop Frye's entry on "Allegory" in the *Princeton Encyclopedia of Poetry and Poetics*, p. 12.

[61]Michael Murrin, *The Allegorical Epic* (Chicago: University of Chicago Press, 1980), pp. 23ff.

20

beyond the text. What is present must direct the reader's attention to what is absent, the real, unspoken concern of the author, which is to be substituted for whatever is given overtly in the text. In the words of Walter Benjamin, allegory is characterized by a fundamental discrepancy between image and meaning, "a dualism of signification and reality." It "means something different from what it is. It means precisely the non-existence of what it presents."[62] In so doing, allegory is quintessentially fiction, or "fictionality foregrounded."[63]

Another way to make this point is to insist on the otherness of allegory, a notion implicit in the earliest definitions. As just cited, Quintilian wrote of allegory that it "presents one thing in words and another in meaning" (*aliud verbis aliud sensu ostendit* [VIII.6.44]; elsewhere *aliud dicere aliud intellegi velle* [IX.2.92], that is, "saying one thing, while intending something else to be understood" [trans. Butler, III, 433]), and this presumption of a fundamental disjunction went unquestioned. This doubled quality, moreover, characterized not only the literary text but also the world-view underlying it. Western allegory creates a hierarchical literary universe of two levels, each of which maintains its own coherence, but only one of which has ultimate primacy. Just as, in the Platonic model, the world of the senses is but a pale imitation of the eternal Forms, so the concrete narrative of an allegorical text is but a pale "shadow" of and vehicle for conveying a more important abstract meaning. Although political allegory, in which the second level of meaning refers to the contemporary reality, has always been an important type within the tradition as a whole,[64] a more common distinction between the visible and the invisible usually separates the two realms. Indeed, the Greek term *allegoria* was actually but a relatively late translation of a much older concept, *hyponoia* ("suspicion," "guess"), which was predicated on a number of dualities:

> it presupposes a relation between two mental contents different in nature: on the one hand, a concrete given is presented to perception; on the other hand, it suggests an idea about the future or transcending the sensible world, posited either as conclusion or as hypothesis; ὑπόγοια designates the operation, often very elementary, which moves from the perceived given to the conjectured idea.[65]

[62] Walter Benjamin, *The Origin of German Tragic Drama*, trans. John Osborne (London: New Left Books, 1977), pp. 194, 233.

[63] Chin-Ten Shu, "Allegorical Structure in Literary Discourse: Western and Chinese," Ph.D. Diss., University of Wisconsin-Madison, 1981, p. 106.

[64] Angus Fletcher, *Allegory: The Theory of a Symbolic Mode* (Ithaca: Cornell University Press, 1964), p. 2.

[65] Pépin, *Mythe et allégorie*, p. 85.

21

Pépin makes clear at great length the intimate connection between this literary practice and the dualism fundamental to Platonic thought:

> If it is true that the visible world is a transient image, the approximate sketch of an exemplary world, the former, for the one who knows how to understand it, must make constant allusions to the latter, constituting a kind of hieroglyph of it. The vulgar being does not see beyond nature; but the spiritual person can discern there, as in a filigree, the indication of the supernatural; the visible world and the invisible world become an exoteric universe and an esoteric universe. But the duality of the sign and of the signified in allegory appears as a particular application of this cosmic hermeticism. (p. 47)

This is not to say, of course, that all allegories are predicated on a fundamental ontological distinction between the seen and the unseen. One influential interpretive tradition linked with the third century B.C. Sicilian Euhemerus, for example, read Greek gods in myths as deified historical figures—whence derives the term euhemerization. For Greek and Roman allegories and allegorists, the invisible could range from meteorological events to psychological impulses to moral principles, all of which were first represented, and thus explained, by divine figures capable of miraculous actions, so that the very presence of gods in a literary work served as a signal: "The medieval and Renaissance writers inherited from Virgil and the Homeric critics a tradition of allegory. They assumed that marvelous scenes symbolized and condensed complex and unseen processes, that such polyvalent figures and actions made epic and romance philosophical."[66] In the course of time, however, these "unseen processes" became increasingly abstract, and the assumption that the allegorist is more likely concerned with suggesting something psychological, philosophical, or moral than concrete events and personages has come to dominate conceptions of the genre. As C. S. Lewis puts it, the writer starts "with an immaterial fact, such as the passions," and "can then invent *visibilia* to express them."[67] This point is echoed by Gay Clifford: "The writer is concerned with recurrent patterns of human experience and the immaterial or metaphysical patterns of which these are supposedly a reflection, but he necessarily relies on particulars to express these abstractions and generalities."[68]

Erich Auerbach has argued at some length that this feature of allegory

[66] Murrin, *Allegorical Epic*, p. 24.
[67] C. S. Lewis, *The Allegory of Love* (London: Oxford University Press, 1936), pp. 44–5.
[68] Clifford, *The Transformation of Allegory*, p. 8.

distinguishes it significantly from another concept particularly important in the medieval interpretive tradition, *figura*. A term with many meanings, including form, shape, model, copy, and rhetorical figure, *figura* came also, in the hands of Tertullian, to be used for "something real and historical which announces something else that is also real and historical. The relation between the two events is revealed by an accord or similarity."[69] Figural or typological interpretation was applied primarily to the Bible, to demonstrate how Old Testament personages and events prefigured those in the New Testament, the sacrifice of Isaac, for example, regarded as the figure or type of that of Christ. Although the latter must be considered to possess the greater ultimate significance for Christian writers, the important point about this type of reading is that it does not diminish or deny the concrete historicity or validity of the former. This is what differentiates it from allegory:

> Since in figural interpretation one thing stands for another, since one thing represents and signifies the other, figural interpretation is "allegorical" in the widest sense. But it differs from most of the allegorical forms known to us by the historicity both of the sign and what it signifies. Most of the allegories we find in literature or art represent a virtue (e.g., wisdom), or a passion (jealousy), an institution (justice), or at most a very general synthesis of historical phenomena (peace, the fatherland)—never a definite event in its full historicity. Such are the allegories of late antiquity and the Middle Ages, extending roughly from the *Psychomachia* of Prudentius to Alain de Lille and the *Roman de la Rose*. We find something very similar in the allegorical interpretations of historical events, which were usually interpreted as obscure illustrations of philosophical doctrines. (p. 54)

Auerbach takes great pains to demonstrate how important it is to realize that figural interpretation involved correspondences between two concrete, historical events, as opposed to love allegory or religious symbolism, where "at least one of the terms does not belong to human history; it is an abstraction or a sign."[70] Yet he must also concede the eventually greater

[69] Erich Auerbach, "Figura," rpt. in *Scenes from the Drama of European Literature* (Gloucester, Ma.: Peter Smith, 1973), p. 29.

[70] "Typological Symbolism in Medieval Literature," *Gesammelte Aufsätze zur romanischen Philologie* (Bern: Francke, 1967), p. 111. Cited by Tzvetan Todorov, "On Linguistic Symbolism," *New Literary History*, 6.1 (Autumn 1974), pp. 131–2.

Jean Pépin suggests a slightly different way of making this distinction, as one opposing the timeless claims of an allegorical interpretation to the temporality of a figural one: "Each time the pagan Greeks suspect a theoretical lesson in the myths, it is a question of atemporal truths envisaged *sub specie aeternitatis*; on the contrary, when the Christians interpret the Jewish Bible spiritually, it is in order to disengage from it the outlines of the history of

power of more spiritualist and Neoplatonic tendencies, influential at the same time, which would read the Bible as an illustration of abstract mystical or ethical systems. The possibility of figural interpretation is important to keep in mind, particularly with reference to traditional Chinese modes of reading, but it seems clear that the assumption of a fundamental ontological dualism, modeled in the cosmos itself, proved powerful enough to ensure the dominance of more traditional types of allegory in the West.[71] The figural mode, moreover, is still a substitutive one, posited on the distinction between what is said and what is meant and privileging the latter.

One way of reconciling these various possibilities of reading was to establish a schema with room for all of them, and this method suggested itself, in fact, at a relatively early stage. A four-part classification of allegory was apparently first developed by John Cassian (ca. A.D. 360–465), who may have been paralleling a system proposed by his contemporary Sallustius for the interpretation of classical myth.[72] The Church fathers were quick to adapt these systems to Biblical exegesis. According to Auerbach, St. Augustine was emphatically committed to the figural mode of interpretation as opposed to pure abstract allegory. His doctrine of the fourfold meaning of Scripture includes the following levels: (1) *quae ibi aeterna intimeatur*—those things which have to do with eternity (anagogical); (2) *quae facta narrentur*—those which narrate historical facts (literal); (3) *quae futura praenunientur*—those foretelling the future (figural); and (4) *quae agenda praecipiantur vel moneantur*—those commanding or advising on actions (ethical). As Auerbach points out, Augustine's model has a strongly "realistic, historical, and concrete character, for three of the four meanings become concrete, historical, and interrelated, while only one remains purely ethical and allegorical."[73]

Whereas Augustine roots his first three levels indisputably in human

salvation, principally under the form of 'types' of the person and work of Jesus. On the one hand, allegory has an eternal claim, for which the notion of a time interval between the myth and its signification has no meaning, no more than it would between a fable of Aesop and its moral. On the other hand, a 'typology' has historical structure, which attaches a fundamental importance to the temporal passage separating the type from the 'antitype.'" From "Le Temps et le mythe," Appendix II to *Mythe et allégorie*, pp. 505–06. Originally published in *Etudes philosophiques*, 17 (1962), pp. 55–68.

[71] Andrew Plaks has made this same point in his discussion of allegory and traditional Chinese fiction in *Archetype and Allegory in the Dream of the Red Chamber* (Princeton: Princeton University Press, 1976), esp. pp. 87ff.

[72] See John MacQueen, *Allegory* (London: Methuen, 1970), p. 49.

[73] Auerbach, "Figura," p. 42. The translation of this article inadvertently omits the second level.

time, the impulse toward a less concretely historical reading is evident in St. Thomas of Aquinas' presentation of the same scheme. The categories are the same, but his description of them contrasts the literal meaning to the other three and diminishes the temporal character of all of them:

That first meaning whereby the words signify things belongs to the sense first mentioned, namely the historical or literal. This meaning, however, whereby the things signified by the words in their turn also signify other things is called the spiritual sense; it is based on and presupposes the literal sense.

Now this spiritual sense is divided into three. For, as St. Paul says, *The Old Law is the figure of the New*, and the New Law itself, as Dionysius says, *is the figure of the glory to come*. Then again, under the New Law the deeds wrought by our Head are signs of what we ourselves ought to do.

Well then, the allegorical sense is brought into play when the things of the Old Law signify the things of the New Law; the moral sense when the things done in Christ and those who prefigured him are signs of what we should carry out; and the anagogical when the things that lie ahead in eternal glory are signified.[74]

Dante's well-known application of this model to secular, vernacular literature replaces the figural with the purely allegorical. The four levels described at the beginning of the second tractate of the *Convivio* are (1) the literal, "that sense which does not go beyond the strict limits of the letter"; (2) the allegorical, which "is a truth hidden under a beautiful fiction"; (3) the moral, the sense "for which teachers ought as they go through writings intently to watch for their own profit and that of their hearers"; and (4) the anagogic or "above the senses," which "occurs when a writing is spiritually expounded, which even in the literal sense by the things signified likewise gives intimation of higher matters belonging to the eternal glory."[75]

Thus the impulse to regard allegorical meaning or meanings as primarily abstract in character can be seen in the evolution of this fourfold doctrine from Augustine to Dante and has persisted, so that Paul de Man, for example, can write that, despite its sequential and narrative character, "more than ordinary modes of fiction, allegory is at the furthest possible

---

[74] From his *Summa Theologiae*, I, 40–41; Question 1, Article 10, Conclusion. Cited by Todorov, "On Linguistic Symbolism," p. 130.

[75] MacQueen, *Allegory*, pp. 54–5. Dante keeps the four terms but revises their definitions somewhat in the possibly spurious but often quoted letter to Can Grande della Scala on the interpretation of the *Divine Comedy* (also translated in MacQueen, pp. 56–57).

remove from historiography...."[76] Theorists also generally concur on a third feature of allegory, namely, its overt self-consciousness. An allegory is supposed to be intentional and obvious, it exists only "when a poet explicitly indicates the relationship of his images to examples and precepts, and so tries to indicate how a commentary on him should proceed. A writer is being allegorical whenever it is clear that he is saying 'by this I also (allos) [allegory < allos (other) and agoreuein (to speak openly)] mean that."[77] There is a certain modus dicendi expected of allegorists, as described by Hans Robert Jauss in his discussion of allegorical genres in Romance vernacular literatures: "aliud verbis, aliud sensu ostendit. They employ an allegorical or typological relationship between form (word, image, event) and meaning, in order to make comprehensible to the reader or hearer that the truth of what is represented lies in the invisible."[78] This is what led Hegel, among others, to distinguish allegory from enigma: for all of its duplicity, its doubleness of meaning, allegory aims "for the most complete clarity, so that the external means it uses must be as transparent as possible with regard to the meaning it is to make apparent."[79]

This is not to say, of course, that allegory does not conceal at the same time it reveals. Indeed, Michael Murrin, who titles one of his books The Veil of Allegory, describes Heraclitus of Ephesus' love of riddles and preference for the hidden over the obvious as expressing "perfectly the typical allegorist's conception of a hidden truth which by its nature excludes the majority of men from its understanding."[80] Certainly the contexts in which many allegories were composed would lead us to expect an urge to conceal, particularly those referring to contemporary situations. The point is, however, that the doubleness of narrative and hence of meaning is generally clearly marked in allegory, even if the precise identity of the second level is obscure or subject to dispute.

The number of questions about the intentionality of a supposedly allegorical work that nevertheless do proliferate calls our attention to one issue frequently overlooked in literature on the subject—the distinction between allegory and allegoresis. Pépin notes several times that ancient

---

[76] Paul de Man, "Pascal's Allegory of Persuasion," in Greenblatt, ed., Allegory and Representation, p. 1.

[77] Northrop Frye, Anatomy of Criticism: Four Essays (Princeton: Princeton University Press, 1957), p. 90.

[78] Hans Robert Jauss, "Entstehung und Strukturwandel der allegorischen Dichtung," in Grundriss der romanischen Literatur des Mittelalters, Vol. VI: La Littérature didactique, allégorique et satirique; Vol. I: Partie historique, ed. Jürgen Beyer (Heidelberg: Carl Winter, 1968), p. 146.

[79] Hegel, Vorlesungen, quoted by de Man, "Pascal's Allegory," p. 1.

[80] Murrin, Allegorical Epic, p. 10.

rhetoricians in fact never clearly distinguished between the two processes and that, if anything, allegory more commonly meant allegorical *interpretation* than expression (p. 488). Nevertheless, it seems clear that critics would be wise to specify which of the two processes they are concerned with. Michael Murrin is only one of several writers who never differentiate between the two. It may well be that, as Northrop Frye argues, "all commentary is allegorical interpretation, an attaching of ideas to the structure of poetic imagery,"[81] but not all literary works are allegories. Maureen Quilligan has been among the most emphatically insistent that there is a difference between "a text designed to manipulate the reader" and an exegetical tradition "focusing on the manipulations the reader can make with a text."[82] This will be an important distinction to keep in mind when we examine the commentary literature in Chinese poetry.

One final issue integral to writings on allegory in the West has to do with critical evaluations of the mode itself. In recent years allegory has become something of a literary fashion, primarily because of the various features I have just delineated: as an extreme in fictional contrivance calling attention to its otherness of reference, it has offered contemporary Western critics convenient examples of the arbitrariness and figurality of all language, the unavoidable distance between signifier and signified, and the illusory assumption of the presence and immanence of meaning in the text. This critical interest represents at the same time a rehabilitation of the trope, for allegory received harsh treatment at the hands of the European romantics, who rejected it in favor of a new conception of the symbol. Whereas earlier writers would have identified the two, Goethe regarded them as antithetical: "There is a great difference, whether the poet seeks the particular for the general or sees the general in the particular. From the first procedure arises allegory, where the particular serves only as an example of the general; the second procedure, however, is really the nature of poetry; it expresses something particular, without thinking of the general or pointing to it."[83] Paul de Man has discussed some of the reasons behind this distinction, calling upon Hans-Georg Gadamer's analysis that the valorization of the symbol and disesteem of allegory were part of a more general attempt to merge experience and its representation and to view meaning as total and universal rather than discrete and pluralistic:

[81] Frye, *Anatomy*, p. 89.

[82] Maureen Quilligan, *The Language of Allegory: Defining the Genre* (Ithaca: Cornell University Press, 1979), p. 281.

[83] From his *Maximen*, no. 279. Cited in René Wellek, *A History of Modern Criticism* (New Haven: Yale University Press, 1955), I, 211.

This appeal to the infinity of a totality constitutes the main attraction of the symbol as opposed to allegory, a sign that refers to one specific meaning and thus exhausts its suggestive potentialities once it has been deciphered. "Symbol and allegory," writes Gadamer, "are opposed as art is opposed to non-art, in that the former seems endlessly suggestive in the indefiniteness of its meaning, whereas the latter, as soon as its meaning is reached, has run its full course."[84]

Defining the symbol as endlessly suggestive represents in fact a radical departure from traditional notions, which would have regarded it as the equivalent of allegory in its reference to one specific meaning, though different in its constancy from context to context. One need only think of the countless dictionaries of symbols in pre-modern art and literature for confirmation of this older view. This earlier conception, moreover, has been a persistent one. C. Day Lewis, for example, defines the symbol as the opposite of an emotionally resonant "intense image" and argues that a "symbol is denotative; it stands for one thing only, as the figure 1 represents one unit."[85] Philip Wheelwright also distinguishes the symbol from imagery and metaphor by virtue of its permanence and universality: "A symbol, in general, is a relatively stable and repeatable element of perceptual experience, standing for some larger meaning or set of meanings which cannot be given, or not fully given, in perceptual experience itself."[86]

Nevertheless, the romantic transformation of the symbol into something more personal, evocative, and philosophically ambitious was to prove of central importance to later developments in European—and especially symbolist and post-symbolist—poetry. This conception underlies William York Tindall's study of the literary symbol, which he opposes to the sign, a term for which one could easily substitute allegory. Alluding to a passage in *The Tempest* that refers to non-discursive though expressive form as "a kind of excellent dumb discourse," Tindall writes that "Unlike the sign, which interests us less for what it is than what it points to, this dumb discourse is interesting in itself. Unlike the sign, it cannot be separated from what it stands for; for it is what it stands for or else part of it by a kind of synecdoche."[87]

[84] De Man, "The Rhetoric of Temporality," rpt. in *Blindness and Insight: Essays in the Rhetoric of Contemporary Criticism*, 2d rev. ed., Theory and History of Literature, Vol. 7 (Minneapolis: University of Minnesota Press, 1983), pp. 188–89. De Man is citing Hans Georg Gadamer, *Wahrheit and Methode* (Tübingen: J. C. B. Mohr, 1960; 4th ed., 1975), p. 70; trans. G. Barden and J. Cumming, *Truth and Method* (New York: Seabury Press, 1975), p. 67.

[85] *The Poetic Image*, p. 40.

[86] *Metaphor and Reality*, p. 92.

[87] William York Tindall, *The Literary Symbol* (Bloomington: Indiana University Press, 1967), p. 11.

It is above all in the writings of Coleridge that we can find the development, in an approach more rhetorical than that of Goethe and other German theorists, of this opposition of symbol as synecdoche to allegory as metaphorical sign. His fullest and best-known statement of this distinction appears in the 1816 *Statesman's Manual*:

> In the Scriptures they [i.e., the histories] are the living *educts* of the Imagination; of that reconciling and mediatory power, which incorporating the Reason in Images of Sense, and organizing (as it were) the flux of the Senses by the permanence and self-circling energies of the Reason, gives birth to a system of symbols, harmonious in themselves, and consubstantial with the truths, of which they are the conductors.... Now an Allegory is but a translation of abstract notions into a picture-language which is itself nothing but an abstraction from objects of the senses; the principal being more worthless even than its phantom proxy, both alike unsubstantial, and the former shapeless to boot. On the other hand a Symbol ... is characterized by a translucence of the Special in the Individual or of the General in the Especial or of the Universal in the General. Above all by the translucence of the Eternal through and in the Temporal. It always partakes of the Reality which it renders intelligible; and while it enunciates the whole, abides itself as a living part in that Unity of which it is the representative. The other are but empty echoes which the fancy arbitrarily associates with apparitions of matter, no less beautiful but not less shadowy than the sloping orchard or hill-side pasture-field seen in the transparent lake below.[88]

Coleridge's conception is based on the classical definition of allegory as extended metaphor, and elsewhere we can find him insisting emphatically on the arbitrary, contrived nature of the similarity yoking the tenor and vehicle of a metaphor, the difference separating them being of fundamental importance. A symbol, he writes, "is always tautegorical, that is expressing the same subject but with a difference, in contradistinction from metaphor and similitudes, which are always allegorical, that is, expressing a different subject but with a resemblance."[89] Coleridge's conception of the symbol had deep roots and was intimately related to other key notions in his thinking. John Hodgson notes, for example, that

[88] Samuel Taylor Coleridge, *The Statesman's Manual* (Burlington: Chauncey Goodrich, 1882), pp. 38–40. Cited in part by Jonathan Culler, "Literary History, Allegory, and Semiology," *New Literary History*, 7.2 (Winter 1976), pp. 262–63.

[89] Coleridge, *Aids to Reflection*, ed. Henry Nelson Coleridge, 4th ed. (1840; rpt. Port Washington, N.Y.: Kennikat, 1971), p. 204. Cited in John A. Hodgson, "Transcendental Tropes: Coleridge's Rhetoric of Allegory and Symbol," in Bloomfield, *Allegory, Myth, Symbol*, p. 285.

synecdoche, and thus symbol, as "the very essence of man's (and nature's) participation in godhead," was an important element in the "one life" philosophy that dominated Coleridge's thinking in the late 1790's (p. 275). Furthermore, as the passage from the *Statesman's Manual* suggests, the valorization of symbol over allegory was based on, and paralleled, that of a truly creative, "esemplastic" imagination over the mechanically associative fancy.[90]

Whether or not this glorification of the symbol represents a typically nineteenth-century attempt at "tenacious self-mystification" that could not, after all, renounce the methods and assumptions of allegory has been the subject of much discussion that need not concern us here.[91] What is important for our purposes is the introduction of yet another conception of imagery that may prove useful in the analysis of Chinese poetry. Differences can be more illuminating than similarities, however, and if the definitions of the various terms discussed in this chapter have wobbled, never quite coming into focus because of important disagreements within the literature itself, the assumptions underlying them, it is to be hoped, have been made explicit. They will serve as a contrastive frame for our examination of the presumptions that shaped the Chinese poetic and critical tradition.

[90] This well-known distinction is given in Chapter XIII of his *Biographia Literaria*: "The imagination then I consider either as primary, or secondary. The primary imagination I hold to be the living power and prime agent of all human perception, and as a repetition in the finite mind of the eternal act of creation in the infinite I AM. The secondary I consider as an echo of the former, co-existing with the conscious will, yet still as identical with the primary in the kind of its agency, and differing only in degree, and in the mode of its operation. It dissolves, diffuses, dissipates, in order to re-create; or where this process is rendered impossible, yet still, at all events, it struggles to idealize and to unify. It is essentially *vital*, even as all objects (as objects) are essentially fixed and dead."

"Fancy, on the contrary, has no other counters to play with but fixities and definites. The fancy is indeed no other than a mode of memory emancipated from the order of time and space; and blended with, and modified by that empirical phenomenon of the will which we express by the word *choice*. But equally with the ordinary memory it must receive all its materials ready made from the law of association." From *Biographia Literaria, or Biographical Sketches of my literary life and opinions*, ed. George Watson (London: E. M. Dent and Sons Ltd., 1975), p. 167.

[91] The citation is from de Man, "Rhetoric," p. 208. For discussions of problematic aspects of Coleridge's distinctions and definitions, see this article, pp. 198–208; Jerome C. Christensen, "The Symbol's Errant Allegory: Coleridge and His Critics," *ELH*, 45.4 (1978), pp. 640–59; and Hodgson, "Transcendental Tropes," esp. pp. 280–83.

The same connection was drawn later in the century by William Butler Yeats, who wrote: "A Symbol is indeed the only possible expression of some invisible essence, a transparent lamp about a spiritual flame; while allegory is one of many possible representations of an embodied thing, or familiar principle, and belongs to fancy and not to imagination: the one is a revelation, the other an amusement." From his *Essays and Introductions* (New York: Macmillan, 1961), p. 116. Cited by Chin-Ten Shu, "Allegorical Structure," p. 89.

IV.

As I mentioned at the beginning of this chapter, the focus on poetic imagery is a relatively late concern of the Western critical tradition, whereas in the case of China it occupies a central position from the earliest commentary literature. Twentieth-century scholars like A. C. Graham have observed that the modern Western interest in the concrete imagery of Chinese poetry can be attributed to the fact that it "travels best"[92] and can be translated literally with frequent felicity, but our concern is with the reasons behind its prominence in the poetry itself. Chief among these, in my view, is its relationship to an important traditional view of the origin of poetry, which is why a study of the imagery and its interpretation takes us to the heart of assumptions about the nature of poetry itself.

As I have argued, while no doubt oversimplifying a long and diverse tradition, certain issues have persisted in Western critical discourse on the lyric that derive from notions going back to Plato and Aristotle: first, that—like all literature—it is mimetic and hence fictive, and, second, that it can only be distinguished from other kinds of literary forms on the basis of the manner or subject matter of its mimesis. Similarly, the Chinese tradition is hardly a monolithic one, yet it has asked a somewhat different set of questions of a poem than those taken for granted in the West. These can be found in the earliest writing on poetry, a passage from the Great Preface (*Da xu* 大序) to the first anthology of poetry, the *Shi jing* 詩經 or *Classic of Poetry*.

The collection itself, in existence by the sixth century B.C., predates this critical preface by several centuries. By tradition the preface was attributed to one of Confucius' disciples, Zixia 子夏, but modern scholars have generally accepted the Han historian Fan Ye's 范曄 (389–445) assignment, in his *History of the Latter Han* (*Hou Han shu* 後漢書), of authorship to the first century A.D. figure Wei Hong 衛宏. Certainly, however, its basic premises have a long heritage and are adumbrated in earlier works like the *Classic of History* (*Shang shu* 尚書).[93] The most cogent passage from the Preface reads as follows:

> Poetry is where the intent of the heart/mind (*xin* 心) goes. What in the heart is intent is poetry when emitted in words. An emotion moves within and takes form in words. If words do not suffice, then

[92] A. C. Graham, Introduction to *Poems of the Late T'ang* (Harmondsworth: Penguin, 1965), p. 13.

[93] For a discussion of these issues, see Zhu Ziqing 朱自清, *Shi yan zhi bian* 詩言志辨 (rpt. Taipei: Kaiming, 1975), pp. 1–48, and Chow Tse-tsung, "The Early History of the Chinese Word *Shih* (Poetry)," in Chow, ed., *Wen-lin: Studies in the Chinese Humanities* (Madison: University of Wisconsin Press, 1968), pp. 151–209.

one sighs; if sighing does not suffice, then one prolongs it [the emotion] in song; if prolonging through song does not suffice, then one unconsciously dances it with hands and feet.

Emotions are emitted in sounds, and when sounds form a pattern, they are called tones. The tones of a well-governed world are peaceful and lead to joy, its government harmonious; the tones of a chaotic world are resentful and anger, its government perverse; the tones of a defeated state are mournful to induce longing, its people in difficulty. Thus in regulating success and failure, moving heaven and earth, and causing spirits and gods to respond, nothing comes closer than poetry.[94]

What we have here is a classical statement of the expressive-affective conception of poetry prevalent in Asian literary theory. While certain assumptions resemble those in the West—the importance of song, emotion, and patterning to poetry—the world-view on which these are based is a significantly different one. Indigenous Chinese philosophical traditions agree on a fundamentally monistic view of the universe; the cosmic principle or Tao may transcend any individual phenomenon, but it is totally immanent in this world, and there is no suprasensory realm that lies beyond, is superior to, or is different in kind from the level of physical beings. True reality is not supernal but in the here and now, and this is a world, furthermore, in which fundamental correspondences exist between and among cosmic patterns (*wen* 文) and operations and those of human culture.[95] Thus the Preface here can assume that what is internal (emotion) will naturally find some externally correlative form or action, and that poetry can spontaneously reflect, affect, and effect political and cosmic order. In other words, the seamless connection between the individual

[94] Although frequently printed separately from the anthology as part of the so-called Great Preface, this passage also appears as part of the Little Preface to the first poem in the anthology, in, for example, Kong Yingda 孔穎達 (574–678), ed., *Mao shi zheng yi* 毛詩正義 (hereafter abbreviated as *Zheng yi*) (Hong Kong: Zhonghua shuju, 1964; 6 vols.), 1A/3a–5a/pp.37–41.

This passage has been translated, in whole or in part, by several other scholars, among them James J. Y. Liu, *Chinese Theories of Literature* (Chicago: University of Chicago Press, 1975), pp. 63, 69.

[95] For an exposition of the view that Chinese thought conceives of the universe as a spontaneously self-generating organism in which all phenomena exist in orderly, mutually implicating, correlative harmonies, see Joseph Needham and Wang Ling, *Science and Civilisation in China*, Vol. II: *History of Scientific Thought* (Cambridge: Cambridge University Press, 1951), pp. 279–344; Frederick R. Mote, *Intellectual Foundations of China* (New York: Alfred A. Knopf, 1971); and Mote, "The Cosmological Gulf Between China and the West," in *Transition and Permanence: Chinese History and Culture*, ed. David Buxbaum and Fritz Mote (Hong Kong: Cathay Press, 1972), pp. 3–21.

and the world enables the poem simultaneously to reveal feelings, provide an index of governmental stability, and serve as a didactic tool. Furthermore, the connections between subject and object or among objects, which the West has by and large credited to the creative ingenuity of the poet, are viewed in the Chinese tradition as already pre-established; the poet's primary achievement often lies in his ability to transcend, rather than to assert, his individuality and distinctiveness from the elements of his world.

The assumption in the Preface—that the poetic emotion is provoked by contact and interaction with the world—was made explicit in slightly later critical texts. Lu Ji's 陸機 (261–303) *Exposition on Literature* (*Wen fu* 文賦), for example, begins with the assertion that the writer "stands at the center of the universe:"

He moves with the four seasons, to sigh at transience,	遵四時以歎逝
And looks at the myriad objects, contemplating their complexity.	瞻萬物而思紛
He laments the falling leaves during autumn's vigor,	悲落葉於勁秋
And delights in the tender branches of fragrant spring.[96]	喜柔條於芳春

Lyric poetry "originates in emotion" (*shi yuan qing* 詩緣情), he writes somewhat later (*Wen xuan*, 17/6a/p.310), a phrase that was to be repeated in countless later texts, and this emotion is engendered by the response of the poet to the external world. Moreover, as this passage suggests, the dimension of the external world that occupies Lu Ji's attention is the realm of nature. The importance of nature as stimulus and source of imagery is certainly evident from the earliest poetry onward, and the connections between the human and the natural were central not only to the Taoist tradition but to Confucianism as well. As Qian Zhongshu 錢鍾書 points out, to Confucius himself is ascribed the observation of affinities between internal quality and external object in this passage from the *Analects* (*Lun yu* 論語): "The wise find joy in water; the benevolent find joy in mountains. The wise are active; the benevolent are still. The wise

---

[96] Included in *Zeng bu liu chen zhu Wen xuan* 增補六臣註文選 (abbreviated hereafter as *Wen xuan*) (rpt. Taipei: Huazheng, 1974), 17/2a/p.308. These lines have also been translated, *inter alia*, by Achilles Fang, "Rhymeprose on Literature," *Harvard Journal of Asiatic Studies*, 14 (1951), rpt. in John L. Bishop, *Studies in Chinese Literature* (Cambridge, Ma.: Harvard University Press, 1965), p. 531; Chen Shih-hsiang, "Essay on Literature," in Cyril Birch, ed., *Anthology of Chinese Literature*, Vol. I (New York: Grove, 1965), p. 205; and James J. Y. Liu, *Chinese Theories of Literature*, p. 72.

are joyful; the benevolent are long-lived."[97] Lu Ji is the first to make such links explicitly relevant to the writing of poetry.

Toward the end of the *Exposition on Literature* Lu Ji also writes that

As for the meeting of stimulus and response and the order of free movement and obstruction,	若夫應感之會通塞之紀
Their coming cannot be hindered nor their departure stopped. (*Wen xuan*, 17/12b/ p.313)	來不可遏去不可止

Similar statements suggesting that I term somewhat inelegantly a "stimulus-response" model of writing also appear in other Six Dynasties texts. The preface to Zhong Hong's 鍾嶸 (469–518) *Classification of Poetry* (*Shi pin* 詩品), for example, opens with the statement that

The vital force (*qi* 氣) moves natural objects, and objects elicit a response in man; thus the stimulation of one's nature and feelings takes shape in dance and song. [This] illuminates the Three Talents [heaven, earth, and man] and makes the myriad things beautifully bright. Spirits rely on this to receive sacrifices, and what is dark and subtle depends on it for elucidation.

And this passage then concludes with a direct citation from the Great Preface: "For moving heaven and earth and causing spirits and gods to respond, nothing comes closer than poetry."[98]

These ideas are also expressed frequently throughout Liu Xie's 劉勰 (ca. 465–523) more comprehensive work, *The Literary Mind: Dragon Carvings* (*Wenxin diaolong* 文心雕龍). "Elucidating Poetry" (*Ming shi* 明詩), the sixth chapter of the volume, explains that "Man is endowed with seven emotions, which are moved in response to objects. When moved by objects one sings of one's intent totally spontaneously."[99] Somewhat later Liu Xie echoes the Great Preface when writing that "Emotions are moved and take form in words; reason emerges and literature appears; for in following the hidden to reach the manifest, one matches the external to the internal" (Fan, 6/p.505; cf. Shih, p. 222).

---

[97] VI.23: trans. D. C. Lau, *The Analects* (Harmondsworth: Penguin, 1979), p. 84. See Qian Zhongshu, *Tan yi lu* 談藝錄 (Shanghai: Kaiming, 1948), pp. 63ff, 283ff.

[98] Included in the *Lidai shihua* 歷代詩話, ed. He Wenhuan 何文煥 (1740; rpt. Peking: Zhonghua, 1982; 2 vols.), I, 2.

[99] Fan Wenlan 范文瀾, ed., *Wenxin diaolong zhu* 文心雕龍注 (rpt. Taipei: Daming, 1965), 2/p.65. Cf. trans. by Vincent Yu-chung Shih in *The Literary Mind and the Carving of Dragons*, bilingual ed. (Taipei: Chung Hwa, 1975), p. 43.

And in Chapter 46 he further develops this correlative thinking by providing specific examples of how, "when phenomena move, the heart/mind is also stirred." Emotions will vary according to seasonal and atmospheric changes, since all natural objects are mutually resonant: "Things all call to one another—how can man remain at rest?" (Fan, 10/p.693; cf. Shih, p. 348). Instead of the mimetic view that poetry is the imitation of an action, then, it is seen here as a *literal reaction* of the poet to the world around him and of which he is an integral part. There are no disjunctures between true reality and concrete reality, nor between concrete reality and literary work, gaps which may have provoked censure in some quarters but which also establish the possibility of poiesis, fictionality, and the poet's duplication of his "heavenly Maker's" creative act.

This is not to say, however, that the Chinese poetic tradition believed, as a rule, that the poem simply mirrored an external scene; the passage from experience to work was deemed considerably more complex. Indeed, there are important sections of these same theoretical texts that might be summoned up in support of arguments other than the one I am proposing. Lu Ji, for example, while stressing literature's origins in the writer's response to the world around him, calls attention in the very same breath to the latter's indebtedness to the written tradition: "He nourishes feelings and mind on the classical greats" (*Wen xuan*, 17/2a/p.308); in other words, he not only responds to the world of nature but also "wanders in the treasure grove of letters" (*ibid.*). In addition, Lu Ji speaks of the writer's necessary transcendence of sensory perception and its spatial and temporal limits. "At the beginning," the critic tells us,

He gathers in sight and turns back hearing,	比收視反聽
Deeply pondering, searching about.	耽思傍訊
His spirit surges to the world's eight reaches,	精騖八極
His mind wanders a myriad miles....	心游萬仞
Past and present observed in a moment,	觀古今於須臾
He touches four seas in the blink of an eye.	撫四海於一瞬
(*Wen xuan*, 17/2b–3b/p.308)	

By suspending the senses the writer gains the focus required to control language and objects:

He clears his mind fully to concentrate thinking,	罄澄心以凝思
Considers all subtlety and puts it in words.	眇衆慮而為言
Heaven and earth he encages in form,	籠天地於形內
Downs a myriad things with the tip of a brush.	挫萬物於筆端
(*Wen xuan*, 17/4a/p.309)	

35

Another passage, furthermore, describes the joys of the writing process in terms that might suggest a notion of creation ex nihilo akin to Western fictionality:

Yes, this business can be enjoyed—	伊茲事之可樂
Always respected by sages and worthies.	固聖賢之所欽
Impose on empty nonbeing to ask forth being,	課虛無以責有
Knock on deepest silence in search of sound.	叩寂寞而求音

(*Wen xuan*, 17/4b/p.309)

We should note, however, that Lu Ji does not actually depict the writer himself here as forging something from nothing, but rather as setting a process in motion. Poetry comes not from within himself alone but as an answer to his "knock" on nature, with which his mind, as a result of attaining the mental emptiness described above, exists in total harmony.

Liu Xie describes a similar state that transcends the limits of space and time in Chapter 26 of *The Literary Mind*, "Spiritual Thinking" (*Shen si* 神思):

> In literary thinking, one's spirit is far-reaching. Thus when one con-centrates and ponders in silence, one's thoughts can touch a thousand years. With a quiet move of the face, one's gaze can pene-trate ten thousand miles. While humming and chanting one spits forth melodies of pearls and jade. Before one's eyebrows and lashes, scenes of windblown clouds furl and unfurl. These are what the order of thought attains. Therefore, when the order of thought is subtle, the spirit and objects wander together. (Fan, 6/p.493; cf. Shih, p. 216)

Here again we see the writer's intuitive contemplation moving beyond the boundaries of his immediate context in imaginative flights that, one might argue, hint at a theory of literary invention. Like Lu Ji, Liu Xie seems intent on asserting that, whatever the primacy of nature as an original stimulus or source of inspiration, the writer is nonetheless free—if not obligated—to offer something more than a literal rendering of physical details. Yet both critics emphasize the momentary withholding of sensory perception primarily in order to insist that only by so doing can the writer penetrate and identify with the essence of objects, not to propose the crea-tion of what does not in fact exist.

Readers of the major poetic genre in the tradition, the short lyric *shi*, would agree that the thrust of such discussions as these centered on the call to go beyond flat description and not, as Western readers might expect, on developing a notion of poetry as fictive artifact. The Chinese poem was assumed to invoke a network of pre-existing correspondences—between poet and world and among clusters of images.

This is not to say, of course, that all poetry was in fact nonfictional. Major genres such as the Music Bureau ballads (*yuefu* 樂府) of the Han dynasty and the early lyric meters (*ci* 詞), for example, typically called for the poet to adopt a persona and/or construct a fictional narrative or dramatic situation. Yet the range of such possibilities was a markedly limited one, attesting to the power of the notion of writing as an exercise in literary convention rather than as invitation to fabrication, although *ci* imagery in particular can be both graphic and innovative. Moreover, as if to prove the rule, the dominant interpretive tradition would draw these exceptions into its accommodating fold by assuming that they, too, were as topically referential as the *shi* was presumed to be. It is this impulse that I shall be tracing throughout this study.

V.

Poetic imagery, then, has been the center of Chinese critical attention from earliest times, although scholars would disagree on the necessarily empirical origin of all images in a poem. Certainly, however, it was never regarded either as mere description or as simple ornament but as the very differentia of poetry itself. Curiously, however, just as in the West the terminology for imagery has proven to be somewhat fluid, so in China no one single word has consistently been used to denote the concept. Moreover, some of the most important presumptions about imagery were not even uttered in reference to poetry itself.

The term commonly translated into English as "image" (*xiang* 象) did not in fact become an important part of the Chinese poetic vocabulary until the Tang dynasty and afterward; before that time it was most commonly associated with the early divination text, the *Classic of Changes* (*Yi jing* 易經). Imagery is central to this work in its very conception and presentation, as Iulian K. Shchutskii has argued:

> Each hexagram is a symbol of some life situation which develops in time. Each text to a hexagram is a short characterization of this situation, basically or completely. Each text to a line is a concrete characterization of some stage in the development of the given situation. With this, one must take into account that, in view of the authors' level of thinking and language techniques, such characterizations almost never are expressed in the form of precise ideas. The elements of the *Book of Changes* are elements of imagery. Instead of speaking of the appropriateness of collective action, the *Book of Changes* says, "When the reed is plucked, the other stalks follow

after it, since it grows in a bunch. Firmness brings happiness. Development." [Hexagram 12.1][100] Instead of speaking of the vanity of an undertaken action, the *Book of Changes* says, "The nobody has to be powerful; the nobleman has to perish. Firmness is terrifying. When the goat butts the fence, its horns stick in it." [Hexagram 34.3; Wilhelm/Baynes, p. 134][101]

The examples Shchutskii presents here are brief texts elucidating the relative significance of particular lines in two different hexagrams, which were themselves viewed as abstracted images of 64 possible life situations. Each hexagram as a whole also carried a brief layer of text called the "Image," which presented a possible concrete embodiment of that situation.

Whereas the *Classic of Changes* itself does not discuss the importance of these images explicitly, the Appended Words Commentary (*Xi ci zhuan* 繫辭傳) or Great Commentary (*Da zhuan* 大傳) to the text does offer several remarks that help to explain how the image was viewed, assumptions that were to underlie attitudes to poetry as well. The commentary was most likely compiled through a process of accretion by many hands during the third century B.C. and thus antedates any major literary-theoretical texts still extant.[102] There are at least three points suggested by this commentary that should be kept in mind. In the first place, it is difficult, if not impossible, to distinguish among an object, one's perception of it, its image or representation, and its significance. Indeed, the first three are all rendered by the same word. Thus *xiang* can denote natural phenomena (*wu xiang* 物象), and in particular the heavenly bodies: "There are no greater primal images than heaven and earth.... Of the images suspended in the heavens, there is none more light-giving than the sun and the moon."[103] In other words, it is important to remember that, as Willard Peterson observes, *xiang* "are independent of any human

[100] Cf. *The I Ching or Book of Changes*, trans. Richard Wilhelm and Cary F. Baynes, Bollingen Series XIX, 3d ed. in new format (Princeton: Princeton University Press, 1969), p. 53.

[101] Iulian K. Shchutskii, *Researches on the I Ching*, trans. William L. MacDonald and Tsuyoshi Hasegawa with Hellmut Wilhelm, Bollingen Series LXII.2 (Princeton: Princeton University Press, 1979), p. 226.

[102] For a discussion of the commentary's authorship, dating, text, and claims, see Willard J. Peterson, "Making Connections: 'Commentary on the Attached Verbalizations' of the *Book of Change*," *Harvard Journal of Asiatic Studies*, 42.1 (June 1982), pp. 67–116.

[103] *Zhou yi zheng yi* 周易正義, in *Shisan jing zhushu* 十三經注疏, ed. Ruan Yuan 阮元 (1764–1849) (rpt. Peking: Zhonghua, 1979; 2 vols.), I, 7/70b/p.82. Trans. Wilhelm/Baynes, p. 319. Subsequent references to the *Classic of Changes* in my text will generally give the page numbers in the Chinese edition followed by those in the Wilhelm/Baynes translation.

observer; they are 'out there,' whether or not we look."[104] At the same
time, however, the authors of the commentary are particularly interested
in the *xiang* as perceived—"What manifests itself visibly they [the sages]
called an image" (I, 7/70a/p.82; p.318)—and translated into the symbols of the eight trigrams, the building blocks of the 64 hexagrams. At one
point the commentary credits the legendary founder of civilization Bao Xi
包犧 or Fu Xi 伏羲 with this process:

> When in early antiquity Pao Hsi ruled the world, he looked upward
> and contemplated the images [*xiang*] in the heavens; he looked
> downward and contemplated the patterns [*wen* 文] on earth. He con-
> templated the markings of birds and beasts and the adaptations to
> the regions. He proceeded directly from himself and indirectly from
> objects. Thus he invented the eight trigrams in order to enter into
> connection with the virtues of the light of the gods and to regulate the
> conditions of all beings. (I, 8/74b/p.86; pp.328–29)

In other passages it is simply ascribed to the ancient sages in general:
"The holy sages instituted the hexagrams, so that phenomena [*xiang*]
might be perceived therein" (I, 7/64b/p.76; p.287); "The holy sages were
able to survey all the confused diversities under heaven. They observed
forms and phenomena, and made representations [*xiang*] of things and
their attributes. These were called the Images" (I, 7/67a/p.79; p.304;
repeated I, 7/71a/p.83; p.324); "Heaven and earth change and transform; the holy sage imitates them. In the heavens hang images that reveal
good fortune and misfortune; the holy sage reproduces these" (I, 7/70b/
p.82; p.320).

The passage from concrete phenomenon to written form is translated
here as "representations" and "reproduces," and, indeed, the commentary itself in one passage defines an image as an imitation or "reproduc-
tion" [*xiang* 像]: "Thus the *Book of Changes* consists of images. The
images are reproductions" (I, 8/75b/p.87; p.336). As such, the process
might appear to resemble the Western concept of mimesis discussed
earlier, but this resemblance is delusory. As I have argued, mimesis is
predicated on a fundamental disjunction between two realms of being,

[104] Peterson, "Making Connections," p. 80. Peterson prefers a translation of *xiang* as
"figure," rather than "image," because "a figure is an image or likeness, but it is also a form
or shape, a design or configuration or pattern, and a written symbol; 'to figure' is to represent as a symbol or image, but also to give or bring into shape" (pp. 80–81). It seems to me,
however, that the term "figure," even more than image, places undue emphasis on the
human acts of representation and interpretation of an object or situation and thereby diminishes the independent status of the *xiang* and its meaning—what Peterson has just argued
for. This is particularly true in view of the Western conception of *figura* discussed earlier.

one of which is replicated in the verbal product, regarded by Plato, for example, as but a pale shadow of some timeless truth. In contrast, implicit throughout the Great Commentary, as in the Great Preface to the *Classic of Poetry*, is the assumption of a seamless connection, if not virtual identity, between an object, its perception, and its representation, aided by the semantic multivalence of the term *xiang*. Such a conception never developed in the West, which preferred to stress the distinction between representation and world—whether to denigrate the former or, on the contrary, to vaunt it as a superior fictional artifact.

This brings us to a second point to be drawn from the commentary. As important as the lack of disjunction between image as object and image as representation is that between image and meaning. The commentary presents one important discussion as a dialogue between a master and his disciples, of which the first section is frequently cited alone as a testament to linguistic inadequacy:

> The Master said: Writing cannot express words completely. Words cannot express thought completely.
> Are we then unable to see the thoughts of the holy sages?
> The Master said: The holy sages set up the images in order to express their thoughts completely; they devised the hexagrams in order to express the true and the false completely. Then they appended judgments and so could express their words completely. (I, 7/70c/ p.82; p.322)

This passage is often cited as testimony to the incommensurability of language and meaning, an idea that also receives powerful expression in early Taoist texts. Yet while apparently agreeing with the notion that *words* may be unable to "express thought completely," the commentary offers a possible alternative in the adequacy of the *image* to meaning. "There is no possibility of reducing these images to simple representations, for they are saturated with a much greater and many-sided content than a representation abstracted from observation."[105] In other words, unlike in the West, where the image began with the mere function of *enargia*, or making one seem to see something, the Chinese image from its first formulations was felt to embody a greater significance.

This is the important "interplay between image and concept" discussed

---

[105] Shchutskii, *Researches*, p. 84. Shchutskii is discussing here the Qing scholar Zhang Xuecheng's 章學誠 (1738–1801) "image theory of meaning," which, among other things, distinguished the images of the *Classic of Changes* from those in poetry: "The images of the *Book of Changes* are understood correctly when they lead, not to an emotional expression, but to the knowledge of ideas invested in them and to the realization of the basic ideas of transformation" (*ibid.*).

at some length by Hellmut Wilhelm, although he begins by positing a somewhat misleading "polarity" between the two.[106] The impulse in the commentary seems instead to move toward asserting the correlations between them, a notion developed somewhat later in an essay entitled "Elucidating the Image" (*Ming xiang* 明象) by Wang Bi 王弼 (226–249), who also annotated the *Classic of Changes* itself. Wang Bi opens by declaring that "The image is that by which meaning emerges, and the word is that which elucidates the image. For exhausting meaning there is nothing like the image, and for exhausting the image there is nothing like the word."[107] It is evident that Wang Bi is thereby modifying the statement the Great Commentary puts in the mouth of the master in the passage cited above: if words cannot express thought completely, they can nevertheless prove fully adequate to the representation of an image. A clear hierarchy does, however, govern the relationship between the three elements Wang Bi discusses, for he then alludes to the Taoist philosopher Zhuangzi's 莊子 (?369–286 B.C.) famous anecdote about fish trap and rabbit snare, developing at some length the ideas that words are to be forgotten once the image has been conveyed, and then the image is to be forgotten once the meaning is obtained.[108]

Somewhat later Wang Bi concludes that the image is grounded in categorical correspondences (*lei* 類) between objects (p. 13b), recalling a third major assumption underlying the Great Commentary. There we find a statement to the effect that "The names given [to objects] are insignificant, but the categorical correspondences [*lei*] that they take hold of are great."[109] Commenting on this passage, the third-century annotator Han Kang 韓康 or Han Kangbo 伯 writes that "The image is recorded to eluci-

[106] Hellmut Wilhelm, "The Interplay of Image and Concept," in *Heaven, Earth, and Man in the Book of Changes: Seven Eranos Lectures*, Publications on Asia of the Institute for Comparative and Foreign Area Studies, No. 28 (Seattle: University of Washington Press, 1979), p. 199.

[107] From his *Zhou yi lue li* 周易略例, included in *Zhou yi zhushu* 周易注疏, ed. Han Kangbo 韓康伯, Lu Deming 陸德明, and Kong Yingda (1871 woodblock ed.), V, 12a.

[108] Wang Bi, p. 12b. The passage in the *Zhuangzi* reads as follows: "The fish trap exists because of the fish; once you've gotten the fish you can forget the trap. The rabbit snare exists because of the rabbit; once you've gotten the rabbit, you can forget the snare. Words exist because of meaning; once you've gotten the meaning, you can forget the words. Where can I find a man who has forgotten words so I can have a word with him?" *Zhuangzi yinde* 莊子引得, Harvard-Yenching Institute Sinological Index Series, Supp. No. 20 (Cambridge, Ma.: Harvard University Press, 1956), 75/26/48. Trans. Burton Watson, *The Complete Works of Chuang Tzu* (New York: Columbia University Press, 1970), p. 302.

[109] *Zhou yi zheng yi, Shisan jing zhushu*, I, 8/77b/p.89. Here I have modified somewhat the translation of Wilhelm/Baynes, p. 345, in order to underline the concept of *lei*. They have: "The names employed sound unimportant, but the possibilities of application are great."

date meaning. One uses the small as a comparison to the great," to which Kong Yingda 孔穎達 (574–678) appends the following notes: "'The names given are insignificant' says that the names of objects given by the words in the *Changes* are mostly minor.... 'The categorical correspondences that they take hold of are great' says that although these objects are insignificant, they can be compared to important situations. The meanings they take hold of can be expanded by categorical correspondence" (*ibid.*). In other words, meaning is not attached externally and arbitrarily to an image but follows logically from the fact that objects and situations were believed traditionally to belong to one or more non-mutually exclusive, a priori, and natural classes.

This concept of category membership or *lei* is fundamental to the *Classic of Changes*, for, as the Great Commentary notes, the trigrams themselves were believed to have been invented "in order to categorize the circumstances of the myriad phenomena."[110] What is important to remember about these classes, moreover, is that they are not static cubbyholes but rather presuppose dynamic interaction or sympathetic responses among constituent members, hence my use of the term "categorical correspondence." This assumption is explained in a passage from the *Wen yan* 文言 (Embellished Words) commentary on the first hexagram, *qian* 乾, which explicates the correspondence between a dragon and a great man:

The Master said: Things of a similar tone respond to one another. Things of similar vital force seek each other. Water flows to what is damp; fire seeks what is dry. Clouds follow the dragon; wind follows the tiger. The sage acts, and the myriad phenomena observe him. What has its root in heaven feels close to what is above. What has its root in earth feels close to what is below. Thus each follows that to which it corresponds by category.[111]

Joseph Needham also describes the concept of responding according to categorical correspondence (*gan lei* 感類) as a "symbolic correlation system" central to many fields of traditional Chinese thought, receiving its classic formulation in Dong Zhongshu's 董仲舒 (ca. 179 to ca. 100 B.C.) statement that "things that categorically correspond move each other."[112]

[110] *Zhou yi zheng yi*, *Shisan jing zhushu*, I, 8/74b/p.86. Wilhelm/Baynes translate this phrase as "to regulate the conditions of all beings" (p. 329).

[111] *Zhou yi zheng yi*, *Shisan jing zhushu*, I, 1/4b/p.16; cf. Wilhelm/Baynes, p. 382. This passage has also been cited by Kiyohiko Munakata in his article, "Concepts of *Lei* and *Kan-lei* in Early Chinese Art Theory," in Susan Bush and Christian Murck, eds., *Theories of the Arts in China* (Princeton: Princeton University Press, 1983), p. 106.

[112] 同類相動, cited in Needham, *Science and Civilisation*, II, 281, as "Things of the Same Genus Energise Each Other."

Because of these mutual correspondences, then, the meaning embodied by one image or object can be applied to a variety of phenomena. Conversely, as Wilhelm notes, an image could be used in more than one way, although, once usages were accepted, they tended to become systematized and stereotyped: "We then find images used almost like tropes, more or less automatically assigned to certain concepts and classifications."[113] The particular applications favored by the Great Commentary and the text of the Classic itself were to human situations, especially those involving decisions of a moral or political nature. Indeed, another commentary attached to the Classic, the Great Image (*Da xiang zhuan* 大象傳) is "systematically occupied with parallels between the images of the text and ethical norms, as if they were reflected in the texts."[114] One cannot overemphasize the conviction of these early thinkers that such norms were not only "reflected" but in fact embodied in the images, by virtue of categorical correlations between different situations. This assumption, as we shall see, was central to the poetic tradition as well, and we shall find references to it cropping up in several later critical texts, though often used in connection with terms other than *xiang*. It lies at the heart of early commentators' interpretations of what have been called the "metaphors" and "allegories" of Chinese poetry.

[113] Wilhelm, "Interplay," p. 214. Shchutskii makes the same observation about the tendency toward standardized or formulaic images in *Researches*, p. 226.

[114] Shchutskii, *Researches*, p. 169.

Imagery in the

Classic of Poetry

I.

Aₗₜₕₒᵤₘ the term "image"
was never used with reference to the earliest poetic anthology, the sixth-
century B.C. *Classic of Poetry*, many of the same concepts spelled out or
implicit in the *Classic of Changes* and associated texts clearly governed
readings of the poetry as well. Imagery is central to the composition of the
305 poems in the collection, performing key formal functions by virtue of
its repetition, usually with slight variations, and role in establishing a
rhyme scheme, and providing the idea structure for most poems, which,
being only minimally narrative, rely on the reader's ability to draw conclusions from the juxtaposition of elements. The connections between image and meaning were taken for granted from the very beginning, unlike
the case in the West. Certainly, the cultural acceptance of a number of
stereotyped images can be confirmed by calling attention, as has Hellmut
Wilhelm, to the many that are shared by both canonical texts.[1] Chia-ying
Yeh Chao has also pointed out that "there is a considerable similarity
between the arbitrary association of an *Yi ching* symbol (*hsiang* 象) with
its referent in the interpretation of the *Yi ching*"[2] and the way in which
images are read in the *Shi jing*, although I would argue that the rela-

---

[1] Hellmut Wilhelm, "The Interplay of Image and Concept," p. 208.

[2] Chia-ying Yeh Chao, "The Ch'ang-chou School of *Tz'u* Criticism," in Adele Austin Rickett, ed., *Chinese Approaches to Literature from Confucius to Liang Ch'i-ch'ao* (Princeton:
Princeton University Press, 1978), p. 162. Professor Chao observes, for example, that both
texts propose an image and then narrate a situation.

   The Song critic Chen Kui 陳騤 (1128–1203) also remarks on the similarities between the
methods of the two texts: "Images in the *Changes* are used to exhaust the meaning. Comparisons in the *Poetry* are used to make feelings go far. In writing literature, how can one do
without comparisons?" See his *Wen ze* 文則, *Congshu jicheng* 叢書集成 ed. (Shanghai:
Shangwu, 1939), *juan shang* 卷上, p. 7.

tionship was by no means construed as an "arbitrary" one by the early commentators, given the assumption of categorical correspondences.

As in the *Changes*, so in the *Poetry* most images are drawn from the natural world, not surprising in an agricultural society whose major philosophical spokesmen looked to nature as the ultimate standard and source of validity. At the same time, in both texts the main interest is with the human world, and the key challenge for commentators, therefore, becomes one of relating the natural image to the human situation—based on the categorical correlation which is believed to link them—and of further clarifying the significance of the latter. Connections between the two are drawn laconically at first, by the annotations to the earliest extant edition of the poems, the Mao 毛 text dating from around the second century B.C. They were even more elaborately detailed in three earlier recensions— long since lost—which, compiled by adherents of the New Text (*jin wen* 今文) school, were more committed to notions of far-ranging cosmological correspondences.[3]

It is this tradition which has been labeled and generally castigated by modern Western sinologists as (unjustifiably) "allegorical." James Legge, in his ground-breaking translation of the *Shi jing* into English, published in 1871, rejects the explanatory prefaces to the poems, "to follow which would reduce many of them to absurd enigmas,"[4] although he himself is not unsusceptible to other "enigmatic" readings. In a 1911 study that attempts to prove that the "Airs of the States" (*Guo feng* 國風), which comprise the first 160 poems in the *Classic*, are of popular rather than aristocratic origin and derive from various rituals and festivals, Marcel Granet declares that he will exclude "all interpretations which are symbolic or which imply subtlety in the poet."[5] "This prejudice in favour of symbolism," he writes, "to which the scholars feel themselves bound as by a professional bond of ethics, leads them into absurdities which they

[3] See Bernhard Karlgren, *Glosses on the Book of Odes* (Stockholm: Museum of Far Eastern Antiquities, 1964), pp. 71–72. The three schools were those of Shen Pei 申培 of the state of Lu 魯, Yuan Gu 轅固 of Qi 齊, and Han Ying 韓嬰 of Yan 燕. They are known as the schools of Lu, Qi, and Han, and their texts had all disappeared by the Song dynasty. See J. R. Hightower, "The *Han-shih wai-chuan* and the *San-chia shih*," *Harvard Journal of Asiatic Studies*, 11 (1948), pp. 241–310.

In the introduction to his translation of the *Bo hu tong* 白虎通 (The Comprehensive Discussions in the White Tiger Hall), Tjan Tjoe Som discusses some of the issues involved in the Han Old Text/New Text controversy. See his *Po Hu T'ung* (rpt. Westport, Ct.: Hyperion Press, 1973), I, 1–178, esp. pp. 137–45.

[4] James Legge, *The Chinese Classics*, Vol. 4: *The She King* (Oxford: Clarendon Press, 1871), "Prolegomena," p. 29.

[5] Marcel Granet, *Festivals and Songs of Ancient China*, trans. E. D. Edwards (London: George Routledge, 1932), p. 27.

sometimes admit," yet he also grants that "these allegorical interpretations of the odes reveal an essential principle of their composition—a law of the species: this is the law of symmetry, the use of *correspondences*. He who knows that law is capable of understanding and translating the *Shih ching*."[6] Arthur Waley includes an appendix to his 1937 translation of the collection, in which he says that an "allegorical interpretation" was applied to over one-third of the songs—mostly those treating courtship and marriage—from which it would otherwise have been impossible to draw the moral principles Confucius and his followers implied they contained. While he agrees with Granet that these readings distort the "true nature" of the poems, he does point out that the treatment was hardly unique to this text or culture, that it was facilitated by the multivalent meanings of words and social practices, and that it led to countless allusions in later literature and even everyday speech.[7] Perhaps the most vehement critic of this tendency has been C. H. Wang in his 1974 study of the *Shi jing* as oral-formulaic poetry. He opens with an attack on the "thematic speculation" of traditional Chinese critics which "aims at allegorization" of the text, "a manifest distortion of this classic anthology, a distortion both of its genetic character and of the original definition of *shih* [poetry] in general." Wang argues that the earliest description of poetry (in the *Classic of History*) links it only with song and "is absolutely unrelated to ethics." Allegorizing commentators ignored the primarily aesthetic function and literal meaning of the songs and saw them instead as "somewhat esoteric and cryptic, with great messages underneath the surface to instruct, to criticize, or to eulogize."[8]

Whether or not the earliest statements about Chinese poetry point to a purely aesthetic function "absolutely unrelated to ethics" is an important question, answers to which will suggest themselves over the course of this study. At the moment, however, I wish to examine the extent to which the way the traditional commentators read the *Classic of Poetry* should be termed allegorization (or allegoresis), as it has been by the Western scholars just cited. Did they themselves believe that they were ignoring the "literal meaning" of the songs? Although the search for an answer may involve a certain amount of hairsplitting, it is nonetheless an important one, primarily because the commentary literature on the *Classic* generated theories and methods which were perhaps even more significant than

[6] Granet, p. 6. In moving so freely between symbolism and allegory, Granet seems not to have recognized the distinctions drawn between the two by Goethe and Coleridge, discussed in Chapter One.

[7] Arthur Waley, *The Book of Songs* (New York: Grove, 1960), pp. 335–37.

[8] C. H. Wang, *The Bell and the Drum*: Shih Ching *as Formulaic Poetry in an Oral Tradition* (Berkeley and Los Angeles: University of California Press, 1974), pp. 1–3.

the collection itself for the later writing and reading of classical Chinese poetry.

How did pre-modern Chinese scholars read the songs? I shall start at the beginning of the Airs of the States, with the first and probably best-known of the songs, whose title (*Guan ju* 關雎) is drawn simply—as are those of the others—from two syllables in the opening line. I use the translation of Bernhard Karlgren, with some modifications.[9]

Guan guan cry the ospreys	關關雎鳩
On the islet of the river.	在河之洲
The beautiful and good young lady	窈窕淑女
Is a fine mate for the lord.	君子好逑
Varied in length are the water plants;	參差荇菜
Left and right we catch them.	左右流之
The beautiful and good young lady—	窈窕淑女
Walking and sleeping he wished for her.	寤寐求之
He wished for her without getting her.	求之不得
Waking and sleeping he thought of her:	寤寐思服
Longingly, longingly,	悠哉悠哉
He tossed and turned from side to side.	輾轉反側
Varied in length are the water plants;	參差荇菜
Left and right we gather them.	左右采之
The beautiful and good young lady—	窈窕淑女
Zithers and lutes greet her as friend.	琴瑟友之
Varied in length are the water plants—	參差荇菜
Left and right we cull them.	左右芼之
The beautiful and good young lady—	窈窕淑女
Bells and drums delight her.	鐘鼓樂之

Formally this poem is fairly typical of the group as a whole, with its tetrasyllabic lines and apparent stanzaic divisions. Typical also is the use of natural images, repeated with variations to open or subdivide each stanza; they are juxtaposed without comment to the human situation—the celebration of a marriage—around which the poem centers and seem, at first glance, unrelated to it. This usage was given the name *xing* 興 ("stimulus") by early commentators and was isolated as one of three rhe-

[9]From *The Book of Odes* (1950; Stockholm: Museum of Far Eastern Antiquities, 1974), p. 2. Unless otherwise noted, subsequent translations from the anthology will also be Karlgren's, although in most cases I shall again be altering them slightly. Page references shall be given in the text. The Chinese text is from Kong Yingda, ed., *Mao shi zheng yi*, 1A/12a–13a/pp.55–57; hereafter usually cited in my text.

torical devices of the *Classic of Poetry*, which were to be discerned in later poetry as well. The meaning and function of the *xing* from the very beginning, however, proved subject to a debate that has continued up until the present, and since it lies at the heart of many early exegeses I shall return to it shortly.

The first comment on this poem was made by none other than Confucius himself in his *Analects*, III.20: "The Master said, '[In the *Guan ju*] there is joy without wantonness and sorrow without self-injury.'"[10] This is one of two brief remarks made on the poem, the second of which (VIII.15) does not concern it as directly. As has often been noted,[11] the Confucian school was responsible for the tendency of much orthodox Chinese criticism to regard not only the *Classic of Poetry* but eventually all literature in general as morally edifying or didactic in some way. Of the several brief references to the *Classic* in the *Analects*, five statements in particular focus on the anthology's ethical propriety and practical utility:

"The Master said, 'The *Odes* are three hundred in number. They can be summed up in one phrase, "Swerving not from the right path."'" (II.2; Lau, p.63)

"The Master said, 'Be stimulated by the *Odes*, take your stand on the rites and be perfected by music.'" (VIII.8; Lau p.93)

"The Master said, 'If a man who knows the three hundred *Odes* by heart fails when given administrative responsibilities and proves incapable of exercising his own initiative when sent to foreign states, then what use are the *Odes* to him, however many he may have learned?'" (XIII.5; Lau, p.119)

"[Bo-yu to Chen Gang:] 'Once my father was standing by himself. As I crossed the courtyard with quickened steps, he said, "Have you studied the *Odes*?" I answered, "No." "Unless you study the *Odes* you will be ill-equipped to speak." I retired and studied the *Odes*.'" (XVI.13; Lau, p.141)

"The Master said, 'Why is it none of you, my young friends, study the *Odes*? An apt quotation from the *Odes* may serve to stimulate [*xing*] the imagination, to show one's breeding, to smooth over difficulties in a group and to give expression to complaints.

'Inside the family there is the serving of one's father; outside, there is the serving of one's lord; there is also the acquiring of a wide knowl-

---

[10] *The Analects*, trans. D. C. Lau, p. 70. Subsequent page references will be given in the text.

[11] See, for example, Zhu Ziqing, *Shi yan zhi bian, passim*; James J. Y. Liu, *Chinese Theories of Literature*, pp. 107ff; and Donald Holzman, "Confucius and Ancient Chinese Literary Criticism," in Rickett, ed., *Chinese Approaches to Literature*, pp. 29–38.

edge of the names of birds and beasts, plants and trees.'" (XVII.9; Lau, p.145)

In other words, the songs in the *Classic* display a moral orthodoxy (presumably why Confucius selected them to compile the anthology from an original pool of three thousand, according to the legend transmitted by the historian Sima Qian 司馬遷 [ca. 145–90 B.C.]) which makes them suitable as sources of information, models for speech, and guides in the performance of administrative and diplomatic duties. The numerous appearances of passages from the songs as indirect means of conveying a speaker's message or opinion in delicate political situations recorded in the anecdotes of two early historical works (the *Zuo zhuan* 左傳 and the *Guo yu* 國語) also attest to what was seen as their practical communicative value. Donald Holzman has argued that the word "stimulate" (*xing*) in the second and fifth citations from the *Analects* above should refer in fact to this practice of using lines from the *Shi jing* to make a point.[12] Indeed, there is reason to believe that these very precedents were responsible for leading the early commentators to their moralizing interpretations, not only because they demonstrated the utility of the songs, but also because they suggested that the opening natural images of a poem should be read in such a way as to create that utility.[13]

There were, however, striking disagreements among various scholars as to how this was to be achieved. To return to the *Guan ju*, which Confucius simply praised for its moderated emotions, the first exegetical tradition saw it as a political critique. Two brief references to the poem appear in the work of the first systematic historian of China, Sima Qian, both of which make essentially the same point: "Alas! When the house of Zhou was in decline, the *Guan ju* was composed."[14] Commentators explain that the poem was seen as criticizing the improper behavior of King Kang 康

---

[12] Holzman suggests that what Lau translates as "stimulate the imagination" should be rendered rather as "make metaphorical allusions," following the pseudo-Kong Anguo 孔安國 interpretation of the term, because he feels that it refers to "the kind of far-fetched analogies we have seen Confucius himself in the act of applying to many passages in the *Shih ching*.... The kind of allusion that was *de rigueur* in diplomatic meetings and the kind of interpretation we find again and again in ancient texts were in fact *hsing* [*xing*]" (p. 36).

[13] On this see Zhu Ziqing, *Shi yan zhi bian*, pp. 66ff. On pp. 68–70 Zhu demonstrates convincingly that, in at least five poems, the interpretations of commentators are indeed based on those implicit in allusions to the works that occur in the *Zuo zhuan*. His entire work argues for the centrality of the ethical function in the earliest theories of poetry in China.

[14] *Shi ji* 史記, "Preface to the Biographies of Confucian Scholars" 儒林列傳序, *juan* 121; *Shi ji hui zhu kaozheng* 史記會注考證 (Taipei: Hongye shuju, 1973), p. 1,253. A similar comment appears in Sima Qian's "Preface to the Chronological Tables of the Twelve Noble Houses" 十二諸侯年表序 (*Shi ji hui zhu kaozheng*, 14/p.227). Also cited in Liu Zhengwu 柳正午, "*Guan ju* zhang yiduan" 關雎章臆斷, *Wenxue pinglun* 文學評論, 2 (1980), p. 77.

and his wife (eleventh century B.C.) by presenting contrasting, positive images of male-female decorum. In making these remarks Sima Qian was apparently influenced by the interpretation of the Lu school in particular, a reading that persisted long enough to make its way into the *History of the Latter Han* of Fan Ye.

This interpretation, obviously, is problematic, not only because the *Guan ju* itself offers no hint of a satirical intent, but also because Sima Qian's own history provides no justification for such a criticism: his account of King Kang's reign records no deficiencies or evidence of decline but describes it as being so peaceful that no punishments needed to be levied for over forty years.[15] Perhaps mindful of these difficulties, the second—and dominant—interpretive tradition, which arose later during the Han dynasty, chose to read the *Guan ju* as a poem of praise, and specifically of the queen of the founder of the Zhou dynasty, King Wen.

This reading begins with the annotators of the earliest extant recension, traditionally identified as Mao Heng 毛亨 and Mao Chang 萇, who were the first to label key introductory images as *xing* and who explain the one here as a purposeful analogy. After noting, among other things, that *guan guan* is the cry of birds responding to each other and that this particular variety observes the separation of the sexes, the Mao comment to the first two lines of the poem continues:

> The queen takes joy in the virtue of her lord, and there is nothing on which she does not accord with him, nor is she wanton about her beauty. Her prudence is firm and her seclusion deep, like the ospreys in their separation.[16] Only afterward can her influence transform the world. When husbands and wives observe the separation of the sexes, then fathers and sons will maintain familial relations. When fathers and sons maintain familial relations, then ruler and minister will respect each other. When ruler and minister respect each other, then all at court will be proper. When all at court is proper, then the king's transforming influence will have been achieved.[17]

The annotation to the third and fourth lines continues by identifying the "young lady" as King Wen's queen, who "possesses the virtue of the

[15]"Annals of the House of Zhou" 周本紀, *Shi ji hui zhu kaozheng*, 4/p.68); also cited by Liu Zhengwu, p. 77.

[16]Mao glosses the binome of the third line, *yao-tiao* 窈窕, which Karlgren translates as "beautiful," as "secluded"; *Zheng yi*, 1A/12a/p.55.

[17]*Ibid.*, p. 55. Hu Puan 胡樸安 points out that reading the poem as a praise of King Wen and his queen is not without its problems as well. For example, since the ruler was only fourteen when he married her, is it likely that he really "tossed and turned" until finding her? See his *Shi jing xue* 詩經學 (Shanghai: Shangwu, 1928), p. 17.

ospreys" by living in seclusion and thus makes a suitable mate for the ruler. Moving on to the second stanza, the Mao editors note that it is she picking the edible water plants (*Nymphoides peltalum*): because (again) she "possesses the virtue of the ospreys" she can begin preparations for the ancestral sacrifices (*Zheng yi*, 1A/13a/p.57). (She has, apparently, been allowed to emerge from the previously laudable seclusion in her chambers.)

The preface to the poem, attributed by Fan Ye to Wei Hong and generally included along with the Mao text, by and large agrees with this reading:

> *Guan ju* speaks of the virtue of the queen. It is the beginning of the Airs (*feng* 風), by which all under heaven was transformed (*feng*) and relations between husband and wife were ordered. Thus they were used by the country people as well as the officials of the states.... Therefore, the *Guan ju* takes joy in obtaining a pure young lady as a mate for the lord and is anxious to present her worth, without being wanton about her beauty. It sorrows for her chaste seclusion and longs for her worthiness and talent without feeling injured by her excellence. This is the meaning of the *Guan ju*.[18]

Furthermore, the prefaces to the remaining ten poems in the first section of the *Classic*, the *Zhou nan* 周南, all describe the songs as referring to one or another aspect of the queen's (and in two cases, King Wen's) virtuous influence. This attempt by the preface writer to unite the poems of a particular geographic section by means of a topical or quasi-narrative structure appears at several other points in the anthology as well.

Only one century later, the renowned Confucian scholar Zheng Xuan 鄭玄 (127–200), who appended "commentaries" (*jian* 箋) to Mao's "annotations" (*zhuan* 傳), had introduced an interesting twist to this interpretation of the *Guan ju*. In his eyes the "pure young lady" refers not to the queen herself, but rather to palace ladies whom their mistress, in her virtuous and jealousy-free seclusion, is seeking as additional mates

---

[18] *Zheng yi*, 1A/2b–3a/pp.36–37; 1A/11a/p.53. These remarks apropos the *Guan ju* envelop the more general discourse on the *Classic of Poetry* as a whole which, since the Song dynasty, has been separated out and labeled the Great Preface (partially cited in the previous chapter), to distinguish it from the prefatory remarks on each individual poem. It has been suggested that the latter, called collectively the Little Prefaces, may have been the accretive work of more than one author at different times. See Jiang Shanguo 蔣善國, *Sanbai pian yanlun* 三百篇演論 (Taipei: Shangwu, 1976), pp. 79–83.

In translating this passage I am following the commonly accepted variant of *you* 憂 ("is anxious") for *ai* 愛 ("loves") but am retaining *ai* 哀 ("is sorrowful") rather than the suggested emendation of *zhong* 衷 ("sincere") because it continues the many echoes in this passage of Confucius' comment on the poem in *Analects* III.20, cited above.

for the king; thus it is she who tosses and turns until finding them. Kong Yingda, who added "notes" (*shu* 疏) to Zheng's commentaries and Mao's annotations and published them all together, elaborates on Zheng's emendation.[19]

This was not, however, the final word. When the Song dynasty scholar Zhu Xi 朱熹 (1130–1200) turned his attention to the *Classic of Poetry*, he did not offer a novel interpretation of the *Guan ju* himself, which is often the case with other poems, but chose to agree in general with Mao, and not with the latter's followers. His annotation to the first stanza, which sets the scene of the poem, reads:

> King Wen of the Zhou possessed a sage virtue from birth and obtained the sage young lady of the Si 姒 clan to be his mate. The people [ladies] of the palace, upon her very arrival, saw her retiring, chaste, and tranquil virtue, and thereupon wrote this poem. It says that those ospreys join together and cry *guan guan* to each other on the islet in the river; how will this secluded young lady not make a good mate for their lord? It says that their joining together in mutual joy and respect is like that of the ospreys, whose feelings for each other are extremely strong yet who maintain the separation of the sexes.[20]

Thus Zhu Xi introduces one new element here, a remark that the song was composed not by some unknown poet but by the ladies of the palace themselves. He also treats the first two lines of the second stanza differently, reading it not—as had Mao—as a literal description of the queen's activities in preparation for ritual sacrifices, but—like the opening couplet—as a juxtaposed, analogical image: just as picking the water

[19] *Zheng yi*, 1A/12a–13a/pp.55–57. Ma Ruichen 馬瑞辰 (1782–1853) points out that neither Mao nor the preface mentions a search for palace ladies, and that Zheng and Kong have misunderstood the phrase in the preface which reads "is anxious to present her worth" 憂在進賢 to mean "is anxious to present worthy ladies." *Mao shi zhuan jian tong shi* 毛詩傳箋通釋 (rpt. Taipei: Zhonghua, 1968), 2/1a. James Legge in his translation of the preface follows this (mis-)reading, p. 37.

[20] Wang Hongxu 王鴻緒, ed., *Shi jing zhuan shuo hui zuan* 詩經傳說彙纂 (hereafter referred to as *Hui zuan*), compiled by imperial authority in 1727 (rpt. Taipei: Dingwen-hua chubanshe, 1967), 1/7a/p.55. In alluding to the extreme feelings of the ospreys for each other, Zhu Xi is accepting a Zheng Xuan gloss on one of Mao's glosses. Mao had written: 鳥摯而有別 (*Zheng yi*, 1A/12a/p.55): "the birds *zhi* yet maintain separation." The meaning of the word *zhi* 摯 was still subject to dispute into the Qing dynasty, but Zheng read it as 至 ("extreme") and thus interpreted Mao to be saying that the birds had an extreme attraction to each other yet maintained their proper distance (*ibid.*). Zhu agrees that these birds "remain faithful to each other without discord, and the mates usually travel together without being improperly intimate" (*Hui zuan*, 1/6b/p.54).

plants requires an arduous search, so a young lady of such rare beauty and virtue will be obtained only after much looking and many sleepless nights (*Hui zuan*, 1/8b/p.55).

Another Song dynasty commentator, Yan Can 嚴粲 (fl. 1248), who usually follows Mao, also rejects the Zheng Xuan/Kong Yingda interpretation and sees the poem as celebrating the marriage of King Wen and his queen. He also expands on Zhu Xi's reading of the comparative aspects of the opening couplet:

> Ospreys by nature mate only once but reside in different places: this is maintaining separation [of the sexes] and not being licentious. Also by nature they like to stay put; once settled they do not move again: this is an image of reclusion and proper quietude. Thus they are used to evoke [*xing*] the queen. The ospreys' cry of *guan guan* on the islet in the middle of the river is far from human habitation; this evokes the queen's virtuous reputation, which is heard of far and wide though she remains deep within the palace.[21]

Not until the work of the Qing dynasty philologist Yao Jiheng 姚際恆 (b. 1647) do we encounter a significantly different interpretation of the *Guan ju*. In his notes to this poem Yao raises several objections to the Zheng/Kong view, which he thinks the preface also shares, that the poem is celebrating the queen's search for other palace ladies, most of which center on the fact that the images (of the ospreys calling to each other) and diction ("young lady" parallel to "lord"; the word "mate" in line 4) suggest a relationship of husband and wife rather than concubine and lord. Against Zhu Xi's idea that the poem was composed by a palace lady praising her queen, Yao argues that it is unlikely such a person would have been capable of the elevated sentiments evident in the poem. He can only conclude, therefore, that it has nothing to do with King Wen or his queen at all but that it is a simple epithalamium for some nobleman and his bride.[22] Yao does, however, attribute a more general significance to this event: the joyful marriage "is an omen that the house of Zhou's fortunes are rising, and can be used to regulate the officials and transform all under heaven" (p. 15). As far as the water plants are concerned, he rejects both notions of earlier commentators that the queen is picking them and that they serve a comparative function; they are simply objects chosen from the same scene—a water-bound islet—from which the ospreys were taken (p. 16).

[21] *Shi qi* 詩緝 (rpt. Taipei: Guangwen [1960]), 1/15a.
[22] *Shi jing tong lun* 詩經通論 (rpt. Hong Kong: Zhonghua, 1963), 1/pp.14–15.

53

Having surveyed these various exegeses, we might ask, first of all, if the *Guan ju* is indeed an allegory. Most modern readers would, I believe, hesitate to respond in the affirmative, at least if judging by Western definitions of the mode. If allegory may be considered to be an extended metaphor, we should search first for the possible implicit comparisons that are being developed in the poem. Are the ospreys a metaphor for a married couple? Most modern commentators reject this idea. Plant-picking for mate-searching? Even the traditional scholars disagree. Are the "pure young lady" and "lord" metaphors for the king and queen or king and palace lady—or simply epithets for them? Certainly none of these pairs "exhibits the normal relation of concretion to abstraction" which Rosamond Tuve has observed is expected of Western metaphor, for in each case the two elements of the correspondence are drawn from the same concrete realm.

It is difficult, moreover, to locate the development of any fictional, sub-stitutive structure in the *Guan ju*. Even if we were to grant a metaphorical relationship between the various natural images and the human situation, we would expect an allegory to speak only of the former and allow them to point obliquely to the real but unstated concerns of the poet. Here, how-ever, both "levels" are present and are simply juxtaposed. In this the *Guan ju* is representative of the great majority of poems in the *Shi jing*, for among the 160 Airs of the States, for example, there are only two for which human referents are not unequivocally present in the text; of these only the second creates the typical fictional "void" of allegory, whose very meaning consists in asserting its function as a series of signifiers for some-thing beyond the text. The first is poem 5, *Zhong si* 螽斯 (*Zheng yi*,1B/7b–8b/pp.84–86), which becomes substitutive only in the hands of Zhu Xi and, following him, James Legge; for that reason I use the latter's translation here:

Ye locusts, winged tribes,	螽斯羽
How harmoniously you collect together!	詵詵兮
Right is it that your descendants	宜爾子孫
Should be multitudinous!	振振兮
Ye locusts, winged tribes,	螽斯羽
How sound your wings in flight!	薨薨兮
Right is it that your descendants	宜爾子孫
Should be as in unbroken strings!	繩繩兮
Ye locusts, winged tribes,	螽斯羽
How you cluster together!	揖揖兮

| Right is it that your descendants | 宜爾子孫 |
| Should be in swarms![23] | 蟄蟄兮 |

The early commentators and preface writer agree that the subject of this poem is present in the third and fourth lines of each stanza, namely, the blessed numerousness of the progeny of King Wen's queen, made possible by her freedom from jealousy and willingness to allow him other concubines. The first two lines of each stanza, then, function simply as comparative images from nature juxtaposed to the human situation with which the poet concerns himself, and the poem does not therefore exhibit the formal structure of allegory. For Zhu Xi, however, although the poem is still seen as a praise of the queen, the "sons and grandsons" in each case refer to the offspring of the locusts, with no actual reference to the queen herself. It thus exemplifies for him a metaphorical comparison (*bi* 比), which he defines in his commentary on the poem: "A comparison compares that object with this object. The queen was not jealous, and her sons and grandsons were numerous. Therefore, the many concubines use the locusts' living together in a group and having numerous sons and grandsons as a comparison to her. [The poem is] saying that [the queen] has this virtue, and thus it is right that she should have this good fortune. All subsequent cases of using comparisons are modeled on this" (*Hui zuan*, 1/20b/p.61). Or as Legge explains it: "The piece is purely metaphorical (比), T'ae-sze [the queen] not being mentioned in it. The reference to her only exists in the writer's mind.... The locusts cluster together in harmony, it is supposed, without quarrelling, and consequently they increase at a wonderful rate; each female laying, some say 81 eggs, others 99, and others 100" (p. 11).

To consider *Zhong si* as an implicit extended comparison requires a willingness to take the "sons and grandsons" as referring to locusts, one which most readers are not likely to possess. It is only in poem 155, *Chi xiao* 鴟鴞 (*Zheng yi*, 8B/1b–3b/pp.708–11) that we find a case where the entire poem more likely involves an otherness of reference:

Barn owl, barn owl,	鴟鴞鴟鴞
You have taken my young ones,	既取我子
Do not destroy my (house) nest;	無毀我室
I have loved them, I have toiled for them;	恩斯勤斯
My young children, for them you should have pity.	鬻子之閔斯
When heaven was not yet clouded and raining,	迨天之未陰雨
I took those mulberry roots,	徹彼桑土
I turned them to make window and door,	綢繆牖戶

[23]Legge, *The She King*, pp. 11–12.

Now you low-down people,	今女下民
Does anyone dare insult me?	或敢侮予
My (hands) claws were grasping	予手拮據
The *tu* herbs I picked,	予所捋荼
The bundles of straw which I hoarded;	予所蓄租
My (mouth) beak was all sore;	予口卒瘏
Do you say that I still have no chamber and house?	曰予未有室家
My wings are worn out,	予羽譙譙
My tail is shrunken;	予尾翛翛
My house is perilously high up,	予室翘翘
It is tossed about by wind and rain;	風雨所漂搖
My cry is alarmed.	予維音曉曉

(Karlgren, p. 100)

What this poem actually concerns is, of course, by no means certain. The preface, Mao and followers, and Zhu Xi all take the speaker to be the duke of Zhou, the paragon of early Zhou history revered by Confucius, the barn owl(s) as his two rebellious brothers who were threatening the stability of the young dynasty, and the poem as an explanation of why he therefore had to kill them. Karlgren, however, believes that here "a lady fights for her rights as wife in the house, for which she has worked so hard. She likens herself to a threatened bird." In any case, it is noteworthy that even here the poem is not as consistently substitutive as it might have been, something evident in the translation above. Each word in parentheses represents the literal original, which Karlgren has seen fit to replace with a word representing the speaker unambiguously as a "threatened bird"; only in the final stanza do we see him/her actually referring explicitly to parts of a bird's body. And this is the clearest case in the Airs of the States of such an extended comparison.

The *Guan ju*, however, does not employ such a potentially allegorical structure. But we might still ask a second question—whether or not we should nevertheless label (and perhaps condemn) the exegetical tradition just surveyed as allegoresis, a process which focuses, as Maureen Quilligan observed, "on the manipulations the reader can make with a text." For an answer, we should take a closer look at those "manipulations."

There are in fact two different though obviously related interpretive processes being performed on poems such as the *Guan ju*, one focusing on the function of the images that tend to open each stanza, and the other involving the situation of the poem as a whole. As mentioned above, the commentators called the images *xing*, one of six terms associated from an early date with the *Classic of Poetry*. Although no evidence exists to prove that the composers of the poems in the anthology were employing such rhetorical devices consciously and intentionally, traditional annotators clearly assumed that to be the case. The early history of these terms is rather complicated and deserves some discussion; later shifts in their definition shall be considered in subsequent chapters.

The terms *fu* 賦 ("exposition"), *bi* 比 ("comparison"), and *xing* 興 ("stimulus") first appear in the *Zhou li* 周禮 (*Rituals of Zhou*), along with *feng* 風 ("air"), *ya* 雅 ("elegance"), and *song* 頌 ("hymn"), as the "Six Song-Methods"[24] (*liu shi* 六詩), and resurface in the Great Preface to the *Classic of Poetry* as the "Six Principles" (*liu yi* 六義) of the poems. Whether or not all six terms originally referred to similar phenomena, the author of the Preface writes only about the latter three, which correspond roughly to our notion of poetic subgenres. Some critics have held that the original order of appearance of the six terms—namely, *feng, fu, bi, xing, ya,* and *song*—does not warrant a subdivision into two groups, such as forms and devices, and that they all therefore should refer to one thing, namely subgenres of the poems (*shi ti* 詩體).[25] Nevertheless, the fact that the Mao editors of the text isolate 116 examples of *xing* within individual *feng, ya,* and *song* scattered throughout the entire anthology suggests that it, at least, should be viewed more correctly as a technique rather than a form.[26] And indeed, the opinion of the Tang commentator Kong Yingda that *fu, bi,* and *xing* are usages or techniques (*shi zhi suo yong* 詩之所用), and *feng, ya,* and *song* are forms or subgenres (*shi zhi cheng xing* 詩之成形) has prevailed.[27]

Until the Tang dynasty, the predominant mode of explicating the exposition, comparison, and stimulus focused on what was seen as their shared purpose of political commentary and on the comparative function of the latter two in particular. Zheng Xuan was the first to define all three within a strictly moralistic framework. In comments on the duties of

[24] *Zhou li zhushu* 周禮注疏, in *Shisan jing zhushu*, I, 23/158a/p.796. Chen Shih-Hsiang translates *liu shi* as "six ways of presenting or performing the *Songs*" (in the *Classic of Poetry*). See "The *Shih-ching*: Its Generic Significance in Chinese Literary History and Poetics," in Cyril Birch, ed., *Studies in Chinese Literary Genres* (Berkeley and Los Angeles: University of California Press, 1974), p. 18n33. Guo Shaoyu 郭紹虞, however, has argued recently that the original meanings of the two sets of terms were not the same. See his "Liu yi shuo kaobian" 六義說考辨 in Zhu Dongrun 朱東潤, ed., *Zhonghua wenshi luncong* 中華文史論叢, 7 (Shanghai: Guji chubanshe, July 1978), p. 210.

[25] See Guo Shaoyu, *ibid.*, for a discussion of this issue.

[26] For precise details on the numbers, percentages, and locations of the *xing* labeled in the Mao text, see Zhu Ziqing, pp. 50ff.

[27] In *Zheng yi*, 1A/7a/p.45. Earlier, in attempting to explain the order of the six terms, he says that *fu, bi,* and *xing* follow immediately after *feng* because they are "used in the Airs" (1A/6b/p.44); they are also, however, used in the Elegances and Hymns.

various court music officials mentioned in the *Rituals of Zhou*, he first remarks laconically that "a stimulus is made through resemblance," and then that "a stimulus uses a good object as a comparison to a good situation,"[28] and somewhat later defines them all:

In an exposition the words are set out; they display in a straightforward manner the goods and evils of present governmental teachings. With a comparison one sees a present failing, does not dare to castigate directly, and selects a categorical correspondence to speak of it. With a stimulus one sees a present excellence, disdains flattery, and selects a good situation to encourage it by comparison.[29]

By focusing on a critical function of the two tropes, Zheng Xuan is deviating from the less specifically political interpretation of his forebear Zheng Zhong 鄭眾 (fl. 58–76), whose definition he provides shortly after giving his own: "A comparison makes a comparison to an object, and a stimulus entrusts a situation to an object."

Kong Yingda first cites Zheng Xuan and then rephrases him:

An exposition displays its situation directly without avoiding anything, thus accomplishments and failings are both spoken of. A comparison is a comparison with an object; one does not dare to speak properly, perhaps because there is something to fear, thus [Zheng Xuan] says that "one sees a present failing and selects a categorical correspondence to speak of it." A stimulus is a word that stimulates intention through praise. Thus [Zheng] says that "one sees a present excellence and uses a comparison to encourage it."[30]

Shortly thereafter he also quotes Zheng Zhong's definitions and explicates them:

"A comparison makes a comparison to an object"; anything that says "like/as" (*ru* 如) is a word that is a comparison.... "A stimulus

---

[28] *Zhou li zhushu*, in *Shisan jing zhushu*, I, 7/46a/p.684 and 22/149c/p.787. Actually, in the *Shisan jing* edition of the *Zhou li*, the first passage, an annotation to 大喪廞裘飾皮車, after explaining that 廞 is equivalent to 興, which in turn is like the 興 of the *Poetry*, says that "it is made by similar adornment" 象飾而作之. In the *Sibu beiyao* 四部備要 edition (*Zhou li Zheng zhu* 周禮鄭注, 7/4b), however, we find the gloss I have given, that a *xing* "is made through resemblance." This is the reading given by Zhu Ziqing, p. 62, who referred me to this passage.

[29] *Zhou li zhushu*, in *Shisan jing zhushu*, I, 23/158a/p.796.

[30] *Zheng yi*, 1A/6a–b/pp.43–44. However, between his citing of Zheng Xuan's definitions from the annotations to the *Rituals of Zhou* and his rephrasing, Kong disagrees briefly with the earlier scholar's most important distinction, stating that "actually praising and blaming can both use comparison and stimulus." (1A/6a/p.43)

entrusts a situation to an object," thus *xing* means to arouse (*qi* 起): to select a comparison which draws forth the categorical correspondence and stimulates one's heart/mind. In the text of the *Classic of Poetry*, all examples of using plants, trees, birds, and beasts to manifest meaning are words that stimulate.[31]

Of the three terms under discussion, it was the stimulus that elicited the most widely varying definitions, no doubt because its meaning was so multivalent, and also because it was the only method Mao chose to point out, without, of course, defining it. The term itself appears sixteen times among the poems in the *Classic of Poetry*, though it is defined only once, as the equivalent of *qi* 起.[32] Since both words possess a variety of meanings, including "to begin," "to arouse," and "to inspire," the gloss is not particularly helpful. Moreover, what is clear in these early discussions is the difficulty of distinguishing between the stimulus and the comparison. These definitions stress the comparative properties of both tropes, each of which is seen as drawing upon the categorical correspondences (*lei*) discussed earlier in connection with the *Classic of Changes*; for Zheng Xuan it is the comparison that "selects a categorical correspondence," whereas Kong Yingda writes that the stimulus "draws [it] forth." As if to confuse the two functions even more thoroughly, Kong also writes, in a note to poem 5, that the stimulus is in fact the same as a comparison (*yu* 喻): "a stimulus and a comparison have different names but in reality are the same" (*Zheng yi*, 1B/8a/p.85). The pseudo-Kong Anguo 孔安國 commentary to the passage cited above from the *Analects* (XVII.9) also defines a *xing* as "drawing forth a comparison and linking the categorically correspondent" (*yin bi lian lei* 引譬連類).[33] Thus the only distinguishing factor, of which Kong does remind us, seems to be the ability of the stimulus to evoke something, to stimulate the reader. As he writes on the opening lines of the *Guan ju*, "*Xing* is the name of a comparison. Its meaning is inexhaustible, hence it is called a stimulus. Other examples of it are modeled on this one [the ospreys]" (*Zheng yi*, 1A/12a/p.55).

However, what precisely is "stimulated" or evoked varies according to the predisposition of the commentator. As we have seen, Confucian scholars argue implicitly or explicitly that such images as the ospreys calling to each other on an islet have been used, because of some inherent similarity

---

[31] *Zheng yi*, 1A/6b/p.44.

[32] This appears in the annotations to poem 236, *Da ming* 大明 (*Zheng yi*, 16B/5b/p.1,312). As cited in Zhu Ziqing, p. 54.

[33] Cited by He Yan 何晏, *Lun yu ji jie* 論語集解; quoted by Hu Nianyi 胡念貽, "Shi jing zhong de fu bi xing" 詩經中的賦比興, *Wenxue yichan zengkan* 文學遺產增刊 1 (1957), p. 4.

to proper conjugal relations, to make a moral and political point on a marriage. In their view, what the *xing* "stimulates" is an awareness of the didactic and illustrative import of the poem. Another later tradition focuses on the *emotionally* evocative power of the stimulus, but it is not generally concerned with the interpretation of poems in the *Classic of Poetry*. Certainly both of these emphases—the didactic and the affective—can be found in the earliest pronouncements on poetry such as the Great Preface; they share a grounding in traditional Chinese cosmological thinking on the organic, correlative relationships among all phenomena in the universe—human and non-human, individual and sociopolitical—and the assumption that what a person feels will be the feeling of the times.

Commentators on poems like the *Guan ju* have not agreed, however, on the provenance of the natural images. Whereas the Han Confucians had assumed a selection process based primarily on categorical correlations, from the Song dynasty onward some scholars began to argue that the images were literal, objective elements of the external world, drawn from the poet's actual experience, thus often undermining claims for both their analogical properties and their morally illustrative functions. Ouyang Xiu 歐陽修 (1007–1072) in his *Mao shi ben yi* 毛詩本義 was the first to question the Han exegeses, and Su Che 蘇轍 (1039–1112) continued this line of investigation, declaring that the stimulus was simply something that the poet had seen and responded to. He cites the opening lines of poem 19 ("*Yin* sounds the thunder/On the south slope of Southern Mountain" 殷其雷 / 在南山之陽 [Karlgren, p. 11]) and writes: "There is nothing to be taken from the thunder here; it must be what was seen at the time and what stimulated the meaning.... This is why it is called a stimulus.... In looking at the *Classic of Poetry*, one must first know that a stimulus cannot be the same as a comparison."[34]

Zheng Qiao 鄭樵 (1104–1162), probably the most vocal opponent of the Han school, presents a similar view: "'*Guan guan* cry the ospreys ...' is what stimulated the writer of the poem at some time. He saw something here, and it happened spontaneously to move his heart/mind. All examples of a stimulus involve seeing something here and obtaining something there: there is no relationship of categorical correspondence between the

[34] From his *Shi lun* 詩論, cited by Zheng Yuqing 鄭郁卿, *Shi ji zhuan zhi fu bi xing yanjiu* 詩集傳之賦比興研究 (Taipei: Wenjin chubanshe, 1976), p. 32. Also in *Hui zuan*, 2/18a/p.79.

For a discussion of various trends in Song dynasty scholarship on the *Classic of Poetry*, see Xia Zhuancai 夏傳才, "Lun Song xue Shi jing yanjiu de jige wenti" 論宋學詩經研究的幾個問題, *Wenxue yichan*, 2 (1982), pp. 97–104.

two situations, nor is there a meaning to be sought."[35] And the Qing scholar Yao Jiheng writes that "A stimulus just involves borrowing an object to arouse; it need not have any connection to the proper meaning itself."[36] Moreover, in his annotations to individual poems he also points out that many examples of the stimulus do not have a comparative dimension but were simply part of the scene observed and described by the poet; his explanation of the plant-picking in the *Guan ju* mentioned above is one such case.

This idea again derives from the early theory, discussed in the preceding chapter, that poetry originates in a stimulus-response relationship between the poet and his/her world, and it answers a pressing need to locate a specific, empirical source for a poem. Indeed, even when commentators—whether Han or Song—interpret the stimulus as primarily a comparison they will do their best to read the images as plausible parts of the scene as well. Poem 69, *Zhong gu you tui* 中谷有蓷 (*Zheng yi*, 4A/6b–7b/pp.366–68), for example, consists of three stanzas, the second two varying only slightly from the first:

In the midst of the valley there are motherworts,	中谷有蓷
Scorched are the dry ones;	暵其乾矣
There is a girl who has been rejected;	有女仳離
Pitiable is her sighing.	嘅其嘆矣
Pitiable is her sighing—	嘅其嘆矣
She has met with trouble from a man.	遇人之艱難矣
(Karlgren, p. 47)	

Here both Han and Song commentators agree that the scorched motherworts are not only comparisons to the abandoned woman, they serve as literal evidence of the situation which has supposedly led to her plight—a severe drought that has devastated the royal domain of Zhou and forced the separation of family members. So go the comments of the preface, Mao, Zheng, and Kong (*Zheng yi*, 4A/6b–7a/pp.366–67), of Yan Can (*Shi qi*, 7/10a), and of Zhu Xi, who sums up this reading succinctly: "During a bad year of famine, families must separate from each other.

---

[35] *Liu jing ao lun* 六經奧論, *juan* 1, "Du Shi yi fa" 讀詩易法; cited in Zheng Yuqing, p. 33. The twentieth-century scholar Chou Ying-hsiung also describes the stimulus as being drawn from the poet's "lived world": it "is used to allow the poet to begin by mentioning objects or scenes nearby which are conducive to the poet's subsequent self-expression." See "The Linguistic and Mythical Structure of *Hsing* as a Combinational Model," in John J. Deeney, ed., *Chinese and Western Comparative Literature Theory and Strategy* (Hong Kong: Chinese University Press, 1980), p. 64.

[36] Yao Jiheng, "Shi jing lun zhi" 論旨, in *Shi jing tong lun, juan qian* 卷前, p. 1.

A wife observes things that stimulate her to narrate these mournful, sighing words" (*Hui zuan*, 5/10b/p.147). This type of interpretation, quite logically, assumes that precisely those natural objects that bear some similarity to the human situation of interest will "stimulate" the poet.

Other writers, however, have argued that there is no empirical basis for the image at all. Some say that it functions simply as a stock, stereotypical formula employed for thematic purposes. Yan Can, for example, notes in his comments on poem 92, *Yang zhi shui* 揚之水 (*Zheng yi*, 4D/5a/p.437), that the opening image of each stanza—which also serves as the title—recurs two other times in the *Guo feng* and is used in each case to evoke weakness (*Shi qi*, 8/36b). Unlike the claim for the empirical origin of the image, this argument supports more directly the earlier assumption of some analogical relationship between the natural image and the human situation. Twentieth-century Western scholars have also advocated this notion, among them Marcel Granet, who declares that natural images like the *xing* are actually stock descriptions, "formulae to be introduced ready-made into the songs. They constitute a sort of stereotyped landscape, and, if they are connected with the sentiments expressed, it is not for the purpose of particularizing them, but rather ... to connect them with general customs."[37] C. H. Wang, arguing for the oral-formulaic basis of the *Classic of Poetry*, also describes these images as stock phrases or "type-scenes":

> Often a *Shih Ching* theme is heralded by some reference to natural objects which in various evocative forms prepares for the fixed realization of the content. The reference to natural objects intensifies the poem by association and reminiscence which the audience can be counted on to recognize. The reference is sometimes explicit and sometimes implicit or even cryptic.... The theme appears not only in the longer, narrative poems as mnemonic device, as some scholars tend to think, but in both long and short poems as a universal means of formulaic composition that asks for spontaneous, fixed response from the audience.[38]

This notion of the image as a stereotypical formula is of course quite compatible with the Han assumption of categorical correspondences between natural object and human situation. A more radical rejection of the empirical origin of the stimulus was suggested by some Song dynasty scholars, who described it as an essentially arbitrary opening to a poem or stanza, selected and varied for purely formal reasons such as rhyme, and

[37] *Festivals and Songs of Ancient China*, p. 86.
[38] *The Bell and the Drum*, p. 102.

simply juxtaposed without any meaningful connection to the human topic which follows. Zhu Xi is responsible for first emphasizing the simple apposition of image to human situation. Indeed, his definitions of all three tropes are strictly formal, as in these comments from his edition of the *Shi jing*: "A stimulus first speaks of another object in order to introduce what you are singing of.... An exposition sets forth the situation and speaks about it directly.... A comparison compares that object with this object."[39]

Several remarks in his *Conversations* attempt to distinguish the stimulus from the comparison, in order to diminish any explicitly comparative functions of the former; again no possible moral purpose is mentioned. Zhu Xi notes that "a stimulus and a comparison are close to each other yet not identical";[40] one involves juxtaposition, the other substitution, and the formal differences give rise to different aesthetic effects. "A comparison compares one object to another, and the situation that one is indicating is usually not mentioned in words. A stimulus borrows that object to introduce this situation, and that situation is usually in the following line. Although the meaning of the comparison is to the point, it is shallow, and although the meaning of the stimulus may be remote, its flavor is long-lasting."[41] In the case of the stimulus Zhu Xi stresses that "one need not have been moved by or seen that object."[42] He also selects its possible meanings of "to begin" and "to arouse" to emphasize the fact that its distinctiveness lies in its preceding formally the subject matter at hand.[43] It is also true, however, that his own exegeses to poems in the *Classic* often posit some comparative relation between the natural image and the human situation.

Yet Zhu Xi's stress on technical or affective factors is clear, and this was true for other Song commentators as well. Zheng Qiao, in particular, argues at great length against any meaningful connection between image and situation: music or sound provides the sole criterion for choosing a stimulus:

Now the basis of the poems is sound, and the basis of sound is the *xing*: birds, beasts, plants, and trees are none other than the fun-

[39] *Hui zuan*, 1/6b–7a/pp.54–55; 1/13a/p.58; 1/20b/p.61.
[40] *Zhuzi yu lei* 朱子語類, ed. Li Jingde 黎靖德 (rpt. Taipei: Zhengzhong, 1962; 8 vols.), V, 80/4a/p.3,345.
[41] *Ibid.*, V, 80/4b/p.3,346.
[42] *Ibid.*, V, 80/5b/p.3,348.
[43] For example: "*Xing* just means to begin/arouse, when saying the following verse directly would not be a [good] beginning, so one uses the preceding verse to carry it in" (V, 80/28a/p.3,373), and "The meaning of the word *xing* is 'to begin'—to begin with an object and arouse a meaning" (VI, 81/1b/p.3,388).

63

damental way to stimulate. When the Han Confucians [e.g., Mao and Zheng Xuan] discussed the poems, they did not discuss sound nor did they understand the stimulus, so their study of birds, beasts, plants, and trees was defective.[44]

Zhu Xi also adopted this view in explicating some poems,[45] and it was argued later enthusiastically and at length by Gu Jiegang 顧頡剛 (b. 1893) and other scholars whose remarks are collected in his *Gu shi bian* 古史辨.[46]

This is not to say, of course, that the ideas of categorical connection and moral purpose to the stimulus died out, for nothing was ever lost in the commodious cupboard of Chinese tradition. Chen Huan 陳奐 (1786–1863) of the Qing, for example, amplified the Mao edition of the *Shi jing* with his own notes and declared that "Using [objects] to clarify one's will is called a stimulus.... If you wish to trace how the will manifests itself and how emotions are unending, you must begin with the stimulus. Thus Confucius said: 'Poetry [the *Shi jing*] can be used to stimulate' (*Analects*, XVII.9). All examples of using birds, beasts, plants, and trees to complete one's words are *xing*."[47] Yet even he grants the possibility of formal considerations as well. In commenting on poem 20, *Biao you mei* 摽有梅 (*Zheng yi*, 1E/2a–b/pp.153–54), for example, he writes that the stimulus fills auditory and semantic needs at the same time. The song's first stanza reads:

Shedding is the plum tree,	摽有梅
Its fruits are seven.	其實七兮
Seeking me are several gentlemen—	求我庶士
May it come to being lucky!	迨其吉兮
(Karlgren, p. 12)	

The two succeeding stanzas decrease the number of fruits remaining on the tree and intensify the wish for some action on the part of the courting gentlemen. Commentators generally concur that the speaker is concerned lest she pass the proper time for marriage, though they differ on when precisely that occurs. They also agree that the state of the plum tree is

[44] "Du Shi yi fa," in *Liu jing ao lun*, 1; cited in Zheng Yuqing, pp. 33–34.

[45] For example, in his comments to the first stanza of poem 21, *Xiao xing* 小星 (*Zheng yi*, 1E/2b/pp.154ff), he explains that the image of the stars was selected simply "on the basis of what was seen," and that other details in the stanza are there simply because of rhyme (*Hui zuan*, 2/22a/p.81). Also cited in Liu Guangyi 劉光義, "Shi Shi fu bi xing zhi xing" 釋詩賦比興之興, *Dalu zazhi* 大陸雜志, 34.2 (Jan. 31, 1967), p. 15.

[46] See Gu Jiegang 顧頡剛, *Gu shi bian* 古史辨 (rpt. Taipei: Minglun chubanshe, 1970), *ce* 冊 3. *xia bian* 下編, entries 179–84, pp. 675ff.

[47] *Shi Mao shi zhuan shu* 詩毛氏傳疏 ([Shanghai]: Shangwu, [1936]), 1/p.3.

being used as a comparison to her own, to which Chen Huan adds a further note: "The plum goes from florescence to decay, just like the lifetime of men and women. Plum [*mei* 梅] is homophonous with matchmaker [*mei* 媒]; it is for this reason that the poet saw the plum to evoke a stimulus."[48]

Despite these many controversies, however, the predominant mode of defining and explicating the stimulus suggests that most traditional commentators on the *Classic of Poetry* believed that some relationship of similarity linked it with the main topic of the poem. The image, then, provides a means of placing the situation at hand within a larger, more general context—of linking it with other members of the category to which it belongs, be it proper (or improper) male-female behavior, as in the *Guan ju* and numerous other marriage and courtship songs, or filial relationships, as in poems 2 (*Ge tan* 葛覃) and 32 (*Kai feng* 凱風), or prolific production of progeny, as in poem 5 (*Zhong si*). But is this allegorization? While some of the connections drawn might seem so absurdly contrived to Western eyes as to merit the term allegoresis, from the Chinese point of view it was not a process of attributing true otherness of reference at all. As with the *Classic of Changes*, natural object and human situation were believed literally to belong to the same class of events (*lei*): it was not the poet who was creating or manufacturing links between them. They were linked by correspondence, but not—as in the Western case of allegory— one between two distinct orders; the critic's task lay simply in identifying the general category to which both belonged. In this respect the traditional readings are perhaps closer to those of typology rather than allegory, as discussed in the preceding chapter. The Chinese practice, however, differs from medieval typology in three crucial ways: first, of the two elements, one is usually drawn from nature and the other from the human realm, rather than both from the latter; second, they are assumed to be simultaneous or immediately sequential rather than distant in time; and, third, neither item is granted precedence as the fulfillment of the other.

This extension—or rejection—of categorical correspondences, with its focus on the stimulus, is only one method of interpretation exercised on songs in the *Classic of Poetry*; the second concerns the poem as a whole, although the reading of the *xing*, of course, remains important. It also moves in the opposite direction from the first—not toward the general, but rather toward the specific. Having identified the category type grounding the comparison, the critics feel compelled to pinpoint the occasion as well. We have seen what the traditional commentators did to the *Guan ju*; yet another example which demonstrates the twin goals of generalizing and particularizing is poem 159, *Jiu yu* 九罭 (*Zheng yi*, 8C/ 4a–5a/pp.733–35):

[48]*Ibid.*, 1/p.40.

The fishes in the fine-meshed net are rudd and bream;	九罭之魚鱒魴
I see this young person—	我覯之子
He has a blazoned jacket and an embroidered skirt.	袞衣繡裳
The wild geese fly along the island.	鴻飛遵渚
When the prince returns, we shall have no meeting-place;	公歸無所
I will stay with you one more night.	於女信處
The wild geese fly along the land.	鴻飛遵陸
When the prince returns, we cannot come here again;	公歸不復
I will pass one more night with you.	於女信宿
Therefore, you with the blazoned jacket,	是以有袞衣兮
Do not return with our prince,	無以我公歸兮
Do not make my heart grieve.	無使我心悲兮

(Karlgren, pp. 104–5)

Traditional commentators agree that this poem is a praise of the duke of Zhou. Indeed, all seven poems in the group to which it belongs, from the state of Bin 豳, ancient home of the Zhou ruling family, are viewed by both Han and Song commentators as having been written either by or about the duke, although only the fourth actually mentions him by name (*Po fu* 破斧 [*Zheng yi*, 8C/1a–2a/pp.727–29)]). *Jiu yu*, according to some, represents the feelings of the people in the eastern part of the kingdom—whither the duke had had to pursue his rebellious brothers (see discussion of poem 155 above)—who are loathe to see him return home to the west. (What Karlgren renders as "prince" above, in the belief that "a young nobleman has come in the suite of the prince, and has a love-affair with a lady and a love-meeting. She promises her beau further love concessions, and implores him not to go away with the prince, leaving her alone" [pp. 103–04], is actually "duke" [*gong* 公] in the original; other changes would also obviously have to be made in the translation to accommodate the traditional interpretations.)

So much for the specific reference of *Jiu yu*. Establishing the comparative dimension of the natural images opening the first three stanzas creates some dissension, but the commentators remain undaunted. Mao laconically notes that the net mentioned in line 1 is usually used to trap small fish, whereas rudd and bream are large, and Zheng, echoed by Kong, elucidates this gloss: "This is saying that catching different objects requires different tools. This stimulus is a comparison to the fact that if King [Cheng 成] wishes to welcome the duke of Zhou's arrival,

66

he should use the proper ceremony" (*Zheng yi*, 8C/4a/p.733). Yan Can, who usually follows Mao, takes issue with him here, pointing out that the "nine-pocketed" net of the line is not particularly small, nor are the fish especially large. His point is that *both* net and fish are common and are being used to suggest the ineffectiveness of ordinary ceremony in persuading the duke to remain in the east; what is needed are the special sorts of garments mentioned in the third line. Other later commentators feel, on the contrary, that rudd and bream are by no means so ordinary; Zhu Xi defines them as beautiful species and sees an implicit analogy between the pleasure of seeing them caught in a net and the joy of the eastern populace at viewing the duke of Zhou in his fine robes. Or, as the Qing commentator Zhu Daoxing 朱道行 succinctly puts it, the stanza "uses the difficulty of netting an uncommon fish to evoke the difficulty of seeing an uncommon man" (*Hui zuan*, 9/39b/p.239).

On the "wild geese" of the second and third stanzas the scholars more or less agree: this type of bird, they explain, does not normally fly among islands, nor is it a creature of the land, and this resembles the fact that the duke is only temporarily in the east, his real home lying elsewhere, to the west. Zheng Xuan insists on even greater specificity, arguing that "the wild goose is a great bird and does not properly fly along islands the way ducks and widgeons and the like do. This is a comparison to the duke of Zhou's living now with common people in the eastern capital and having lost his proper place" (*Zheng yi*, 8C/4b/p.734).

III.

Despite these numerous disagreements as to detail, however, the commentators on the *Classic of Poetry* usually concur on three points. First, their readings are moral or tropological; like the third of Dante's four levels of meaning, they are concerned with the conduct of life, with isolating the moral implications of a particular situation. And there is certainly no doubt that some of the poems in the *Classic of Poetry* do have lessons to impart. Poem 52, *Xiang shu* 相鼠 (*Zheng yi*, 3B/1b–2a/pp.298–99), for instance, whose first stanza (echoed with variations by the second and third), runs

Look at the rat, it has its skin;	相鼠有皮
A man without manners—	人而無儀
A man without manners,	人而無儀
Why does he not die?	不死何爲
(Karlgren, pp. 33–34)	

is clearly a moral piece. Yet the commentators persist in extracting similar readings from more recalcitrant songs. Thus they must often argue that a particular poem's lesson is present only implicitly, as in poem 20, *Biao you mei*, cited in part earlier, which would strike a modern reader as expressing the speaker's anxiety over possible spinsterhood rather than a breach of marriage rules, or made by way of contrast, as in poem 82, *Nü yue ji ming* 女曰雞鳴 (*Zheng yi*, 4C/2b–3b/pp.410–12), an aubade which its preface claims depicts a scene from the good old days "in order to criticize a present which delights not in virtue but in sex" (*Zheng yi*, 4C/2a/p.409). It is also true even when they differ so widely as to infer opposite moral lessons. We have already seen many cases in which their accounts of the meaning of a poem differ profoundly, to the point of being mutually exclusive, as in poem 84 above. Other notable examples of such incompatible commentaries include several courtship songs scattered throughout the collection, which are viewed by Mao as critical of licentious behavior yet by Zhu Xi as embodying that very "depravity."

Second, however, despite the tendency toward abstraction inherent in such tropological readings (no matter what the message), traditional exegetes read individual images as concretely as possible, ignoring other plausible purposes. For example, poem 101, *Nan shan* 南山 (*Zheng yi*, 5B/1b–3b/pp.474–78), mentions pairs of dolichos shoes and cap pendants, which Karlgren believes perform a symbolic or ritual function to emphasize the coupling of which this marriage song speaks.[49] The early commentators, however, in addition to identifying the couple involved, read these items simply as part of the bride's literal dowry, note their inappropriateness to each other and to the season of the marriage, and draw appropriate moral inferences from those facts (in their view, the poem speaks of the incestuous relationship between Duke Xiang of Qi 齊襄公 and his sister Wen Jiang 文姜, who had married Duke Huan of Lu 魯桓公 in 708 B.C.; see *Zheng yi*, 5B/1a–b/pp.473–74). Similarly, in poem 104, *Bi gou* 敝笱 (*Zheng yi*, 5B/5b–6b/pp.482–84), which speaks of the journey of "a young lady of Qi" to "her new home," they would not agree with Karlgren that the images of fish bursting their traps that open each stanza are fertility symbols: "The fishes are so plentiful as to burst the wicker fishing-baskets in the water to catch them; so numerous will be the offspring of the bride" (p. 67). Rather, because in their view this poem also speaks of the illicit relationship between Duke Xiang and Wen Jiang, they see the fish traps that are too weak to contain their catch as a comparison to Duke Huan's inability to prevent the scandalous behavior of his wife (*Zheng yi*, 5B/5b/p.482). In other words, the images are not symbols

---

[49] *The Book of Odes*, p. 65.

in the Western sense, which are timeless, context-free, and are believed to embody some transcendent meaning.

Finally, with but a handful of exceptions, these tropological readings are not *generally* didactic but are rooted by the commentators in specific historical contexts. In other words, in their view the *Classic of Poetry* is not just a "textbook of personal morality," as Waley expresses the traditional view,[50] it is one conveying the lessons of specific historical situations. Thus, where references to a particular poem in a historical work like the *Zuo zhuan* can be found, the editors of the Qing dynasty imperial edition of the *Shi jing* will cite them to show that the poem in turn should be read as a historical document.[51] A good example of this is poem 76, *Jiang Zhongzi* 將仲子 (*Zheng yi*, 4B/4b–5b/pp.392–94), whose first stanza reads:

I pray you, Zhongzi	將仲子兮
Do not leap into my hamlet;	無踰我里
Do not break our planted *qi* willows—	無折我樹杞
It is not that I dare regret them,	豈敢愛之
But I fear my father and mother.	畏我父母
You, Zhong, are worth loving,	仲可懷也
But the words of father and mother	父母之言
Are also worth fearing.	亦可畏也
(Karlgren, p. 51)	

Rather than view this as a woman's cautionary word to an overly ardent suitor, the preface to the poem declares that it is criticizing Duke Zhuang of Zheng 鄭莊公 for not disciplining his younger brother, who had "lost the Way" but happened to be his mother's favorite, and for failing to heed the remonstrances of Ji Zhong 祭仲, one of his ministers; the poem supposedly represents Zhuang's response and self-defense to the latter. Kong Yingda notes that the story of the complex relationships among Zhuang, his mother, and his younger brother Duan 段 is given in the *Zuo zhuan*, Yin 隱 1, although that hardly proves that the poem is telling the same tale (*Zheng yi*, 4B/4b/p.392). And, as Legge points out, though the imperial editors recognize the strained nature of this interpretation, they include a citation by Huang Zuo 黃佐 of the following entry in the *Zuo*

---

[50] *The Book of Songs*, p. 336.

[51] For a comprehensive discussion of the numerous references to the *Classic of Poetry* in the *Zuo zhuan* and *Guo yu*, see Zhu Ziqing, esp. pp. 65ff. The Ming critic Yang Shen 楊愼 (1488–1559) argues that this practice of making veiled allusions to a current political situation in fact goes back to the *Spring and Autumn Annals* (*Chun qiu* 春秋); see his *Sheng an shihua* 升庵詩話, in *Xu Lidai shihua* 續歷代詩話, ed. Ding Fubao 丁福保 (rpt. Taipei: Yiwen yinshuguan, 1974; 2 vols.), II, 5/p.881.

zhuan (Xiang 襄 26), which might support the Han dynasty historicist view (*Hui zuan*, 5/25b/p.155): "In B.C. 548, the marquis of Wei was kept a prisoner in Tsin, and the lords of Ts'e and Ch'ing went to the court of that State to intercede for him; and in their negotiations for that purpose, the minister, who was in attendance on the earl of Ch'ing, sang this piece, as suggesting a reason why the prisoner should be let go."[52]

Furthermore, not only are individual poems read as historically referential, but entire groups of songs are interpreted as miniature chronicles of the states from which they were said to originate. Thus just as the *Guan ju* and the other ten poems in the *Zhou nan* section are said to celebrate the virtue of King Wen and his queen, first rulers of the Zhou dynasty, so similar operations are performed on other geographically linked groups of poems: several of the songs of Bei 邶 are seen as dealing with a Zhuang Jiang 莊姜, the wife of a marquis of Wei; the odes of the Royal Domain (*Wang feng* 王風) supposedly reveal the progressive decay of the Zhou ruling household; many of the songs of Zheng are said to speak of Duke Zhuang and his brother Duan (as is poem 76); and the songs of Tang 唐, Qin 秦, Chen 陳, and Bin are all said to record different aspects of the mores in their respective states.

A particularly illuminating example of this process can be seen in the commentaries on the following five Airs of Tang, which appear in this order among the twelve songs supposedly collected from the feudal state of Jin in North China (present-day Shanxi province).

115. *Shan you ou* 山有樞
(*Zheng yi*, 6A/4a–b/pp.527–28; Karlgren, pp. 74–75)

On the mountain there are thorn-elms,	山有樞
In the swamp there are white elms.	隰有榆
You have robe and skirt	子有衣裳
But neither drag nor trail them.	弗曳弗婁
You have horse and carriage	子有車馬
But neither gallop nor spur them on.	弗馳弗驅
You wither and die.	宛其死矣
Another will enjoy them.	他人是愉
On the mountain there are mangroves,	山有栲
In the swamp there are *niu*-trees.	隰有杻

---

[52] *The She King*, p. 126. The imperial editors quote another *Zuo zhuan* entry to show that the preface's interpretation of poem 87, *Qian shang* 褰裳, was the one accepted by the people of Zheng, its state of origin (*Hui zuan*, 5/43a/p.164). And while agreeing with Zhu Xi's reading of poem 94, *Ye you man cao* 野有蔓草, as a description of an illicit tryst in the wilds, the editors also cite two passages from the *Zuo zhuan* to show that it was viewed as a praise of worthy men (*Hui zuan*, 5/52a/p.168).

You have courtyards and chambers	子有廷內
But neither sweep nor sprinkle them.	弗洒弗埽
You have bells and drums	子有鐘鼓
But neither beat nor strike them.	弗鼓弗考
You wither and die.	宛其死矣
Another will preserve them.	他人是保

On the mountain there are lacquer trees,	山有漆
In the swamp there are chestnuts.	隰有栗
You have wine and food—	子有酒食
Why not daily play your zither?	何不日鼓瑟
You should enjoy them,	且以喜樂
And prolong the day with them.	且以永日
You wither and die.	宛其死矣
Another will enter your chamber.	他人入室

116. *Yang zhi shui* 揚之水
(*Zheng yi*, 6A/5a–6a/pp.529–31; Karlgren, p. 75)

Amid stirred waters	揚之水
The white stones shine.	白石鑿鑿
With ecru robe and vermilion collar	素衣朱襮
I will follow you to Wo.	從子于沃
When I have seen my lord,	既見君子
How could I not be happy?	云何不樂

Amid stirred waters	揚之水
White stones gleam.	白石浩浩
With ecru robe and vermilion embroidery	素衣朱繡
I will follow you to Gu.	從子于鵠
When I have seen my lord,	既見君子
How could I be sad?	云何其憂

Amid stirred waters	揚之水
White stones are fretted.	白石粼粼
I have heard the call	我聞有命
And dare tell no one of it.	不敢以告人

117. *Jiao liao* 椒聊
(*Zheng yi*, 6A/6a–7a/pp.531–33; Karlgren, p. 76)

The fruits of the pepper plant	椒聊之實
Spread luxuriantly and fill a pint.	蕃衍盈升
That person there	彼其之子
Is very great and peerless.	碩大無朋

Ah, the pepper plant!	椒聊且
How far its branches reach!	遠條且
The fruits of the pepper plant	椒聊之實
Spread luxuriantly and fill my hands.	蕃衍盈匊
That person there	彼其之子
Is very great and generous.	實大且篤
Ah, the pepper plant!	椒聊且
How far its branches reach!	遠條且

118. *Chou mou* 綢繆
(*Zheng yi*, 6B/1a–2b/pp.539–42; Karlgren, p. 76)

Bound round is bundled firewood;	綢繆束薪
Three stars are in the sky.	三星在天
What evening is this?—	今夕何夕
To see this fine person.	見此良人
Oh thee! Oh thee!	子兮子兮
Wherefore this fine person?	如此良人何
Bound round is bundled hay;	綢繆束芻
Three stars are in the corner.	三星在隅
What evening is this?—	今夕何夕
To see this happy meeting.	見此邂逅
Oh thee! Oh thee!	子兮子兮
Wherefore this happy meeting?	如此邂逅何
Bound round is bundled thornwood.	綢繆束楚
Three stars are at the door.	三星在戶
What evening is this?	今夕何夕
To see this beautiful one.	見此粲者
Oh thee! Oh thee!	子兮子兮
Wherefore this beautiful one?	如此粲者何

119. *Di du* 杕杜
(*Zheng yi*, 6B/2b–3b/pp.542–44; Karlgren, p. 76–77)

There is a solitary russet pear;	有杕之杜
Its leaves are luxuriant.	其葉湑湑
Alone I walk and friendless.	獨行踽踽
How could there be no others?	豈無他人
They are not like my siblings.	不如我同父
Alas, you travelers—	嗟行之人
Why do you not join me?	胡不比焉

| A man without brothers— | 人無兄弟 |
| Why do you not aid me? | 胡不佽焉 |

There is a solitary russet pear;	有杕之杜
Its leaves are abundant.	其葉菁菁
Alone I walk and helpless.	獨行睘睘
How could there be no others?	豈無他人
They are not like my kinsmen.	不如我同姓
Alas, you travelers—	嗟行之人
Why do you not join me?	胡不比焉
A man without brothers—	人無兄弟
Why do you not aid me?	胡不佽焉

As is the case throughout most of the collection, the preface writer interprets each poem as praise or condemnation (and generally the latter) of some situation or personage in the state represented. These Airs of Tang are said to trace a rough chronology—the first in the group (no. 114) supposedly being directed against Duke Xi 僖公, who reigned from 839–822 B.C., and the last (no. 125) said to criticize Duke Xian 獻公 (r. 675–650 B.C.); various other rulers are mentioned along the way. The five poems given here, with the exception of no. 118, are believed to be explicit criticisms of Duke Zhao 昭公 (r. 744–738 B.C.), and in the following ways:

115. "On the mountain there are thorn elms" is a criticism of Duke Zhao of Jin. He was unable to cultivate the Way and order his state; he had resources but was unable to use them; he had bells and drums but was unable to take pleasure in them; he had courtyards yet was unable to sprinkle and sweep them. Government was neglected and the people dispersed. He was on the verge of ruin, and neighbors on four sides were plotting to seize his state without his knowledge. The people of the state made this poem in order to criticize him. (*Zheng yi*, 6A/3b/p.526; cf. Legge, p. 55)

116. "Amid stirred waters" is a criticism of Duke Zhao of Jin. Duke Zhao divided the state to enfeoff [his uncle with] Wo 沃. Wo flourished and grew strong, while Duke Zhao grew smaller and weak. The people of the state were about to rebel and go over to Wo. (*Zheng yi*, 6A/4b/p.528; cf. Legge, p. 55)

117. "Pepper plant" is a criticism of Duke Zhao of Jin. The lords saw Wo flourishing and strong and [its ruler's] ability to regulate his government. They knew that it would grow in prosperity and greatness and that its descendants would possess the state of Jin. (*Zheng yi*, 6A/6b/p.531; cf. Legge, p. 56)

118. "Bound round" is a criticism of the chaos in Jin. The state was in chaos, thus marriages did not take place at the proper time. (*Zheng yi*, 6B/1a/p.539; cf. Legge, p. 56)

119. "Solitary russet-pear" is a criticism of the times. The lord was unable to maintain the affection of his clansmen; his bones and flesh left him and scattered. Living alone without brothers he was about to be annexed by Wo. (*Zheng yi*, 6B/2b/p.542; cf. Legge, p. 56)

The Mao annotations label each one of the opening images here as *xing*, with varying degrees of explanatory comments. About "On the mountain there are thorn-elms," Mao notes simply that "the ruler of the state has resources yet is unable to use them, like the mountains and swamps which are unable to use their resources by themselves" (*Zheng yi*, 6A/4a/p.527). Yan Can refers this reading explicitly to the failings of Duke Zhao and the impending threat to his control of Jin by his uncle Huanshu 桓叔, whom he had enfeoffed with the territory of Wo (*Shi qi*, 11/7a–b). Zhu Xi, however, writes that this poem simply repeats the *carpe diem* message of the one preceding it (no. 114, *Xi shuo* 蟋蟀, *Zheng yi*, 6A/2b–3b/pp.524–26; Karlgren, p. 74). He cites poem 115 as an example of how the stimulus is merely a way of introducing the subject of a poem; its first two lines "have no meaning other than to stimulate or introduce as stimulus" the next couplet (*Hui zuan*, 7/4a/p.188).

In the case of poem 116, "Amid stirred waters," major commentators agree with the preface that it is alluding to Duke Zhao and his uncle and that the opening images are implicit comparisons, but they do not concur on the precise referents, thereby producing mutually contradictory readings. Mao is silent, but Zheng Xuan writes that

> stirred-up waters quicken the current and the rushing swirl rinses away filth and turbidity, causing the white stones to gleam brightly. This stimulus is a comparison to Huanshu, prospering and strong, who eliminated what the people abominated so that they were able to attain the possession of propriety and righteousness. (*Zheng yi*, 6A/5a/p.529)

Zhu Xi, however, reads this as a comparison likening Zhao to the soft, weak waters and his uncle to the firm, prominent rocks. Ouyang Xiu and Yan Can agree (*Hui zuan*, 7/5b–6a/p.189). On "Pepper plant," Zheng Xuan again expands on the preface and writes: "The pepper plant is by nature fragrant yet has few fruits. Here the fruits contained by one plant spread extensively and fill a pint, which is unusual. This stimulus is a comparison to Huanshu, who is a relative of the lord of Jin yet his progeny are numerous and will prosper more every day" (*Zheng yi*, 6A/6a/p.531).

Zhu Xi is unsure of the reference but mentions the preface's allusion to Huanshu; his Yuan dynasty descendant Zhu Gongqian 朱公遷 and Yan Can accept the earlier identification unequivocally (*Hui zuan*, 7/8a/p.190).

"Bound round" elicits a particularly interesting group of disharmonious interpretations. Mao, followed by Yan Can, believes that the poem presents a positive image of couples waiting until proper ritual times for marriage, "like firewood and hay awaiting human action to be bound." The "three stars" are placed by them in the constellation Shen 參 (Orion), which is said to be "just appearing in the eastern quadrant" of the sky (in the tenth lunar month, according to Legge [p. 180]), thereby marking a permissible time to marry (*Zheng yi*, 6B/1a/p.539). Kong Yingda explains that this image is meant to indicate the absence of such proper observances in the state of Jin; he also assumes that Mao takes the speaker throughout the poem to be a man (*Zheng yi*, 6B/1b/p.540), an assumption warranted by the fact that Mao glosses the word for "beautiful one" (*can zhe* 粲者) in stanza three (lines 4 and 6) as "a great minister's one wife and two concubines" (*Zheng yi*, 6B/2b/p.542). In opposition to Mao, Zheng Xuan believes that the three stars refer to the constellation Xin 心 (Scorpio), which is not seen in the eastern sky until the end of the third lunar month or beginning of the fourth; hence the poem is chronicling the *failure* to be married at the proper time, a reading confirming in a more direct manner than Mao's the preface writer's opinion. Zhu Xi accepts Zheng Xuan's identification of the three stars as part of Scorpio, but finds that the thrust of the poem is to celebrate a marriage that has occurred, however late, rather than to criticize a breach of propriety. In this vein he argues for three shifts in speaker: from the wife alone in the first stanza, to both husband and wife in the second, and to husband alone in the third.[53] We should note that, whatever their disagreements, the traditional commentators all read the "three stars" as a specific temporal reference for the song; it would not occur to them to assume with Karlgren (who bases himself on the gloss of *can zhe* as the three wives of a dignitary) that the constellation "of course symbolizes the three beautiful girls" (p. 76).

Finally, Mao, Zheng Xuan, and Kong Yingda agree with the preface that "Solitary russet-pear" uses its opening natural image to criticize by contrast the increasing isolation of Duke Zhao. The latter two are forced to perform some exegetical contortions to arrive at this reading, because of what Karlgren has convincingly demonstrated to be a likely corruption of the text—the insertion of a negative (*bu* 不) into Mao's gloss on *xu xu*

---

[53] *Hui zuan*, 7/9a–10a/p.191. On this he has the support of Qian Zhongshu, who explains that the poem thereby follows a typical "ternary thematic scheme" (*san zhang fa* 三章法). See his *Guan zhui bian* 管錐編 (Peking: Zhonghua, 1979; 4 vols.), I, 120–21.

湑湑: "branches and leaves joining" (hence "luxuriant").[54] Kong, for example, must explain it in the following way:

> This speaks of a solitary russet-pear growing by itself whose leaves are luxuriant and flourishing yet whose branches are sparse and distant and do not join each other. This evokes the ruler of Jin, who is distant from his clansmen and is not intimate with them, resembling the russet-pear's branches and leaves not joining each other. Because the ruler is not close to his brothers he causes bones and flesh to separate and disperse; the ruler thus walks alone within the land, friendless and without any intimates. (*Zheng yi*, 6B/3a/p.543)

Zhu Xi and Yan Can both agree on the abundance of the russet-pear's leaves (*Hui zuan*, 7/10b/p.191; *Shi qi*, 11/16b), but Zhu rejects the specific reference to Duke Zhao, preferring instead to read the poem as "the words of a man without brothers who laments his being alone and seeks help from people."

IV.

The interpretations we have considered are moralizing, but didacticism alone is not the same as allegoresis. More importantly, they make the poems topically allusive, which again I see as something different from Western allegoresis. The traditional commentators read the poems in the *Classic of Poetry* not as fictional works composed ad hoc to create or correspond to some historical reality or philosophical truth, but as literal vignettes drawn from that reality. They are not making the poems refer to something *fundamentally* other—belonging to another plane of existence—than what they say, but are revealing them to be specifically referential. The process is one of *contextualization*, not allegorization, and one that proved to be the dominant tradition in later criticism as well, which preferred to read a poet's works as literal records of actual experience, from which a biography could be constructed. Thus the moral lesson is not accidental or arbitrary, but one that arises from a specific context, and for a specific historical reason.[55]

---

[54] Karlgren, *Glosses*, pp. 205–06.

[55] This preference for the specific is illustrated by a contrast made for different purposes by C. H. Wang in an article on the imagery of the Airs of the States. Wang points out that the Greek myth of Atys' self-castration and bleeding to death under a pine in response to Rhea's love-crazed pursuit of him led to the sanctification and worship of *all* pine trees. In the *Classic of Poetry*, on the other hand, a type of pear tree is celebrated because Prince Shao 召伯 once rested under it (poem 16, *Gan tang* 甘棠), but the reverence is attached to that

Why did they do this? The reasons for the moralizing are fairly clear: to rationalize the praise lavished by Confucius on a collection that included some apparently inconsequential and often alarmingly forthright love songs; to explain why, as historical sources had it, he had troubled to compile the anthology at all, as a supposed gauge of the sentiments of the people; and to justify its position as a work of scripture, to which it ascended during the Han along with historical, ritual, and divination texts. This process is one with which the West is not unfamiliar, as in exegeses of the *Song of Songs*. It is also possible that the puzzling relationship of many of the opening natural images to the rest of the poem led commentators to search far and wide for ways to explain the apparent arbitrariness of their appearance. Having discovered some emblematic function for the images, they might have gone on to apply it to the poem as a whole. Why the poems should also have been made topically referential is a slightly more complex question, to which I can only suggest some possible answers.

In the first place, some of the poems in the *Classic of Poetry* are indisputably historical. Poem 131, *Huang niao* 黃鳥 (*Zheng yi*, 6D/3b–4b/ pp.592–94), for example, refers to the documented burial of Duke Mu of Qin 秦穆公 in 621 B.C., during which three noblemen were buried alive with him (*Zuo zhuan*, Wen 文 6), and is therefore one of the few datable poems in the anthology. The poem exhibits the typical form of the Airs of the States—three stanzas, each opened by a natural image varied slightly each time and followed by the human situation at hand, or the classic *xing* method:

---

particular tree only. See Ye Shan 葉珊 (C. H. Wang), "Shi jing Guo feng de cao mu he shi de biaoxian jiqiao" 詩經國風的草木和詩的表現技巧, *Xiandai wenxue* 現代文學, 33 (1967), pp. 124–25.

Actually, the myth Wang alludes to is Phrygian in origin, Atys is more commonly spelled Attis (to distinguish this figure from another Atys, who in Lydian myth was killed by a boar), and the woman is more properly known as Cybele—who did occupy the same position as mother of the gods in Phrygian and Lydian mythology as did Rhea for the Greeks, and who may even have been Attis' mother. In most versions of the legend Attis does not seek to escape Cybele's clutches and the two are described rather as mutual lovers; the self-castration was therefore caused by a jealous, hermaphroditic Agdistis, who was actually Attis' grandfather, for from his own severed genitals had sprouted an almond tree, by which Attis' mother Nana had been miraculously impregnated. The cult of Attis and Cybele as god and goddess of vegetation and fertility developed into an elaborate spring festival by Roman times (not attested to until A.D. 354 but certainly imported several centuries earlier). The week-long ritual involved fasting, purification, the bringing of a pine tree into the temple, orgiastic rites leading to the self-mutilation of the cult's priests, and a joyous celebration of Attis' subsequent resurrection. See *The Oxford Classical Dictionary* (London: Oxford University Press, 1970), entries for "Attis," pp. 146–47, and "Cybele," pp. 303–04, and Sir

Crosswise fly the yellow birds,	交交黃鳥
They settle on the jujube trees.	止于棘
Who follows prince Mu?	誰從穆公
Ziju Yanxi....	子車奄息

Crosswise fly the yellow birds,	交交黃鳥
They settle on the mulberry trees.	止于桑
Who follows prince Mu?	誰從穆公
Ziju Zhonghang....	子車仲行

Crosswise fly the yellow birds,	交交黃鳥
They settle on the thorn trees.	止于楚
Who follows prince Mu?	誰從穆公
Ziju Qianhu....	子車鍼虎

(Karlgren, p. 84)

Although Zhu Xi believes that the image simply represents something the author of the poem happened to see (*Hui zuan*, 7/33b/p.203), most other commentators attribute some comparative function to it. Mao writes: "The yellow birds come and go according to the seasons and attain what is rightfully theirs; a man's death should also be that which is rightfully decreed for him," and Zheng elaborates on this:

The yellow birds settle on the jujube to seek peace for themselves; if this jujube is not peaceful then they move. This stimulus is a comparison to the similar way a minister serves his ruler. Here Duke Mu makes his ministers follow him into death, and the poem criticizes [the ministers'] inability to attain the original purpose of the yellow birds in setting on the jujube. (*Zheng yi*, 6D/3b/p.592)

For the Song commentator Cao Cuizhong 曹粹中 (*jinshi* 進士 1119–26) the grounds for comparison are slightly different: "What men delight in

---

James George Frazer, *The Golden Bough*, Part IV, Vol. I: *Adonis, Attis, Osiris: Studies in the History of Oriental Religion* (London: Macmillan, 1913; rpt. 1980), 263ff. Frazer also mentions an account in Ovid (*Metamorphoses* X) of Attis' changing into a pine tree after his death. (p. 265)

Chin-Ten Shu has made much the same point as I in a dissertation which I came across only after substantially completing this chapter: "Allegorization, Western and Chinese, both operate from the premise that literature is referential. Allegorical critics in the West tend to view a literary work as a reference to experiences of the sensible world which, in turn, refer to a more abstract structure of reality. While taking a referential view of literature, Chinese allegorical critics—the exegetes of the *Book of Poetry*, generally do not see the hidden meaning as necessarily more removed from the pale of common sense. Instead, it still refers to the experiences of the sensible world. It gains its significance because it fulfills the peculiarly culture-bound conditions for significance: capability for historical verification or moral/political edification." "Allegorical Structure," p. 39.

are the beautiful cries and color of the yellow birds, just as what they loved were these three good men" (*Hui zuan*, 7/33/p.203). Whatever the case, perhaps this served as a model for or granted license to similarly topical readings of other poems, in which natural images were read as illustrative emblems.

Second, it is possible that the frequent usage of passages from the *Classic of Poetry* as a means of capping an argument or conveying information obliquely in the *Zuo zhuan* and *Guo yu* inspired the later commentators on the songs to make them as morally pointed and specifically historical as possible. As I mentioned earlier, they could turn a reference in a historical text around to serve as proof that a song was historically referential. And, third, many of the poems are so brief and elusive that they literally cry out for a context, one which in some cases could be supplied only by linking them with other songs in their group. Given the spareness of obvious expressive or narrative function in the text itself, history leaped to the rescue.

Indeed, I would argue that the tendency on the part of the preface writer and commentators to view poems within a regional group as comprising some kind of narrative sequence comes close to creating the functional equivalent of the epic in the West. Quite aware of the controversial nature of this claim, I should state from the outset that it has not been motivated by any desperate urge to locate an epic in China's literary history, as was the scholarship of many twentieth-century Chinese intellectuals. Certainly, the very meaning of the term "epic" is still being argued, but for the moment I am working with definitions given in the *Princeton Encyclopedia of Poetry and Poetics*: the epic "imitates men as they are and as they ought to be"; is "concerned with actions consequent upon good moral choices, but also with errors and frailties, with happiness and unhappiness"; characteristically presents "outstanding and noble people"; and may be "deliberately conceived ... to give meaning to the destiny of a people, asserting the implications of their history" (p. 243).

An epic is an extended narrative that can provide origins, structure, and meaning to a culture, something that certainly did not exist in any comprehensive form by the time the *Shi jing* annotators began their work during the Han dynasty. While I certainly have no intention of arguing that these scholars were consciously seeking to create such a culturally unifying work, it does seem that they treated the *Classic of Poetry* as if it were. As we have seen, a look at almost any group of Han glosses on the songs of an individual state reveals that the commentators read the poems as comprising a more or less coherent, chronologically arranged document of universal human tendencies and concerns and of the fate of the specific government at hand. In particular, their readings of the imagery of the poems resemble quite closely those most appropriate to Western epic. Mikhail Bakhtin has written of the important fusion of individual and collective life in the epic and the consequent focus on the surface level of events:

> *Individuums* are representatives of the social whole, events of their lives coincide with the events of the life of the social whole, and the significance of such events (on the individual as well as the social plane) is identical. Internal form fuses with external: man is all on the surface....

And he observes that this affects the status of the imagery in the epic:

> Metaphors, comparisons and in general tropes in the style of Homer have not yet lost their unmediated meaning, they do not yet serve the purposes of sublimation. Thus an image selected for comparison is worth just as much as the other member of the comparison, it has its own independently viable significance and reality....[56]

Bakhtin's remarks here describe with remarkable precision the assumptions behind the traditional commentators' readings of the evocative imagery of the *Classic of Poetry* and their adherence to interpretations asserting the empirical provenance of an image and relying on the principle of categorical correspondence, which attributes equal reality and ontological importance to each member of a relationship. The poems themselves, of course, were not written with any epic function in mind, although taken as a whole their scope is certainly comprehensive. Unlike the great Western works, moreover, the songs were not viewed as imitations of human actions but as records of actual events or actual responses to them. Nevertheless, the scholars were entrusting the poems with a very similar purpose. History alone could function as revelation, offering the kinds of lessons and models that classical epic gave to Western culture.

In conclusion, then, I would suggest that the Confucian commentators on the *Classic of Poetry* were validating the anthology in the only way allowed by a non-dualistic cosmology—by attesting to its roots in history. Where Western allegorists attempted to prove that Greek myth possessed a deeper philosophical or religious meaning—an abstract, metaphysical dimension[57]—so the Chinese exegetes had to demonstrate the literal truth

---

[56] Mikhail Bakhtin, "Forms of Time and of the Chronotope in the Novel: Notes toward a Historical Poetics," in *The Dialogic Imagination: Four Essays*, ed. Michael Holquist, trans. Caryl Emerson and Michael Holquist (Austin: University of Texas Press, 1981), p. 218.

[57] Cf. Northrop Frye's comment that the rationalization of Greek myth represents one of the earliest forms of allegorical interpretation, one that attempted to diminish the apparent foolishness of divine behavior and interpret the gods instead "as personifications either of

value of the songs: not a metaphysical truth, however, but the truth of this world, an historical context. Tropological discourse, the elucidation of the moral and social value of the text which they shared with Western allegorists,[58] was not enough, for morality had to have a context. Thus, whereas didactic literature in the West commonly aims to present a vision of the world as it ought to be, Chinese didactic criticism sees literature as inferring lessons from the world as it actually is or was.[59] This practice was grounded in the earliest Confucian doctrines on the identity of ethics and politics (sociopolitical interaction as simply individual and family behavior writ large), ideas which were developed by Han dynasty thinkers into cosmological systems linking all moral, historical, and natural phenomena by elaborate correlative networks. These same concepts certainly also motivated the interpretation of the stimulus as a comparison to the human event.

Traditional Chinese poetics and criticism continued to operate under these assumptions, insisting on specifying concrete historical sources and references for any poet's work. Indeed, given the de-emphasis on such notions as creation ex nihilo and fictionality (owing perhaps to the conspicuous lack in indigenous Chinese cosmogonic thinking of a creator-figure), these were the most plausible explanations for the genesis of a literary text. Moreover, like the stimulus-response model from which it derives, this empirical explanation of the origin of a poem could provide a ready-made, supposedly irrefutable meaning for it as simply a record of that experience. As Jonathan Culler has pointed out in discussing the subjectivism of romantic poetry, when the source of poetry can be explained

---

moral principles or of physical or natural forces." Frye also notes that "Judaism had similar difficulties, and the extensive commentaries of Philo on the Pentateuch are the most ambitious of the earliest Jewish efforts to demonstrate that philosophical and moral truths are concealed in the Old Testament stories." "Allegory," *Princeton Encyclopedia of Poetry and Poetics*, p. 13.

[58] See Michael Murrin, *The Veil of Allegory: Some Notes Toward a Theory of Allegorical Rhetoric in the English Renaissance* (Chicago: University of Chicago Press, 1969), p. 62: "One cannot speak of a person as a lion without passing a value judgment on that person. In this sense all tropological discourse functions as a medium for moral value and continues the late classical tradition, in which the poet molds the invisible standards by which his society lives. Moral exegesis is inherent in allegorical form and particularly apparent in hyperbole."

[59] Siu-kit Wong makes a similar point when he argues that the word *ci* 刺, which appears frequently in the prefaces to individual poems and which I translate as "criticize," should not be rendered—as has been done by others—as "satirize": "it seems to me that English satire is much less personal that what *ci* connotes, much more concerned with *general* human folly and vices, even exemplified in particular persons, whereas the Chinese verb usually implies some individual human target." See his *Early Chinese Literary Criticism* (Hong Kong: Joint Publishing Co., 1983), p. 8.

as follows: "when standing before this particular scene I felt this; I thought that," then "the relationship between object and meaning is given a history, assimilated to a model of stimulus and response which cannot be easily questioned," and this is a "strategy designed to protect the attribution of meaning, to assert that the object is a natural cause of its meaning...."[60]

Thus the "secular" poetic tradition would continue to regard a poem not as a work of fiction but as what Barbara Hernnstein Smith has called a "natural utterance," which

> not only occurs *in* a particular set of circumstances—what is often referred to as its *context*—but is also understood as being a response *to* those circumstances. In other words, the historical "context" of an utterance does not merely surround it but *occasions* it, brings it into existence.

This occasion *is* the meaning of a poem, ascertained from asking

> *why it occurred*: the situation and motives that produced it, the set of conditions, "external" and "internal," physical and physiological, that caused the speaker to utter that statement at that time in that form—in other words, what we are calling here its *context*.[61]

Although such an approach might be dismissed as "shallow, reductive, or 'literal-minded'" (*ibid.*, p. 34) to critics working within a different set of norms, it was, I maintain, perhaps the only possible option for a tradition based on a stimulus-response method of poetic production rather than a mimetic one.[62] Poetry chronicled the life of an individual as naturally as it did the fate of a feudal state. As I mentioned in Chapter One, there were, of course, several subgenres of poetry—most notably *yuefu*, or the Music Bureau folk songs which were first collected during the Han dynasty and then imitated by literati for centuries afterward, and the lyric meters (*ci*) of the late Tang and Song—which often employed personae and depicted clearly fictional situations. Yet even in those cases the critical tradition would persist in its attempt to read them as referring, however, obliquely, to the life history of the poet.

The development of such forms does suggest, however, that the most common imagistic practices of the *Classic of Poetry* came to be augmented and modified in important ways over the course of the next

---

[60] Culler, "Literary History, Allegory, and Semiology," p. 265.

[61] Barbara Hernnstein Smith, *On the Margins of Discourse*, pp. 16, 22.

[62] For a discussion of how such presumptions of nonfictionality might affect the reading of later poetry, see Stephen Owen, "Transparencies: Reading the T'ang Lyric," *Harvard Journal of Asiatic Studies*, 34.2 (Dec. 1979), pp. 231–51.

several hundred years. In particular, the typical juxtaposition of elements whose relationship required the elucidation of the exegete and the equally typical reluctance to employ the substitutive methods so familiar to Western metaphor were to undergo significant changes in the hands of poets and critics. Indeed, when we turn now to the major work of the next great poetic anthology, we shall see the prototype for a use of imagery that represents an important complement to that of the *Classic of Poetry*.

CHAPTER THREE

Imagery in

"Encountering Sorrow"

I.

To MOVE from the *Classic of Poetry* to the *Songs of Chu* is to encounter the poetry of a culture with, at first glance, markedly different literary, religious, and material roots. It is not difficult to summon up the hoary clichés that contrast the two anthologies, a distinction that goes back to Zhong Hong's *Classification of Poetry*, which singled them out as the sources of the two main traditions in Chinese poetry. Thus, for example, the *Shi jing* is the compilation of songs from the northern "cradle" of Chinese civilization, down-to-earth, emotionally restrained, and concerned with the unpredictable conditions of everyday life for its rural society. The *Chu ci* 楚辭 anthology, on the other hand, originating in the state of Chu on the Yangzi River, was southern and hence tangential to the ancient Chinese cultural and political sphere; it was, therefore, prone to literal and figurative flights inspired by the importance of shamanism within the culture, and filled with highly subjective outpourings of unrelieved self-pity and lament. The meters of the poems are also dissimilar, perhaps owing to differences in the types of musical instruments accompanying them: in contrast to the predominantly tetrasyllabic line of songs in the *Shi jing*, one can find in the *Chu ci* poems written in a double line of five substantive syllables each. As might be expected, these later works tended to be longer as well. All of these generalizations have been applied in particular to the longest poem in the *Songs of Chu*, the *Li sao* 離騷 or "Encountering Sorrow," attributed to Qu Yuan 屈原 (?343–278 B.C.) and, unlike most of the other works in the anthology assigned to his authorship, probably genuinely of his hand; it is on that poem that this chapter shall focus.

Of all the many contrasts that have been drawn between the *Classic of Poetry* and the *Songs of Chu* as products of northern and southern cultures respectively, the most important and, to modern eyes, the most striking is one that was strangely scarcely remarked upon by traditional commentators: the latter collection's use of imagery. As we have seen, poems in the first anthology typically juxtapose their imagistic material drawn from natural and human worlds in an unspecified relationship, to be explained by exegetes as connected by virtue of analogy, rhyme, empirical experience, or perhaps as not related at all. The number of instances in which overt mention of one member of the relationship is suppressed— the method so familiar to readers of Western poetry—is negligible indeed. In the *Li sao*, on the other hand, this substitutive method apparently becomes the key mode of discourse, such that large sections of the poem could, it seems, be claimed to exemplify the practice of *aliud verbis, aliud sensu ostendit*, "presenting one thing in words, another in meaning," what has been singled out since Quintilian as the hallmark of extended metaphor or allegory.

In stressing the apparently substitutive mode of imagery in the poem I am not attempting to claim that it employs exactly the type of Western metaphor defined by Christine Brooke-Rose. Indeed, as I argued in Chapter One, such a formulation is not only rigid but is also usually applied without attention to the broader implications of such a method. It is precisely upon those implications that I shall be focusing, which requires not only determining if in fact the *Li sao* really is using an imagery of replacement; second, what that would mean; and, third, whether or not it was interpreted along those lines. Curiously, whereas, in contrast to the poems in the *Classic of Poetry*, "Encountering Sorrow" would appear to present a ready-made case for a Western-style consistently allegorical interpretation, one that would assume the purely fictional status of the elements explicitly given in the text and that would seek to replace them by the poet's "real," unspoken, and abstract meaning, this is precisely what the traditional critics do not commit themselves to undertaking.

What unity they do display is evident primarily in their shared assumption that the true subject matter of the poem is the poet's autobiography, centering on his political life at the court of Chu. In one sense, this can be viewed simply as an example of the urge to contextualize, to make a poem historically referential, that we have observed in the commentary literature on the *Classic of Poetry*. Yet there is no poem in the earlier anthology that roots itself so specifically in the subjective feelings and experiences of one known individual, thus lending itself to the identification between author and speaker that was to become one of the hallmarks of traditional Chinese criticism. The 2,469 words of "Encountering Sorrow"—the earliest surviving long poem—develop a narrative that begins with an account of the speaker's birth and ends with a resolution to leave the world, both of which naturally frame a life's course and seem to correspond in particular to that of Qu Yuan. The profligate use of the first person pronoun—in marked contrast to both earlier and later poetry—also encourages an autobiographical reading. At the same time, however, this interpretation must take shape in the distinct absence of an unambiguous or coherent set of guidelines within the poem itself.

For all of the valiant attempts by commentators, particularly during the Qing dynasty, to divide "Encountering Sorrow" into sections and discern in it a logical pattern of events, no arrangement emerges as necessarily more convincing than any other. To be sure, there is a consistency of emotion that propels the work forward to its conclusion, and the final decision to depart makes sense coming where it does, but the sequence of episodes and the shifts in mode of discourse throughout the poem remain as bewildering and unrecalcitrant as ever. These oscillations are mirrored, if on a different plane, in the exegetical vacillations of the critics as well.

To summarize the poem briefly: Qu Yuan opens by establishing his credentials—a divine ancestry, an auspicious date of birth (although commentators have disagreed on when precisely this occurred), and an equally propitious name. Inner, moral beauty has been bestowed on him from birth, he says, and he spends much of the poem providing suitable external counterparts to it: planting, plucking, plaiting, weaving, donning, and ingesting a profusion of exotic herbs and flowers. His "Fairest," however, chooses to take the word of slanderers and refuses to pay heed to him, thereby provoking countless laments on the speaker's incompatibility with his times. He invokes legendary historical figures to justify his position, undertakes a fantastic journey to all corners of the cosmos, only to find the door of heaven closed to him, and engages in a number of unsuccessful suits of other women. Two favorable oracles, one of which again chronicles a number of historical precedents, attempt to assure him that, somewhere, he will find a suitable mate and/or ruler. Disgusted by the inconstancy and corruption of those around him and inspired by the auspicious predictions, he sets off on a second dragon-borne journey to the highest heavens, only to find that his groom and steeds, homesick, balk and refuse to carry him further. The poem concludes with the four-line envoi that grounds most autobiographical readings yet is still subject to debate:

186. Enough! There are no true men in the state: no one to understand me.	已矣哉！國無人莫我知兮
Why should I cleave to the city of my birth?	又何懷乎故都
Since none is worthy to work with in making good government,	既莫足與為美政兮

I will go and join P'eng Hsien in the place where he abides.[1]　　　　吾將從彭咸之所居

The word "government" (*zheng* 政) suggests, retrospectively, the context within which to place the rest of the poem, and, depending on how one identifies Peng Xian 彭咸, Qu Yuan is either resolving here, after much faltering and hesitation throughout the narrative, to drown himself as did a virtuous minister of old (the traditional interpretation), or deciding to abandon politics and study the occult with a shaman (Hawkes).

Certain constants do emerge from the frequent confusion of the narrative. As Chen Shih-hsiang observed, the poet's sense of time provides a kind of "leitmotif" to "Encountering Sorrow" as a whole.[2] There is a pervasive sense of panic at the swiftness of time's passage and corresponding changes in moral standards and behavior; the poet, on the contrary, steadfastly upholds the honorable ways of the past (and, as just mentioned, calls upon legendary precedents to validate himself). Statements attesting to the agonizing contrast between two time frames recur throughout the poem:

38. I take my fashion from the good men of old:　　謇吾法夫前修兮
A garb unlike that which the rude world cares for:　　非世俗之所服

48. But I am sick and sad at heart and stand irresolute:　　忳鬱邑余侘傺兮
I alone am at a loss in this generation.　　吾獨窮困乎此時也

90. Many a heavy sigh I heaved in my despair,　　曾歔欷余鬱邑兮
Grieving that I was born in such an unlucky time.　　哀朕時之不當

154. The age is disordered in a tumult of changing:　　時繽紛其變易兮
How can I tarry much longer among them?　　又何可以淹留

162. Since, then, the world's way is to drift the way the tide runs,　　固時俗之流從兮
Who can stay the same and not change with all the rest?　　又孰能無變化

[1] David Hawkes, "Li Sao," in *Ch'u Tz'u: The Songs of the South* (Boston: Beacon, 1959), p. 34. Further translations from this work will be his, identified in the text simply by line numbers.
[2] See his "The Genesis of Poetic Time: The Greatness of Ch'ü Yüan, Studied with a New Critical Approach" (published posthumously), *Tsing Hua Journal of Chinese Studies*, New Series X.1 (June 1973), pp. 1–44.

The contrast between two time frames and their corresponding ethical systems not only helps to explain the emotional situation of the poet, it also suggests the pertinence of looking for other discrepancies in the poem, i.e., between what is said and what is meant. The legitimacy of this search is then confirmed by the presence of other sections in the poem that suggest that they be taken at other than face value. For one thing, the unsuccessful pursuit of a loved one clearly serves as the narrative frame of the poem yet strikes one as the unlikely actual topic of the work because of the several political references. The object of desire even shifts in gender: from being, apparently, male at the beginning of the poem it becomes female in the second half (the suitor's sex presumably changes as well). The important point, though, is the failure of the quest—whether because of inept matchmakers, machinations of other jealous lovers, or, simply, the inconstancy of the loved one. Moreover, the flower imagery—in garden and garb—is striking for its profusion, particularly in contrast to other poems in the Chinese tradition—and is central to an interpretation of the poem, for it immediately invites what we would be tempted to call a metaphorical reading. And, finally, the two major journeys on which the poet embarks introduce elements of the mythological and supernatural that are apparently difficult to reconcile with what should be a straightforward autobiography, once again suggesting the appropriateness of a non-literal interpretation. Commentators have certainly proven receptive to this invitation, extended only rarely by the *Classic of Poetry*. Yet while they tend to read the objects and figures in the poems as substitutive images for moral and/or political qualities and situations, their commitment to this mode is by no means thoroughgoing, and the differences and disagreements among them are illuminating.

II.

The first eight lines of "Encountering Sorrow" provide a brief genealogy for the poet as someone descended from the divine founder of the Chu royal house and blessed with an auspicious birth. This section appears relatively unproblematic and has elicited few comments outside of attempts to specify the date and precise astronomical configuration at the time, yet the fact that in the fourth distich Qu Yuan puns on his name rather than mentioning it directly provides an important clue to the method of the rest of the poem. In other words, whereas in the poems of the *Classic of Poetry* one is confronted directly with all the necessary elements of the situation at hand, there is evidence in the *Li sao* from the very beginning of a possibly more elliptical method of presentation. Only Wang Fuzhi notices this, observing further that "concealing a name yet talking hold of its meaning in order to compose the text is like what the genre of exposition (*fu*) does."[3] And indeed, this sort of punning—semantic, auditory, and ideographic—was to become one of the hallmarks of later works in that genre.[4] The poet thus makes explicit here the kind of comparison between inner virtue and external object that runs throughout the entire poem.

In the next two lines Qu Yuan provides the justification for reading much of the imagery in the poem as external correlates for internal states:

5. Having from birth this inward beauty,   紛吾既有此內美兮
I added to it fair outward adornment: 又從之以修能

and follows it with the first of many examples:

6. I dressed in selinea and shady angelica,   扈江離與辟芷兮
And twined autumn orchids to make a garland. 紉秋蘭以爲佩

Thus Wang Yi 王逸 (fl. 110–120), the first major annotator of the text, not surprisingly explains that this "garland" or girdle (*pei* 佩) is "an image [*xiang*] for virtue,"[5] one of the earliest instances, to my knowledge, where this term is taken from its context in the *Classic of Changes* and applied to a literary text. Most commentators agree with him, although Wang Yuan 汪瑗 (fl. 1600) argues that "the ancients actually did use orchids to make garlands, so this is not just a metaphor, and scholars should know this."[6] This is only the first of many disagreements between commentators on the extent to which images should be taken literally.

Wang Yi, however, remains undaunted, and his method prevails. When Qu Yuan speaks of gathering angelica and plucking sedges, the Han commentator explains: "Angelica sheds its skin and does not die, and sedges do not wither in winter: these are used as comparisons for the fact that, though slanderers may wish to make things difficult for him, he has received his nature from heaven and it can never be altered" (1/5b/p.18). Noteworthy is his determination to offer as concrete—in this case botanical—an explanation as possible for the comparison, to demonstrate

[3] In his *Chu ci tong shi* 楚辭通釋, preface dated autumn 1685 (rpt. Shanghai: Zhonghua, 1965), p. 2.

[4] For an example of readings exploiting these possibilities, see Friedrich Bischoff, *Interpreting the Fu: A Study in Chinese Literary Rhetoric*, Münchener Ostasiatische Studien, Vol. 13 (Wiesbaden: Franz Steiner Verlag, 1976).

[5] Wang Yi, *Li sao jing zhang ju* 離騷經章句, in Hong Xingzu 洪興祖 (1070–1135), ed., *Chu ci bu zhu* 楚辭補註 (rpt. Taipei: Yiwen, 1973), 1/4a/p.15. Subsequent page references are generally given in the text.

[6] From his *Chu ci ji jie* 楚辭集解, cited in You Guoen 游國恩, *Li sao zuan yi* 離騷纂義 (Peking: Zhonghua, 1980), p. 33. Further page references from this compendium, abbreviated as *Zuan yi*, will usually be given in the text.

that there is nothing far-fetched or fictional about it at all. Zhu Xi, as is the case with his annotations to the *Classic of Poetry*, is much less insistent on providing a specific basis for the image, explaining simply that Qu Yuan is "speaking of picking objects whose fragrance is long-lasting as a comparison for his conduct, which follows the eternal path of loyalty and goodness."[7] When the poet goes on to speak of the swift passage of time and the fading, falling foliage, Wang Fuzhi assumes that "the alternation of springs and autumns is a comparison to the prosperity and decline of the state" (p. 3), and Zhu Xi agrees that the poet's worries about the fading of his "Fairest's" beauty express "the mind of a minister" who fears that his ruler will not have time to thrive (1/14b/p.14). Wang Yi identifies this "Fairest" (*mei ren* 美人) specifically as King Huai of Chu 楚懷王, explaining that he is so called because "a ruler's clothes and adornment are beautiful and fine," once again insisting both on the precise basis for the image and the historical specificity of its reference, although Hong Xingzu adds that Qu Yuan elsewhere also uses "Fairest" as an epithet for other virtuous men and for himself (1/5b/p.18). Huang Wenhuan 黃文煥 (*jinshi* 1625) and Qian Chengzhi 錢澄之 (1612–1693) believe that he is referring to himself here, whereas Lu Bi 魯筆, also of the seventeenth century, explains that "the method of comparing a beautiful person to a ruler is one bequeathed by the Three Hundred Poems":

> It begins with the praise of one's wife which in time is borrowed as a comparison for a virtuous ruler, but in the case of the wife one is indicating her beautiful appearance, whereas with the virtuous ruler one is indicating his beautiful virtue. Because this verbal method is intriguing and is close to the emotion of the poem, both the Airs and the *sao* employ it.[8]

More to the point, of course, would be the statement that this is the legacy of the exegetical tradition of the *Classic of Poetry*, and not of the anthology itself. In any event, the putative relationship between the two collections is an issue to which I shall return shortly.

The next section is generally read as a chastisement of the "Fairest," who has failed to heed the speaker's counsel, refusing to gallop forth with the "brave coursers" (i.e., "virtuous wisdom" [*Chu ci bu zhu*, 1/6a/p.19]) harnessed for him and to utilize properly his "fragrant flowers" (i.e., "virtuous officials" [*ibid.*]). Hence the poet fears lest his lord's "chariot" ("the state" [*ibid.*]) be dashed and laments, "20. But the Fra-

[7]Zhu Xi, *Chu ci ji zhu* 楚辭集注 (rpt. Taipei: Huazheng, 1974), 1/4b/p.14. Subsequent references to be given in the text.

[8]Excerpts from Huang Wenhuan's *Chu ci ting zhi* 聽直, Qian Chengzhi's *Qu gu* 屈詁, and Lu Bi's *Chu ci da* 達 are all given in *Zuan yi*, pp. 43–44.

grant One refused to examine my true feelings." Here Wang Yi again provides a concrete explanation for this epithet: "The ruler of the people dresses in sweet-smelling clothes, thus fragrant plants are used as a comparison" (1/7b/p.22), but Zhu Xi disagrees, arguing (somewhat obscurely) that this Fragrant Plant is too insignificant to stand directly for the ruler, that it was a common mutual appelation among people at the time and is being borrowed merely to suggest the ruler.[9] Again, the disagreement between the two most famous commentators on the *Li sao* here is typical, with Wang Yi interested in demonstrating the specificity both of the comparison and of the historical referent, and Zhu Xi concerned merely with indicating the presence of a more general political or moral critique.

Qu Yuan continues to attest to his unwavering devotion and worth, describing his assiduous cultivation of orchids, melilotus, sweet lichens, and other fragrant flowers (26–27), which are interpreted either as his own virtuous conduct (Wang Yi, *Chu ci bu zhu*, 1/8b/p.24) or other upright officials whom he has attempted to recommend for service;[10] in either case, however, they waste in the "rank weeds" of calumny and corruption. After a brief declamation on the greed, envy, and malice of others, the poet gives evidence of his own purity:

34. In the mornings I drank the dew that fell from the magnolia;	朝飲木蘭之墜露兮
At evening ate the petals that dropped from chrysanthemums.	夕餐秋菊之落英

Here Wang Yi reveals the influence of cosmological theories of correspondence flourishing during the Han, explaining that by naming the two times of day Qu Yuan is indicating his absorption of the essence of both *yang* and *yin*, the complementary forces of light and dark, male and female, etc. (1/10a/p.27). Wang Yuan, however, dismisses this and all other such comparisons, stating that the poet is simply chronicling the untiring extent of this efforts at self-purification (*Zuan yi*, p. 106). Other commentators engage in a heated controversy over whether or not chrysanthemums really do drop their petals (*Zuan yi*, p. 105), suggesting the power of a general reluctance to allow a substitutive image to depart from the realm of strict accuracy. Hu Yinglin's 胡應麟 (1551–1602) retort in his *Shi sou* 詩藪 that Qu Yuan is simply using the object as a comparison and that even if chrysanthemums do not drop their blossoms, it is perfect-

---

[9] In his *Chu ci bian zheng shang* 楚辭辯證上, included in the *Chu ci ji zhu*, 7a/p.330.

[10] Jiang Ji 蔣驥, *Shandaige zhu Chu ci* 山帶閣注楚辭, preface dated 1713 (rpt. Shanghai: Zhonghua, 1962), p. 36.

ly permissible for him to say that they do (*Zuan yi*, p. 106), may sound reasonable to Western ears, but the rarity of this argument within the Chinese context provides a convincing index of the forces operating against truly allegorical interpretation. In any event, the poet goes on plucking, trimming, plaiting, and knotting his aromatic plants—activities that are read as indirect indications of moral virtue by most scholars, although Wang Yuan typically is less eager than others to jump to such comparisons. At one point, for example (in a comment on distich 36), he issues a blanket refutation of all such interpretations. Wang Yi and Hong Xingzu had explained the poet's mention of tree roots (*gen* 根) as referring to the root (*ben* 本) of his character, and Wang Yuan states flatly that "the two scholars' explanation that takes this comparison is wrong. [The poet] does nothing more than speak of pulling out the roots of a fragrant tree in order to tie up valerian to make a girdle, and that is all. How could he ever have meant to compare this to the basis [of his character]? Reasoning from this example, then how can subsequent mentions of varied objects also be comparisons?" (*Zuan yi*, p. 113) Wang Yuan's wariness here is generally evidenced by his comments throughout "Encountering Sorrow," which are intent on demonstrating the literal basis of the poem's many images, although instances do occur where, despite the stance just taken, he also discerns certain comparisons at work.

The poet continues by declaiming against the inconstancy of his Fair One, who has been deluded by the jealous chatter of other ladies—the first direct indication of the speaker's assumed sex. Wang Yi notes that these women are other officials and explains the appropriateness of the metaphor: "Women are *yin* and do not act on the principle of independent responsibility, just as, when the ruler acts, the minister follows. Thus they have been used as a comparison to ministers" (1/12a/p.31). The correspondence here has a long tradition; as You Guoen points out, it is spelled out in the *Wen yan* commentary to the second hexagram *kun* 坤, where one finds the principle of *kun* described as that of *yin* in the complementary pair of forces, *yin* and *yang*: "Though it has its beauty, it conceals it in order to follow along in service to the king and does not dare fulfill it [alone. *Kun/yin*] is the way of the earth, the way of the wife, the way of the minister."[11] This recalls again the belief in fundamental cos-

[11] *Zhou yi zheng yi*, in *Shisan jing zhushu*, I, 1/7a/p.19. Cf. trans. of Wilhelm/Baynes, p. 394. Cited in You's *Chu ci lunwen ji* 論文集 (Peking, 1965; rpt. Hong Kong: Wenxing, n.d.), p. 192. Laurence A. Schneider also calls attention to the importance of this equation, referring us to this citation, which, however, he states is from the *Zhou li* rather than the *Zhou yi*. He also cites Herrlee G. Creel, *Shen Pu-hai* (Chicago: University of Chicago Press, 1974), p. 45, as a source providing earlier examples of this king-husband, minister-wife imagery. See Schneider's *A Madman of Ch'u: The Chinese Myth of Loyalty and Dissent* (Berkeley and Los Angeles: University of California Press, 1980), p. 218n27.

mological correlations underlying the *Classic of Changes*, its commentary literature, and notions of the image which were to be transferred to the realm of poetry as well. In other words, the comparison was not construed as an arbitrary one.

Whatever the case, Qu Yuan emphasizes his uniqueness and isolation among this crowd, offering two further analogies to his inability to fit in:

50. Eagles do not flock like birds of lesser species;　　鷙鳥之不群兮

...

51. How can the round and square ever fit　　何方圜之能周兮
together?

After a brief and unsuccessful journey to visit his loved one he returns to his dressmaking:

58. I made a coat of lotus and water-chestnut　　製芰荷以爲衣兮
leaves,
And gathered lotus petals to make myself a skirt.　　集芙蓉以爲裳

Wang Yi takes this completely literally, for a change, seconded by Hong Xingzu's expatiation on the appropriateness of leaves for the upper garment and petals for the lower (1/14a/p.35), an explanation rejected out of hand by Hu Yinglin in the passage cited above. The word "fragrant" (*fang* 芳) appears three times in the next five distichs as Qu Yuan describes himself, and Wang Yi observes that "fragrance is the smell of virtue" (1/14b/p.36), citing a passage from the Great Commentary to the *Classic of Changes*: "Its fragrance is like orchids."[12] In other words, the epithet is true both literally and metaphorically. Zhu Xi, however, believes that these are simply literal descriptions of the poet's garb (1/10b/p.26).

After a sudden decision to travel to all four quarters of the world, Qu Yuan receives a visit from his "maidens" (variously identified), who urge him to tone down his insistence on his purity in isolation. In response he delivers a lengthy plaint that invokes a number of legendary sages and villains in order to validate his conviction that, in the past, only the righteous have been entrusted to govern. Grieving that his age alone seems not to adhere to this rule, he at last departs:

93. I yoked a team of jade dragons to a phoenix-　　駟玉虬以桀鷖兮
figured car
And waited for the wind to come, to soar up on my　　溘埃風余上征
journey.

[12] *Zhou yi zheng yi*, in *Shisan jing zhushu*, I, 7/67c/p.79; cf. Wilhelm/Baynes, p. 306.

What follows, over the next several distichs, is the description of a trip whose dimensions, destinations, and encounters are of supernatural proportions. David Hawkes has argued quite convincingly that this section—and indeed the poem as a whole—represents a "cannibalization" of Chu shamanistic rituals involving an unsuccessful quest of a deity and enacting a magical circuit through the cosmos to acquire and demonstrate power.[13] Wang Yi at first seems to take the account literally, making sure that we know that these dragons, for example, are of the hornless variety (*qiu* 虬) rather than horned (*long* 龍) (1/30b/p.48). Somewhat later, however, it becomes clear that he reads this section as yet another veiled description of an attempt to make contact with the ruler, for he notes that the word "fairy" (*ling* 靈) in distich 95 ("I wanted to stay a while in those fairy precincts") refers obliquely to the ruler; Hong Xingzu further explains that "the dwelling place of the spirits is a comparison to the ruler" (1/21b/p.50). Other commentators whose remarks are collected in the *Li sao zuan yi* engage in a lively debate, either supporting Wang Yi's contention or arguing that the mythological elements should be taken at face value, rather than as political images (pp. 255–56). Zhu Xi, however, displays the least literal cast of mind, for he advises us that the entire account of the journey is in fact fictional: "these words mostly simulate—these objects and events do not really exist" (1/25a/p.35). Such a statement, along with Hu Yinglin's remark on the chrysanthemum debate cited above, is quite rare in the commentary literature, alerting us to the tremendous power of those assumptions within the classical exegetical tradition which would not allow readers to stray far from the literal bases of a comparison.

Thus Wang Yi goes on to read the succeeding denizens of the heavens as governmental figures. The charioteer of the moon, Wang Shu, becomes a minister, presumably because both are linked with the category of *yin*; the Wind God becomes the ruler, recalling an association which goes back to a passage in the *Analects* likening the moral influence of the ruler to that of wind over grass (XII.19); and the Bird of Heaven announcing the poet's arrival becomes a virtuous man (1/33a/p.53). Natural phenomena are interpreted in a similar fashion. Where Qu Yuan writes, for example,

103. The whirlwinds gathered and came out to meet me,   飄風屯其相離兮

Leading clouds and rainbows, to give me welcome,   帥雲霓而來御

---

[13] David Hawkes, "The Quest of the Goddess," *Asia Major*, New Series, XIII.1–2 (1967), pp. 71–94.

Wang Yi explains that the "whirlwinds are irregular and are used to evoke [*xing*—one of the few times this term appears in his commentary] evil groups," and the clouds and rainbows possess "an evil atmosphere as a comparison for flatterers" (1/33b/p.54). Zhu Xi argues against this whole chain of interpretation, in the first place because he feels that no distinctions between good and evil are at work here, and, second, because even if there were, Wang Yi has them wrong. The Song philosopher cites a passage from Mencius which mentions the people regarding the dynastic founding king Tang as they would a rainbow (after a great drought; IB.11) and asks how this could then be serving as an image (*xiang*) for petty or evil men (*Bian zheng shang*, 12b/p.340). Nevertheless, he also subscribes to the dominant political reading of a subsequent distich:

105. I asked Heaven's porter to open up for me;   吾令帝閽開關兮
But he learnt across Heaven's gate and eyed me   倚閶闔而望予
    churlishly.

as "a comparison to seeking a great ruler and not meeting him" (*Ji zhu*, 1/16b/p.38).

What follows this rejection, after a moment of indecision devoted to knotting orchids, is a series of frustrated suits of various "fair ladies." It is here that the sex of the persona in the poem appears to shift from the feminine to the masculine, if, as some commentators (e.g., Zhu Xi) argue, the women being sought are all images for the ruler. Others, however, among them Wang Yi, interpret them as referring to virtuous officials or recluses whom the speaker is seeking as like-minded worthies committed to serving the throne. In any event, the suits are unsuccessful, whether through capriciousness on the part of the women, the presumed competition of other lovers, or ineptitude on the part of matchmakers. A direct statement concluding this section encourages the political reading of the love stories:

128. Deep in the palace, unapproachable,   閨中既以邃遠兮
The wise king slumbers and will not be awakened;   哲王又不寤

an invitation accepted gladly, of course, by the exegetes.

Two oracles follow and seem to promise a turn in the speaker's fortunes. One, a divination offered by Ling Fen 靈氛, returns to the flower imagery in an attempt to persuade the poet that he can seek successfully for love and recognition if he leaves home. Elsewhere, he hears, likings and loathings are attached to their proper objects, and only here (read Chu) have they been reversed:

137. For they wear mugwort and cram their
   waistbands with it;   戶服艾以盈要兮

While the lovely valley orchids they say are not fit
   to wear....   謂幽蘭其不可佩

139. They gather up muck to stuff their perfume-
   bags with;   蘇糞壤以充幃兮

But the pepper-shrub they say has got no fragrance.   謂申椒其不芳

Faltering, the poet solicits a second prediction, this time offered by the
deified ancient Shaman Xian 巫咸, who again urges him to look elsewhere
and not to worry about a "matchmaker," citing numerous legendary
examples of sage ministers accidentally discovered by their rulers while
engaged in humble occupations.

Qu Yuan responds to these auspicious oracles with a renewed lament on
his topsy-turvy age in which time-honored standards have been stood on
their heads:

155. Orchid and iris have lost all their fragrance;   蘭芷變而不芳兮
Flag and melilotus have changed into straw.   荃蕙化而爲茅

Previously fragrant flowers have "all transformed themselves into worth-
less mugwort," and some have surprised him with their treachery. These
are particularly good examples of the type of substitutive imagery which
distinguishes "Encountering Sorrow" from poems in the *Classic of Poetry*. The poet mentions two betrayals in particular, that of Orchid, whom
he had thought "was one to be trusted, / But he proved a sham bent only
on pleasing his masters" (158), and Pepper, who "is all wagging tongue
and lives only for slander" (160). Typically, commentators have ex-
pended great energy on providing the specific identities of these two figures. Wang Yi writes that Orchid (*lan*) refers to Zilan 子蘭, "the younger brother of King Huai," although Hong Xingzu cites the *Shi ji* to emend
this to read King Huai's younger son, younger brother of his successor
King Qingxiang 頃襄 (1/43a/p.73), an annotation that has proven per-
suasive. Pepper (*jiao*) is identified by Wang Yi as a great minister of Chu
named Zijiao 子椒, although there is no historical record of such a person's existence (Hawkes, *Ch'u Tz'u*, p. 214). More cautiously, Wang
Fuzhi suggests that these "all are used as comparisons for men who had
once been involved in the same activities as [Qu] Yuan before they fell
into evil. At the time they must have had specific references but now we
cannot seek them" (*Chu ci tong shi*, p. 20). Zhu Xi, however, resists the
search for a specific historical figure and writes that these lines simply

develop the motif of times and flowers changing introduced earlier (1/22b–23a/pp.50–51), once again demonstrating his preference for more general readings of references. In any event, the poet reassures himself of the constancy of his "garland's" perfume and resolves to act on Ling Fen's favorable oracle and travel afar in search of a lady.

Once again Qu Yuan embarks on a fantastic journey, inspiring equally daring flights of fancy in the commentary literature. Where the poem reads

170. "Harness winged dragons to be my coursers;　　爲余駕飛龍兮
"Let my chariot be of fine work of jade and ivory!"　　雜瑤象以爲車

the critics offer a number of possibilities. Wang Yi simply observes that in harnessing flying dragons, Qu Yuan is "riding animals of bright wisdom," but the Five Ministers' note in the *Wen xuan*, cited in the same edition, expands on this: "Flying dragons are a comparison to the Tao. Jade and ivory are comparisons to the virtue of the ruler. This is saying that in my distant journey I am only harnessing this Tao and this virtue as my chariot." Hong Xingzu, perhaps daunted by these readings, takes the distich at its word: "This is saying that he is using jade and ivory in his chariot and harnessing flying dragons" (which Hong has just helpfully glossed as "having wings") (1/44b/p.76). Other commentators offer further variations. The Ming scholar Zhang Fengyi 張鳳翼 writes in his *Wen xuan zuan zhu* 文選纂註 that "Dragons are divine objects, and ivory and jade have been finely worked to make a chariot. This is a comparison to driving a divine spirit with the principle of the Tao as chariot." Wang Yuan, resolutely literalist to the end, argues that the poet is simply "speaking of the beauty of his chariot, and there is no further meaning to be taken from it. The ancient commentators' explanations of comparisons are erroneous." Heedless of this admonition, Wang Kaiyun 王闓運 (1833–1916) notes in his *Chu ci shi* 楚辭釋 that "'Flying dragons' are a comparison to King Huai.... 'Jade and ivory' refer to jade and ivory paths. Being 'finely worked' means uniting the feudal lords to oppose Qin" (all in *Zuan yi*, p. 454).

The journey then takes on mythical proportions, encompassing legendary locations in far reaches of the cosmos and carrying the poet higher and higher into the heavens. Once again he is betrayed, however, but this time not by churlish gatekeepers or fickle lovers—rather, his own groom and horses, longing for home, refuse to take him farther, and the poem ends with the envoi cited earlier declaring the poet's resolve to join Peng Xian.

97

III.

What can we make of this summary of "Encountering Sorrow" and its commentaries, which is by no means exhaustive but should give some indication of general exegetical trends? In the first place, it is worth noting that few traditional commentators feel impelled to remark explicitly upon the numerous direct and indirect comparisons in the poem—quite different from imagery in the *Classic of Poetry* and remarkable for their form, variety, and profusion. In addition to the many uses of historical allusion to point out overt similarities and contrasts to the present, Qu Yuan employs, as we have seen, imagery and narratives which also establish, implicitly, a second level of reference—the flowers, the travels, the use of a persona, the pursuit of a loved one. Whereas in the *Shi jing* scholars generally confronted images from nature juxtaposed to a human situation in a relationship whose purpose and meaningfulness often eluded even the most imaginative minds, here they are blessed with a text in which the "metaphorical" intent, at least, seems indubitable.

The substitutive method so familiar to Western metaphor and so demonstrably rare in the *Classic of Poetry*, then, seems to constitute a striking feature of "Encountering Sorrow." Indeed, the extent and repetition which characterize much of the imagery would at first glance appear to justify the appelation of allegory to the text, defined traditionally, as discussed in Chapter One, as continuous metaphor. Yet there seem to be few references in the critical literature to the novelty of this method. The Qing commentator Jiang Ji 蔣驥 (fl. 1713) makes passing comment on what he sees as the systematic nature of some of the comparisons: "The *Li sao*'s use of the woman as a comparison to a virtuous ruler and of fragrant plants as a comparison to virtuous officials is a thread that runs throughout from beginning to end."[14] Twentieth-century scholars also remark upon their importance. Lu Kanru 陸侃如 observes, for example, that two distinctive characteristics of the *Li sao* are its use of personification (as in the magpie as matchmaker) and implicit comparison (as in the use of flowers). And You Guoen discusses at some length the *Chu ci*'s innovative use of the woman as metaphorical image, as compared with the *Shi jing*'s use of plants, animals, objects, and natural phenomena.[15]

[14] Jiang Ji, *Chu ci yu lun shang* 語論上, in *Shandaige zhu Chu ci*, p. 190.

[15] See Lu's *Qu Yuan pingzhuan* 屈原評傳; cited in Huang Jiusheng 黃究生, "Liushi nian lai de Chu ci xue" 六十年來的楚辭學, Ph.D. Diss. National Taiwan Normal University, 1977, p. 85. For You Guoen's discussion, see his "Chu ci nüxing zhongxin shuo" 楚辭女性中心說, in *Chu ci lunwen ji*, p. 191. Jao Tsung i 饒宗頤 in his *Bibliography of Chü Tzu (sic)* 楚辭書錄 (Hong Kong: Tong Nam, 1956), also cites an article by Xiao Difei 蕭滌非 on this subject, "Li sao de yong bi" 離騷的用比, *Qinghua zhoukan* 清華周刊, 35.2, which I have not seen.

How sustained and how truly "allegorical," however, is Qu Yuan's use of metaphor? Only a modern commentator like You Guoen is concerned about this problem, taking great pains to demonstrate what he sees as the consistency of Qu Yuan's use of the woman as image for himself. Thus he argues that the "Fairest" in distich 10 does not, as Wang Yi and many other commentators have it, refer to King Huai but to the poet; the fragrant plants are not selected arbitrarily as images of virtue and integrity but because they are appropriate for the feminine persona he has chosen; the various women whom the poet seems to pursue after his first journey are not objects of love for a presumably male protagonist—they are fellow women whom the speaker is entreating to speak to her loved one on her behalf (*Lunwen ji*, pp. 193–99). Yet these efforts are hardly convincing, for we have seen how difficult it is to determine a consistent sex for the speaker. Indeed, despite the fact that the *Li sao*'s use of any one substitutive image or set of images is certainly more developed than is the case with the *Classic of Poetry*, the poem as a whole does not display any discernible systematic pattern to their appearance. From section to section the poet not only shifts between substitutive and nonsubstitutive modes of expression, but he also moves freely back and forth between the various possibilities of the former: gardening, weaving, traveling, wooing, etc. These segments are collocated, juxtaposed to one another rather than contributing toward the development of a continuously allegorical narrative, one which would establish two levels of narrative or distinctly different orders.

These vacillations in mode of discourse are reflected in similar shifts in exegetical strategy. We have seen in the previous section how the commentators couple a willingness in most cases not to take any utterance in "Encountering Sorrow" at face value with, in certain instances, a surprising literalness of their interpretation. Wang Yi's handling of the dragons pulling the poet's carriage, the care he takes to alert us about the presence or absence of horns, is only one of the more memorable examples of this cast of mind. This impulse is related to the wish to identify the elements of the poem as actual historical personages, a tendency we have already observed in the commentary tradition of the *Classic of Poetry*. In other words, as with the earlier anthology, the images are not construed as vehicles for some general, abstract statement but rather as referring to a specific historical context. There is always a concrete basis for an image—thus the references to fragrance or aromatic plants must be explained by the fact that the ruler, for example, actually did dress in sweet-smelling garb. Only Zhu Xi takes exception to this practice—as he frequently does in his annotations to the *Shi jing*—arguing, for example, that Wang Yi's gloss just mentioned on the correspondence between literal and figurative garments is "a great error" and that Qu Yuan's use of the male-female relationship is not meant literally to refer to any particular ruler and official, although it may imply something about them (*Bian zheng shang*, 7a–8a/ pp.330–31). Furthermore, he complains, Wang Yi and other scholars have misled generations into thinking that Orchid and Pepper were actual historical figures rather than a means for Qu Yuan to comment on the degeneracy of his times (16b/p.348).

Zhu Xi's isolation in making these arguments only demonstrates the persistence of the literal frame of mind in traditional readers of both anthologies. Yet the distinctiveness of the *Li sao*'s use of substitution as opposed to the methods of the *Shi jing* was also undeniable. Nevertheless, rather than argue for the differences between the two anthologies, early commentators were more inclined to demonstrate the similarities between them. Certainly, the contrasts which were to become so popular for various reasons in the twentieth-century[16] often overlooked the common cultural ground shared by the two texts. The state of Chu by the fourth century B.C. was no longer merely marginal to Chinese civilization proper and played a key role in politics following the demise of the Zhou ruler's power. Moreover, the mythological and legendary figures named explicitly in "Encountering Sorrow" were those central to the culture of the north, and, as an upright minister devoted to the welfare of his ruler and his country, Qu Yuan is a paragon of Confucian virtue—in fact more so, explicitly, than the speakers of songs in the pre-Confucian *Shi jing*. Traditional critics thus attempted to prove similarities in both content and style between the two works, an effort that raises an important issue and thus merits some discussion.

The earliest extant text in which we can see these links being drawn is Sima Qian's biography of Qu Yuan in his *Shi ji*. This account, paired with a biography of the other early poet associated with Chu, Jia Yi 賈誼 (?201–169 B.C.), has been shown to be in large part a pastiche of quotations from a variety of texts; its veracity has been questioned by many scholars but their accusations have been equally effectively countered.[17] Sima Qian opens by mentioning Qu Yuan's membership in the Chu royal family, the skill with which he acquitted his responsibilities at court, and the respect granted him by the king. When the slander of another jealous official succeeded in estranging the ruler from him, Qu Yuan, "full of sorrowful grief and dark thoughts, composed the *Li sao*." Sima Qian goes

[16] For a discussion of the reasons behind some twentieth-century Chinese critics' advocacy of the north/south contrast, see Schneider, *A Madman of Ch'u*, pp. 94ff.

[17] E.g., by Hawkes, *Ch'u Tz'u*, pp. 15–19, and by Lin Geng 林庚, *Shi ren Qu Yuan ji qi zuopin yanjiu* 詩人屈原及其作品研究 (Shanghai: Gudian wenxue chubanshe, 1957), pp. 30–43.

on to emphasize the poet's righteousness amid difficulty and explains the roots of his song:

> Qu Ping's [his given name] conduct was morally correct and un-swerving; he devoted all of his loyalty and wisdom to serving his ruler, yet slander came between them: this can be called being in difficulty. To be faithful yet doubted, loyal yet slandered—could he be without complaint? Qu Ping's composition of "Encountering Sorrow" was born from this complaint.[18]

As is well known, Sima Qian was convinced of the links between great writing and great suffering—hence his interest in and sympathy for Qu Yuan. By stressing the poet's need to repine or complain (*yuan* 怨), he also recalls the passage in the *Analects* which mentions giving "expression to complaints" (XVIII.9, cited in Chapter Two) as one of four functions of quotations from the *Shi jing* and thus legitimates "Encountering Sorrow" from a Confucian point of view.

The biography continues by making the connection explicit:

> "The Airs of the States love beauty without being licentious; the Les-ser Elegances complain and condemn without being seditious. As for 'Encountering Sorrow,' it can be said to combine both [virtues]!" It praises first [the legendary sage king] Di Ku 帝嚳 and then speaks of [Duke] Huan of Qi 齊桓 [r. 685–643 B.C.], telling of Tang 湯 [first ruler of the Shang dynasty] and Wu 武 [first ruler of the Zhou] in between, in order to criticize events of its times. In its elucidation of the boundless dignity of true morality and the principles of regulat-ing disorder, there is nothing that cannot be seen in its entirety. His writing is terse, his language subtle, his intention is pure, and his conduct incorrupt. What he speaks of is insignificant but it suggests something much greater; he brings forward categorical correspon-dences close at hand yet manifests far-reaching meaning. His intention is pure, thus the objects he names are fragrant, his conduct incorrupt, thus he died rather than bear to give in. He cleansed himself of sick-eningly foul mud, "cast off from amidst corruption and filth in order to soar beyond the dust and dirt." He did not accept the foul defile-ments of the world, "unblemished by dregs from the mire. One can conclude that his intention was equal in brilliance to the sun and the moon." (*Shi ji*, 84/pp.983–84; cf. Hawkes, p. 12)

[18]"Biographies of Qu Yuan and Master Jia" 屈原賈生列傳, *Shi ji hui zhu kaozheng*, 84/p.983. Cf. Hawkes, *Ch'u Tz'u*, p. 12.

The emphasis on Qu Yuan's moral integrity and forthrightness here is familiar enough in Confucian texts, but what is particularly noteworthy is Sima Qian's allusion to the passage from the Great Commentary to the *Classic of Changes* on the symbolic function of the hexagram and, by extension, of the poetic image ("what he speaks of is insignificant ..."), the first instance to my knowledge of such an application, one that was to become frequent in subsequent literature. The historian goes on to detail Qu Yuan's further troubles with the powers of Chu and his eventual banishment; he cites two poems from the *Chu ci* anthology and concludes with the poet's suicide by drowning, a brief mention of his literary legacy, and an indirect vindication of his political policies.

The overt comparison between parts of the *Classic of Poetry* and "Encountering Sorrow" on the basis of their moral qualities was not original to Sima Qian. The Han scholar Ban Gu 班固 (39–92) wrote a preface (*xu* 序) to his no longer extant edition and commentary (*Li sao zhang ju* 章句) in which he attributes the passages enclosed by quotation marks in the excerpt above to Liu An 劉安 (?179–122 B.C.), a Taoist adept and philosopher, the grandson of Liu Bang 劉邦, founder of the Han dynasty, and the second king of Huainan 懷南. Liu An was the author of a now lost *Li sao zhuan* 傳,[19] from which other sections of the *Shi ji* biography were taken as well. Unlike Sima Qian, however, Ban Gu takes issue with the comparison, arguing that it "appears to go beyond the truth," for Qu Yuan should have been able to retreat and complain without being so severely affected by adversity:

> But now Qu Yuan vaunted his talents and praised himself, struggling among the petty groups endangering the state. Because he encountered slander and abuse he upbraided King Huai repeatedly and complained about the misdoings of Pepper and Orchid. His grieving spirit and bitter feelings violently condemned his people, he could not

[19] According to Liu An's biography in the *History of the Former Han*, he received his commission to write the work from the emperor Han Wudi 武帝 in the morning and completed it by the evening meal of the same day (*Han shu* 漢書 [rpt. Hong Kong: Zhonghua, 1970], 44/p.2,145). Cited, *inter alia*, by Fan Wenlan, *Wenxin diaolong zhu*, p. 49n3. The exact nature of his *zhuan* has been subject to some dispute. The Tang commentator Yan Shigu 顏師古 (581–645) noted that the term meant to explicate and discuss, as in the Mao annotations to the *Classic of Poetry* (*Han shu*, 44/p.2,146n6). Wang Niansun 王念孫 (1744–1832), however, in his *Du shu za zhi, Han shu Li sao zhuan* 讀書雜志漢書離騷傳, argued that "*zhuan* 傳 should actually read *fu* 傅, which in ancient times meant the same as *fu* 賦. To be commissioned to write a *Li sao fu* meant that he was asked to approximate [the *Li sao*'s] general meaning and compose it as a *fu* 賦 (exposition)." Fan Wenlan cites these and other remarks and concludes, after a long discussion, on the side of Yan Shigu (pp. 49–50).

102

contain his resentment, and he drowned himself in the river and died.[20]

Although Ban Gu rejects as "excessive" equating "Encountering Sorrow" with the virtues of the *Classic of Poetry*, he does grant its words "breadth, beauty, and elegance" and credits Qu Yuan with having provided the prototype for the *fu* 賦 (exposition), the main literary form of the Han dynasty and of which he himself was a practitioner.

Ban Gu's criticism reflects a kind of backlash against an admiration for Qu Yuan and his work that "had grown to cult proportions" by the first century A.D. and led people, among other things, to label it, like the *Shi*, a "classic" (*jing*).[21] The Han historian himself, in addition to this critical preface, wrote another "Eulogistic Preface" (*zan xu* 贊序), in which there is no hint of condemnation of Qu Yuan's excessive behavior. Speaking of King Huai's refusal to heed his minister's advice not to ally with the state of Qin, for example, Ban Gu writes there:

> Qu Yuan was pained by his ruler's failure to understand the situation and his trust in coteries of petty men. The state was about to be destroyed, and feelings of loyalty and integrity were inexhaustible in his bosom, so he wrote "Encountering Sorrow." From above he brings forth the models of [the sage kings] Yao 堯, Shun 舜, Yu 禹, Tang, and Wen; from below he speaks of the misdeeds of Yi 羿, Jiao 澆, Jie 桀, and Zhou 紂 [all of whom paid for their sins], in order to admonish King Huai. In the end [the king] was unenlightened and believed those who advised the contrary.... After Qu Yuan died Qin did indeed destroy Chu, and his words were mourned over by all virtuous people and thus have been transmitted to later generations.[22]

But the impulse to criticize Qu Yuan's overweening self-righteousness and suicide had its precedents, going back to Jia Yi's "Lament for Qu Yuan" (*Diao Qu Yuan* 弔屈原), which, even as it sympathizes with his predecessor, suggests that the latter might have avoided some of his problems by emigrating to another state, a common strategy at the time. Somewhat later Yang Xiong's 揚雄 (53 B.C. to A.D. 18) "Contra *Li sao*" (*Fan sao* 反騷) proved significant as the

[20] Ban Gu, *Li sao xu*, reprinted, *inter alia*, in Hong Xingzu, *Chu ci bu zhu*, 1/50b–51a/ pp.88–89.

[21] See Schneider, *A Madman of Ch'u*, pp. 23ff.

[22] Ban Gu, *Li sao zan xu*, included in *Chu ci bu zhu*, 1/52a–b/pp.91–92. Jiang Liangfu 姜亮夫 notes that this is "the earliest complete explanation of the meaning of the *Li sao* still extant," in his *Chu ci shumu wu zhong* 楚辭書目五種 (Shanghai: Zhonghua, 1961), p. 313.

first overt condemnation of Ch'ü Yüan's suicide. One must remember that Ch'u poetry was still in vogue (Liu Hsiang's *Chiu t'an* was written only a few years before the *Fan sao*) and that Ch'ü Yüan still represented the paragon of Confucian conduct. Yang Hsiung's position is not that of an iconoclast but of a Confucian who finds Ch'ü Yüan's suicide incompatible with Confucian doctrine.[23]

When Wang Yi prepared his *Li sao jing zhang ju*, the oldest extant edition at present (although he mentions two earlier versions by Liu An and Liu Xiang 劉向 [77–6 B.C.], now lost),[24] he argued eloquently against these attacks on Qu Yuan and insisted on the double filiation of the poet to Confucian models and of his poem to the *Classic of Poetry*. Wang's Postface 敍 following "Encountering Sorrow" opens by mentioning the accomplishments of Confucius and his major disciples and places his fellow native of Chu directly in this line: "And Qu Yuan's conduct was loyal yet he was slandered. With melancholy and mournful thoughts he based himself solely on the principles (*yi* 義) of the authors of the *Poetry* and wrote the *Li sao* in order to admonish those above and console himself below" (*Chu ci bu zhu*, 1/48b–49a/pp.84–85). After discussing briefly earlier editions of the text and then his own, Wang links Qu Yuan with other legendary martyrs like Wu Zixu 伍子胥, Bi Gan 比干, Bo Yi 伯夷, and Shu Qi 叔齊, and argues against Ban Gu's accusation that the poet's interest in "parading his talent and vaunting himself" and his petulant, self-pitying complaints impugned his purity and integrity.[25] Returning to the poem, Wang Yi insists on its resemblance not only to the *Classic of Poetry*, but to the other four as well—"The text of the *Li sao* relies on the Five Classics to establish its meaning" (1/50a/p.87)—and he goes on to compare individual lines with passages in the Classics of Poetry, Changes, and History.

Wang Yi's preface to "Encountering Sorrow" glosses what had come to be the title of the work in a way that does not necessarily define it as a scripture though certainly associates it with the canonical texts. After briefly recounting the poet's background and the beginning of his troubles, he writes:

[23] David Knechtges, "Two Han Dynasty *Fu* on Ch'ü Yüan: Chia I's *Tiao Ch'ü Yüan* and Yang Hsiung's *Fan Sao*," in *Two Studies on the Han Fu, Parerga*, 1 (Seattle: Far Eastern and Russian Institute, 1968), p. 29.

[24] In his "Postface" 敍 to "Encountering Sorrow," *Chu ci bu zhu*, 1/49a/p.85.

[25] Hong Xingzu supplements Wang Yi's implicit defense of Qu Yuan's suicide by stating that, as a member of the Chu royal family, he did not have the option of emigrating to another state, as Jia Yi and Yang Xiong had suggested he could have done (*Chu ci bu zhu*, 1/51a/p.89).

Qu Yuan maintained the loyalty and integrity of his conduct yet was slandered maliciously. His heart was grieved by the troubles and disorder and he did not know how to make a plaint, so he wrote the *Li sao jing* 經. *Li* is "to leave," *sao* is "grief," *jing* is a "path" (*jing* 徑). This means that after his banishment and departure, his heart was filled with sorrowful thoughts yet he still held to the path of the Tao in order to admonish his ruler.[26]

More important, however, is the direct connection Wang Yi draws at the conclusion of the preface between the imagistic methods of "Encountering Sorrow" and those which had been imputed to the *Classic of Poetry*. He had hinted at this earlier in writing that Qu Yuan "had based himself solely on the principles of the *Poetry*," which include the rhetorical tropes of *fu*, *bi*, and *xing*.

> The writing of "Encountering Sorrow" takes the method of *xing* from the *Poetry* and draws out categorical correspondences as comparisons. Therefore, beneficial birds and fragrant plants are used to correspond to loyalty and integrity; noxious birds and foul-smelling objects are used as comparisons to slander and deceit. The Divine Beauty and Fairest One equal the lord; intimate consorts and beautiful maidens are used as analogues to virtuous officials. In dragons and phoenixes is invested the ruler; whirlwinds, clouds, and rainbows are used for petty men. His language is mild and refined, his

---

[26] *Chu ci bu zhu*, 1/1b–2a/pp.10–11. Hong Xingzu, however, provides other explanations of the meaning of the title offered by Sima Qian, Ban Gu, and Yan Shigu and states that none of them mention the word *jing*. Later generations, he says, had called it a *jing*, but this was not Qu Yuan's intention and Wang Yi's gloss was therefore mistaken (1/2a/p.11).

The late Ming scholar He Yisun 賀貽孫 wrote a commentary on the poem, *Sao fa* 騷筏 (*Li sao* the Great Raft [Classic]), which resumes Wang Yi's contention that the text is canonical. In his General Preface to the *Chu ci* (*Chu ci zong xu* 總序) he offers an ingenious defense of this position: "The *Songs of Chu* in their entirety go from 'Encountering Sorrow' to the 'Great Summons' (*Da zhao* 大招). The songs of Chu are not among the Airs of the States, but when we look at the *Chu ci* today, then we can see to what extent Chu did write airs. Scholars distinguish *shi*, *sao*, and *fu* into three categories, yet they do not know that the *Poetry* had *bi*, *xing*, and *fu*; thus *fu* is none other than a genre of *shi*. As for *sao*, it is based on the *Shi* poets' wish to express themselves compassionately, and it speaks with profound pain.... Later generations venerated "Encountering Sorrow" by calling it a classic, and some have doubted this as being excessive. A classic is what is constant, and sorrow involves change. Certainly what changes could never be a classic. Yet 'Encountering Sorrow' has been, from antiquity to the present, the first and greatest text expressing loyal love. Loyal love is the official's constancy. Qu Yuan's conduct changed yet did not lose its constancy; the Changed Airs and Changed Elegances are all included in the *Classic*. Thus, as far as venerating the 'Encountering Sorrow' as a classic is concerned, were the sages to arise again, would they prefer a different term?" Cited in Jiang Liangfu, *Chu ci shumu wu zhong*, pp. 329–30.

meaning is pure and lucid. Among the hundred lords there is none who does not respect his clear loftiness, delight in the beauty of his writing, mourn his lack of fulfillment, or grieve over his intentions. (1/2b/p.12)

This passage is significant not only because it elucidates the principles behind Wang Yi's own exegetical methods, but because it represents the first attempt to extend the domain of the Six Principles terminology beyond the text of the *Shi jing*. Sima Qian's account, with its allusion to the Great Commentary on the *Classic of Changes*, had suggested the important meaning-bearing functions of Qu Yuan's images, but Wang Yi makes this explicit; even more important is his elucidation of what the stimulus does.

The extent to which Wang Yi's interpretation of the term *xing* corresponds to earlier or later usages remains to be seen. Nevertheless, other critics echoed his application of this terminology to "Encountering Sorrow." Liu Xie in his *Wenxin diaolong* had obviously been impressed by the movement to place Qu Yuan's work in the Confucian tradition and to relate it in various ways to the *Classic of Poetry*, for he titles his fourth chapter "Distinguishing the *Sao*" (*Bian sao* 辨騷), i.e., from the *Shi jing*. After opening by describing the *Li sao* as the greatest literary achievement since the *Poetry*, Liu Xie reproduces arguments we have seen supporting or denying the connections between the two: the passage from Liu An's *Li sao zhuan* included in Sima Qian's biography; Ban Gu's criticisms in his preface; Wang Yi's line-by-line comparisons with various classics; and other references attesting to the similarities between them. Liu Xie observes that the statements on both sides are arbitrary and exaggerated and suggests that only concrete examples from the *Songs of Chu* can clarify the situation. He writes that in four respects it is "the same as the Airs and Elegances": its use of history (*dian gao* 典誥), admonishment (*gui feng* 規風), comparison and stimulus (*bi xing*), and loyal complaint (*zhong yuan* 忠怨).[27] In four other respects, however—its use of the fantastic, of the unbelievable, its choice of suicide, and favorable attitude to certain licentious behavior—it is not, so he concludes that, while not the equal of the Classics, it is certainly superior to other literature of the Warring States period.[28]

Perhaps the fullest discussion linking "Encountering Sorrow" to the methods and subgenres of the *Classic of Poetry* can be found in Zhu Xi's

[27] Fan Wenlan notes that *dian gao* is not one of the methods of the *Classic of Poetry* and suggests that Liu Xie's statement that these are the "same as the Airs and Elegances" should be emended to read "same as the *History* and the *Poetry*" (*Wenxin diaolong zhu*, p. 53n11).

[28] *Wenxin diaolong zhu*, 1/pp.46–47.

preface to his edition of the text. The preface proper actually does not differ significantly from Wang Yi's, but it contains a lengthy note that expatiates on the "six song-methods" mentioned in the Rituals of Zhou and used for "instructing the sons of the state":

These are called *feng, fu, bi, xing, ya,* and *song.* And the Great Preface to the Mao edition of the *Poetry* calls them the Six Principles. Now from antiquity to the present the methods for poetry have not diverged from these. Thus the Airs are words expressing the customs of communities and the feelings and thoughts of men and women. Elegances are the compositions of nobles and great officials for court gatherings, feasts, and rituals. Hymns are the music of songs and dances for sacrifices to ghosts and spirits in the ancestral temple. These have all been distinguished on the basis of the different rhythms of the individual works.

Exposition means to display an event or situation directly. Comparison means to select an object for comparison. Stimulus means to entrust in an object to start the words. These have also been distinguished on the basis of differences in how they use words to imply a meaning. When those who chant poetry first distinguish these then the Three Hundred Poems [of the *Shi jing*] will have principles, be ordered and not confused.

These are not unique to the *Poetry*. The words of the people of Chu also use them, and one can seek them out. Thus [the *Chu ci*'s] lodging feelings in plants and trees and investing meaning in men and women in order to give the full measure of events observed on travels is in the tradition of the Changed Airs.[29] Its narrating events and displaying feelings, being moved by the present and recalling the past in order not to forget the principles of ruler and minister resemble the Changed Elegances.... Those words which are filled with sacrificial songs and dances to the spirits approximate the Hymns, although there are great changes.

The use of exposition is like the first stanza of the *Li sao* classic; comparison includes the categorical correspondences of fragrant plants and noxious objects; a stimulus entrusts in objects to start the words and does not take hold of the meaning at the beginning, as, in the *Nine Songs*, "the Yuan River angelicas and the Li River orchids"

---

[29]Like He Yisun in the excerpt cited in n. 26, Zhu Xi is alluding to the early theory, first mentioned in the Great Preface to the *Classic of Poetry*, that the "Changed" (*bian* 變) Airs and Elegances, which by common agreement make up the majority of each group, are so called because they were written during a period when the kingly way had already begun to decline; they are therefore characterized by their melancholy, nostalgia, and admonishment.

are used to evoke thoughts of the ruler without yet daring to utter them. Yet in the *Poetry*, the stimulus is more frequent than the comparison, and exposition is least common; in the *Sao*, the stimulus is rare and comparison and exposition are common. One must distinguish these in order to seek out the meaning of the text; the reader cannot fail to examine them. (*Ji zhu*, 1/4b–5a/pp.10–11)

For all of Zhu Xi's insistence on an adequate understanding of these devices, he was taken to task by the Qing scholar Jiang Ji for not having done his job completely. In a discussion following his edition of the *Songs of Chu*, Jiang writes:

The *Sao* evolved from the *Shi*. The *Shi* had exposition, comparison and stimulus, and only the *Sao* does as well. However, the Three Hundred Poems are short and concise in length, and [the principles] are easy to seek out and discern. But the *Sao* as a whole is full of changes; exposition, comparison, and stimulus emerge only irregularly and can certainly not be sought out by using one rule. When I look at Master Zhu's annotations of the comparison and exposition and the like in the *Sao* classic, then I must say that they are not exhaustively appended. Also, when the whole book is examined, then [the annotations] are only in the first sections [i.e., "Encountering Sorrow" and the *Nine Songs*].[30]

Nevertheless, Jiang Ji does grant the pertinence of this rhetorical terminology to the *Li sao* even if his own annotations do not focus on the same kind of analysis of imagery practiced by Wang Yi and Zhu Xi. The passage cited above, furthermore, suggests a third way in which scholars sought to demonstrate the filiation of "Encountering Sorrow" with the *Classic of Poetry*. As we have seen, first, they could place Qu Yuan within the Confucian tradition by citing his unswerving righteousness, loyal yet not uncritical devotion to his ruler and state, and decision to write during a period of adversity to express his grievances. Second, they could discern the same imagistic principles supposedly deduced from the *Classic of Poetry* being put to work in "Encountering Sorrow" to make the author's point indirectly yet more effectively. And, finally, they could claim that the later work was simply a blood relation of the *Shi jing*, as it were, a direct descendant in the evolution of genres.

The Song scholar Zhao Buzhi 晁補之 (1053–1110) presents one of the fuller explications of this idea in the preface to his edition of the *Songs of*

---

[30] Jiang Ji, *Chu ci yu lun shang*, in *Shandaige zhu Chu ci*, p. 180.

Chu. After placing the origin of the *Classic of Poetry* during "the glorious times of the Former Kings," he discusses the evolution of the Changed Airs and Elegances as conditions began to deteriorate and poets began to lament the present and long for the past. When the *Poetry* had died out, it was reborn as the *Songs of Chu* in an unbroken cycle of evolution, depletion, and rejuvenation:

> From the Airs and Elegances there was a change into the *Li sao*, which by the Han became the exposition.... It is said that "the exposition is a strain of ancient poetry."[31] Thus "Embracing the Sand" (*Huai sha* 懷沙, the fifth of the *Nine Declarations* [*Jiu zhang* 九章]), is called an exposition; "Hymn to the Orange" (*Ju song* 橘頌, eighth of the *Nine Declarations*), is called a hymn; the *Nine Songs* are called songs (*ge* 歌); the *Heavenly Questions* (*Tian wen* 天問) are called questions (*wen*)—these are all poetry and "Encountering Sorrow" includes them all. Thus the tradition of the *Classic of Poetry* arrived in Chu to become "Encountering Sorrow," then by the Han became the exposition, then it changed again to become poetry, and then again to become mixed prose, ballads, dialogues, inscriptions, songs in praise of constancy, and ditties—whatever varieties have developed from the words of the Chu poets with few changes can be known a hundred generations later.[32]

Jiang Ji also alludes to this idea in the statement cited above. It is one which has been traced to Mencius, resurfaces in the chronology Li Bo 李白 (701–762) outlines in the first of his 59 "Ancient Airs" (*Gu feng* 古風) and in Bo Juyi's 白居易 (772–846) account of the history of poetry ("the Airs of the States changed to become the *Songs of Chu*"),[33] and becomes particularly popular during the Ming and Qing, as in Gu Yanwu's 顧炎武 (1613–1682) claim that "the Three Hundred Poems could not but come down to the *Songs of Chu*, and the *Songs of Chu* could not but come down to [literature of] the Han and Wei."[34] These writers were not just concerned with the *Chu ci*, of course, but with testifying to the irrecoverable

---

[31] This statement is given, unattributed, by Ban Gu in the preface to his "Exposition on the Two Capitals" (*Liang du fu* 兩都賦), included in the *Wen xuan*, 2/2b/p.21.

[32] From the preface to his *Chong bian Chu ci* 重編楚辭, cited in Jiang Liangfu, *Chu ci shumu wu zhong*, pp. 27–28.

[33] Bo Juyi, *Yu Yuan Jiu shu* 與元九書, in Wang Rubi 王如弼, ed., *Bo Juyi xuanji* 白居易選集 (Shanghai: Guji chubanshe, 1980), p. 346.

[34] Gu Yanwu, *Ri zhi lu* 日知錄, 21; cited in *Wenxin diaolong zhu*, p. 49n2. Fan Wenlan, among others, cites this passage from the *Mencius* (4B.21): "When the traces of the kings were obliterated then the *Poetry* died out, and thereafter the *Spring and Autumn Annals* were written."

greatness of a golden age while validating at the same time the legitimacy of new forms.[35]

IV.

The reasons behind the urge to demonstrate the connections between the *Classic of Poetry* and "Encountering Sorrow" are not difficult to fathom. Scholars like Sima Qian who were sympathetic with the figure of Qu Yuan would of course be interested in deflecting attention from the less orthodox aspects of the poem and in situating the poet within the mainstream of upright official behavior. They sought to justify his plaintive—if not downright petulant—verse as heir of the classical obligation to remonstrate and to provide lofty precedents for his otherwise problematic choice to commit suicide. In most cases, moreover, their desire to vindicate Qu Yuan was motivated as much by intensely personal as by more abstract considerations. We have already mentioned the strong appeal for Sima Qian of historical examples demonstrating the intimate connection between suffering and great writing, understandable given his own tragic situation.[36] Noteworthy as well is the evidence that compilers of later editions of the *Chu ci* were also impelled to their efforts by a powerful personal identification they sensed with the misunderstood, resolutely critical, and profoundly frustrated figure. Laurence Schneider has argued that Wang Yi was attracted to Qu Yuan not only as a fellow native of Chu, but also because he sensed not unflattering affinities between his own role in the transmission of a putative classic and that of Confucius, according to legend, vis-à-vis the *Classic of Poetry*.[37] More common in prefaces to later editions, however, are testaments to the particular appeal of Qu Yuan to scholars experiencing similar personal difficulties—whether owing to illness and old age (Zhu Xi, Jiang Ji), political disregard or disfavor (Wang Yuan, Huang Wenhuan), or political protest (Ming loyalists such as Wang

---

[35] For a discussion and critique of this notion of genre depletion, see Qian Zhongshu, *Tan yi lu*, pp. 32–38, and Theodore D. Huters, *Qian Zhongshu* (Boston: G. K. Hall, 1982), pp. 40–48.

[36] The story is well known: when the historian attempted to defend the general Li Ling 李陵 (d. 74 B.C.), who, vastly outnumbered, was defeated in battle against the Xiongnu 兇奴 tribes and captured, to an angry emperor, he was charged with treason. He made the humiliating choice to be castrated rather than the more honorable and conventional one of death because of his commitment to completing the grand history project begun by his father. Sima Qian explains his agonizing decision in a famous letter to his friend Ren An 任安, translated by James Robert Hightower and included in Cyril Birch, *Anthology of Chinese Literature*, I, 95–102.

[37] Schneider, *A Madman of Ch'u*, pp. 27–31.

Fuzhi and Qian Chengzhi). At the least, their statements testify eloquently to the power of the autobiographical assumptions of the poem's origin and its literal truth-value.

For our purposes, however, a more important question is the extent to which the scholars' claim that the imagistic practices of "Encountering Sorrow" are identical to those of the *Classic of Poetry* is justified. Had they argued that the Chu text employed the rhetorical trope of *bi* or comparison, one might have few bones to pick, but they chose instead to argue for the shared use of the *xing* or stimulus. We find this implicitly in Sima Qian's biography and then discussed at length in Wang Yi's preface. His claim that the *Li sao* used the method of stimulus from the *Shi* was resumed, for example, by Liu Xie in his *Wenxin diaolong*, for, despite the critic's wish to "Distinguish the *Sao*" in the fourth chapter of that work, in chapter 36 on *"Bi and Xing"* he affirms the rhetorical links between the two anthologies: "King Xiang [of Chu] trusted the toadies and the Sanlü [minister—Qu Yuan's title before his troubles began] was loyal and ardent. He based himself on the *Shi* to create the *Sao*, which in its remonstrance employs both comparison and stimulus."[38] And critics down to the twentieth century have accepted the filiation as well.[39]

To be sure, Zhu Xi does entertain some doubts about the application of the term "stimulus" to the *Li sao*. He refers to Wang Yi's string of examples of *xing* in the poem and takes issue with some of the analogies deduced by the Han scholar:

> Now in my judgment Yi's statement here has some correct aspects and some errors. What he says about correspondences to loyalty and integrity, comparisons to slander and deceit, the Divine Beauty and Fairest One are correct. These are all what in the *Shi* are called comparison. As for intimate consorts and beautiful maidens, they are also the Fairest One. Dragons and phoenixes are also in the category of beneficent birds and should not be considered separately as establishing a different principle. Whirlwinds, clouds, and rainbows are also not comparisons to petty men. Yi's explanations here are all wrong, and the arguments against them should be discussed in detail for later generations. (*Bian zheng shang*, 3b/p.322)

Yet though he disagrees with Wang Yi's interpretations of some of the images, Zhu Xi here only implicitly questions the earlier scholar's use of the term stimulus to refer to them, when he says that "these are all what

---

[38] *Wenxin diaolong zhu*, 8/p.602.

[39] E.g., You Guoen, *Chu ci lunwen ji*, p. 192, and Ferenc Tökei, *Naissance de l'élégie chinoise: K'iu Yuan et son époque* (Paris: Gallimard, 1967), p. 173.

in the *Shi* are called comparisons." Only in his own preface to "Encountering Sorrow," cited earlier, do we see him explicitly acknowledging the paucity of examples of the stimulus as opposed to the comparison in the *Songs of Chu*, and, indeed, his own annotations bear this out. As he had done with the *Classic of Poetry*, he identifies each section of the text as one of the three rhetorical tropes or a combination of two, and he finds no examples of the stimulus in the *Li sao* at all. The term only appears once in the *Nine Songs* as a note to the line in the fourth poem, "The Lady of the Xiang" (*Xiang furen* 湘夫人) about the Yuan River angelicas and Li River orchids cited in his preface, and even there questions have been raised about its applicability.

Another traditional commentator challenged the transfer of this terminology to "Encountering Sorrow" from a different point of view. In a lengthy preface entitled "Principles of the *Songs of Chu*" (*Chu ci tiao li* 楚辭條例) to his edition of the anthology, Lu Shiyong 陸時雍 (fl. 1633) explicitly takes issue with Zhu Xi's mode of analysis:

> There are six principles in the *Classic of Poetry*, three of which are comparison, stimulus, and exposition. Zhu Huiweng 晦翁 [Xi] in annotating "Encountering Sorrow" came up with principles based on the *Poetry*; he distinguished among comparison, stimulus, and exposition and explicated them. I say "Encountering Sorrow" and the *Poetry* are not the same. In the *Sao* comparison and exposition appear intermingled: there are comparisons in the midst of exposition and exposition within comparison. If one adheres steadfastly to one principle then the meaning will decay and the language will stagnate. Thus there is nothing to be gained from it.[40]

Nevertheless, for all of this quibbling over fine points, the *fu bi xing* terminology as a whole is never seriously questioned and, more important, these two exegetes are outnumbered by those who maintain the opinion that the *Li sao*'s use of the stimulus is identical to that of the *Classic of Poetry*.

The term *xing*, however vague, is generally associated with evocative juxtaposition rather than systematic substitution. One might argue that the juxtaposition of substitutive or quasi-metaphorical sections of the *Li sao* to straightforward ones represents the *xing* method writ large, but this would be straining to make a point. There is no doubt that "Encountering Sorrow" employs imagery apparently intended to be replaced by the un-

[40] From his *Chu ci shu* 疏, woodblock edition of 1705. Jiang Liangfu asserts that the title printed on the edition I have seen (in the Rare Book Collection of Princeton University's Gest Oriental Library), *Qishier jia ping zhu Chu ci* 七十二家評註楚辭, is erroneous (*Chu ci shumu wu zhong*, p. 104).

spoken subject matter of the poem—sustained or not—and that the poem is thus the first major example of such methods in the Chinese poetic tradition. Two important questions continue to arise, however: first, what are the likely influences, if any, on the development of this practice, and, second, why did traditional commentators fail to acknowledge its novelty and choose instead to identify it as the *xing* method of the *Classic of Poetry*?

It is only in the work of modern scholars that we can find fruitful suggestions about some of the possible precedents for this practice. Certainly, the influence of shamanistic ritual is undeniable,[41] for the very situation of the shaman as ritual impersonator would encourage the development of a literature that employed a similar device of impersonation or donning of a persona. Various critics have remarked upon the importance as well of flower-bedecked costumes, decorations, and props in providing the lexicon of objects to be mentioned in the poem. The *Li sao* poet's obsession with purity and plants may also be directly linked with ritual practices, for one scholar has noted that in the case of the American shaman, cleanliness "may be attained by frequent bathing in remote lakes or streams, by the use of the sudatory, or by either of these means, with the added requirement of rubbing the body or scenting it with fragrant herbs and roots."[42] As mentioned earlier, David Hawkes' important study on the "Quest of the Goddess" also argues convincingly for tracing the sources of the mythical journey and the frustrated love-suit to common patterns in shamanistic ritual and liturgical traditions.

Other literary forebears have been suggested as well, in particular the tradition of enigmatic expressions (*yin yu* 隱語), also known as *sou ci* 廋辭 or riddles in rhymed verses. You Guoen proposes this fondness for camouflaged yet pointed expressions, along with the well-documented practice of reciting poems from the *Classic of Poetry* on diplomatic missions, as the two major precedents for a poetry employing the comparison and stimulus or images conveying political admonishment in an indirect

[41] This has been argued at length by David Hawkes in his *Ch'u Tz'u* and "The Quest of the Goddess"; by Arthur Waley in *The Nine Songs: A Study of Shamanism in Ancient China* (San Francisco: City Lights Books, 1973); and by Chan Pingleung, "Ch'u Tz'u and Shamanism in Ancient China," Ph.D. Diss. Ohio State, 1972.

Li Jiayan 李嘉言 also makes the point that the comparative images of "fragrant plant" and "fair one" trace their origins to the shamanistic mythology of Chu but does not develop it. See "Qu Yuan 'Li sao' de sixiang he yishu" 屈原離騷的思想和藝術, in *Chu ci yanjiu lunwen ji* 楚辭研究論文集, Vol. II; *Zhongguo gudian wenxue yanjiu lunwen ji huibian* 中國古典文學研究論文集滙編, Vol. II, ed. Zhongguo yuwenxue she 中國語文學社 (1969), p. 62.

[42] Roland B. Dixon, "Some Aspects of the American Shaman," *Journal of American Folklore*, 21 (1908), p. 4. Cited in Chan Pingleung, "Ch'u Tz'u and Shamanism," p. 129n88.

113

way,[43] although Li Qi argues that the latter is simply one of several varieties of the former.[44] The three most important characteristics of these riddling expressions, You points out, were the use of an object as comparison, a correspondence of rhyme between tenor and vehicle, and a purpose of veiled remonstrance (p. 217). These were all to characterize the early development of the exposition, of which the writings of Qu Yuan and his followers were viewed as precursors. Both You and Li cite "Encountering Sorrow" as a poetic prototype of these methods, although the first poem to employ them in a systematic fashion was another work in the *Songs of Chu*, the "Hymn to the Orange," which uses one object—the orange tree—from beginning to end as an image for the self. Li Qi writes that this poem clearly exemplifies the method of *tuo wu* 托物, "which means to invest the description of an object with an ulterior meaning, which is the real theme. Thus a fashion started of seeking the real meaning of a poem not in the poem itself but in between lines or outside of the poetical utterance" (p. 347).

These suggestions as to possible sources of the *Li sao*'s imagistic practice, however, are relatively recent ones. Traditional critics from Wang Yi on simply carried over the *xing* terminology from the *Classic of Poetry* without acknowledging, it seems, the distinctiveness of the later text. Laurence Schneider argues, following many twentieth-century Chinese critics, that the impulse to demonstrate this and other areas of filiation between the two anthologies was motivated primarily by the urge to mold the Chu text in the Confucian image: "Ch'ü Yüan and his poetry were largely co-opted by the Han Confucianists in a fashion similar to the co-optations of the *Odes*. Wang I was central in this process, which he accomplished through his polemics with Yang Hsiung and Pan Ku, and through his application in his commentaries of the principles used for interpreting the *Odes*" (p. 29). But both of these views are not without problems. To say that "Encountering Sorrow," a text dating from the early third century B.C., uses the stimulus and comparison, terms which do not appear with any certainty in the literature until the second century B.C. at the earliest, is to make the mistake, as almost all scholars have done, of assuming that they can actually be shown to go back to the sixth-century B.C. anthology, rather than to significantly later—certainly, later

[43] You Guoen, *Chu ci lunwen ji*, pp. 211ff. This argument runs the risk, of course, of suggesting that the terms *bi* and *xing* are, after all, most properly associated with ways of using or interpreting the poems in the *Classic of Poetry* rather than with their actual composition, a point which I have been advocating but which has not been granted by most writers on the subject, You Guoen himself included.

[44] See Li Chi (Li Qi 李祁), "*Yin-yü* and *Tai-yü* in Chinese Poetry," *Tsing Hua Hsüeh-Pao*, New Series II.2 (June 1961), pp. 343–59.

than Qu Yuan—exegetical imaginations. And to say that the commentaries on the southern anthology simply repeat the "co-optation" of those on the earlier one misjudges crucial differences between the poem and the interpretive traditions, not to speak of the impulses behind those readings.

For one thing, the degree of "co-optation" of "Encountering Sorrow" is significantly less than is the case with poems in the *Shi jing*. To modern eyes, the later poem does employ an oblique mode of presentation, contains clear hints of reference to political concerns, and expresses at heart a more conscious and easily demonstrable Confucian moral vision than any Air of the State in the Classic. And Wang Yi's glosses reflect the prevalence of substitutive imagery by calling attention to the comparisons (*yu* 喻) he sees throughout the text. Early commentaries on the *Classic of Poetry*—the Mao glosses and the prefaces—do not, in contrast, emphasize this comparative function of that anthology's imagery explicitly, being more concerned with providing historical contexts for the poems. It is not until Zheng Xuan, who follows Wang Yi in time and adds his notes to those of Mao, that the word *yu* enters with any frequency into the exegetical literature on the earlier text. Indeed, it would make more sense to say that it was the *Songs of Chu*, with their intentionally substitutive images and Wang Yi's explications of them, that influenced the commentaries on and theories of imagery in the *Classic of Poetry*, rather than the reverse. In other words, the later text may either have inspired or justified the ideas about imagistic practice attributed to the earlier.

But the question to which we keep returning centers on why the traditional commentators took no notice of what strikes us as a new use of imagery, however inconsistent, in "Encountering Sorrow." Why did they—until Zhu Xi—simply affix the label of "stimulus" to what, if anything, should have been called comparisons? The answer lies, I think, in the fact that, despite the many attempts at distinguishing the two tropes, the functional similarities between them were ultimately of greater importance. This was not the case with all critics, but for these commentators, at least, all natural imagery fulfilled the same purpose: using one thing to suggest something that was of greater significance yet was viewed as belonging to the same natural, pre-existing order. As in the case of the *Classic of Poetry*, and in marked contrast to most of the Western tradition, they did not construe correspondences between two objects or between an object and an idea as artificial or contrived in any way, the ingenious creation of the poet as maker of fictions. Rather, links between things were always already there, grounded by shared membership in an a priori category (*lei*) antecedent to any individual artifice. From this derives the frequent insistence on the literal or concrete basis of a comparison and the curious vacillation between their literal and less

115

literal readings of what we might see as clearly metaphorical episodes: the flowers may or may not be symbols of virtue, and the dragons are often simply dragons—horned, hornless, or flying. Real and supernatural in this view are not two absolutely differentiated levels, nor are past and present in historical time; the same linkages pertain to the fragrance of flora and virtue and the yielding, receptive ways of wife and minister.

The assumption that poetry represented at base a non-fictional response to an experienced stimulus also fueled the overpowering impulse to take words, in the last analysis, at face value, as an actual historical document, erasing the formal differences between the substituted and the juxtaposed. The power of this assumption may also help to explain why the commentators never take explicit note of the fact that "Encountering Sorrow" is the first poetic text to use substitution extensively and intentionally and to permit interpretations predicating an otherness of reference without the strain necessary in the case of the *Classic of Poetry*. Certainly, the belief in cosmological correlations was so strong during the Han dynasty, to which the first glosses on both anthologies date, that the exegetes may simply have taken such imagistic practices for granted. In other words, the poetry's confirmation of a widespread belief did not have to be acknowledged. Hence the curious lack of any remarks on the innovative techniques of Qu Yuan. He was simply, in their eyes, calling upon pre-established, self-evident, and literally true correlations—between woman and minister, fragrance and virtue, spirits and ruler—provoked by his experience and belonging to the same realm of being. Thus the substitutive form of his poem, though superficially similar, was based on a fundamentally different set of assumptions from those of metaphor or allegory in the West. Qu Yuan was not writing in the mode familiar to such discourse, i.e., "presenting one thing in words and another in meaning." Closer to the mark would be a revision of this formulation: "presenting the same meaning in different words," with both elements simultaneously present, even if not mentioned explicitly. Their presumptions exemplify notions fundamental to the Confucian worldview: that politics was simply ethics writ large, and that it was impossible for any individual, when speaking of himself, not to implicate a larger context as well. The holistic assumption grounding this view came to underlie, in some form, all later poetic theory.

Whatever the attempts to identify them, the *Classic of Poetry* and the *Songs of Chu*—of which "Encountering Sorrow" is clearly the most important work—can be seen to have established two different models for imagery in classical Chinese poetry. The juxtaposition of two elements related in some unspecified way that is typical of the earlier anthology appears frequently in later works, although the connections came to be

116

more and more cogent, if not standardized. The *Li sao*, on the other hand, offered a precedent for substitutive, politically relevant imagery that was central to the development of the exposition and resurfaced at times in poetry as well, beginning with other works in the *Songs of Chu* like the "Hymn to the Orange." The legacies of both examples will be discussed in subsequent chapters.[45] And the presumptions of the early commentaries on the two anthologies—of a second level of meaning that was not truly "other," of the moral and political purposes of poetry, of the source of the poem in empirical experience and its consequent literal truth-value—also left their mark on the poetic and critical tradition. Indeed, although some of these notions receded at times or were supplemented by others, one might very well argue that these scholars' readings of the first anthologies were of equal, if not ultimately of even greater, influence in later times than the poems themselves.

[45]Zhu Ziqing in *Shi yan zhi bian*, however, does argue that the *Chu ci*'s "drawing out categorical correspondences as comparisons" 引類譬諭 influenced the development of four later types of poetry involving veiled allusions or substitutive imagery: poems on history, on traveling immortals, on love, and on objects (pp. 88ff). He also opens this discussion by asserting categorically that "the *Songs of Chu* actually do not have the so-called stimulus" (p. 88).

Six Dynasties Poetry
and Criticism

I.

Howᴇᴠᴇʀ the actual influence of the poems in the *Classic of Poetry* and *Songs of Chu* compares to that of their commentaries—a problem whose examination would take us far beyond the scope of this study—what does become clear over the succeeding centuries is the critical interest in constructing genealogical charts linking later poets and these first anthologies, much as had been done between the two works themselves. As E. Bruce Brooks has noted, the assumption that all poetry could trace its filiation to one or the other of the two collections along essentially unrelated lines of descent developed into a "critical commonplace" of Six Dynasties literary theory, finding its fullest expression in Zhong Hong's *Classification of Poetry (Shi pin)*.[1] Although Zhong Hong himself was more interested in what he perceived to be the general stylistic qualities of the early poems and their influence—the political and moral loftiness of the one group and the emotional profundity of the other—he did pay heed to the rhetorical legacy of the *Classic of Poetry* as well. The relevance of the *fu bi xing* terminology in the analysis of imagery in poems of this period by other traditional commentators is equally apparent. As I have suggested, however, not only do the distinctions between these terms become increasingly blurred, but critical conceptions of their functions also undergo significant changes in contemporary theoretical writings—shifts that go hand in hand with developments in the imagistic practice of Six Dynasties poetry itself. In this

---

[1] E. Bruce Brooks, "A Geometry of the *Shr Pin*," in Chow Tse-tsung, ed., *Wen-lin: Studies in the Chinese Humanities* (Madison: University of Wisconsin Press, 1968), p. 141. Brooks provides a chart of Zhong Hong's genealogical efforts on p. 140, a slightly different version of which can also be found in Luo Genze 羅根澤, *Zhongguo wenxue piping shi* 中國文學批評史 (rpt. Hong Kong: Dianwen, n.d.; 3 vols. in 1), p. 248.

118

chapter, then, I shall be taking a close look at a sample of poems, commentaries, and critical literature of this period in order to trace these changes in the usage and interpretation of imagery and in the corresponding terminological definitions.

The Song critic Zhang Jie 張戒 opens his *Suihantang shihua* 歲寒堂詩話 with the following assessment of classical poetry:

> The poetry of the Jian'an 建安 period (196–220), Tao [Qian 陶潛 (365–427)], Ruan [Ji 阮籍 (210–63)], and before solely speaks of one's intent (*yan zhi* 言志). Poetry after Pan [Yue 潘岳 (d. 300)] and Lu [Ji] solely sings of objects (*yong wu* 詠物). Those who have both are Li [Bo] and Du [Fu 杜甫 (712–70)]. Now speaking of one's intent is none other than the fundamental purpose of the poet, and singing of objects is only a secondary affair. Of ancient poets, Su [Wu 蘇武 (fl. 81 B.C.)], Li [Ling], Cao [Zhi 曹植 (192–232)], Liu [Zheng 劉楨 (d. 217)], Tao [Qian], and Ruan [Ji] did not basically plan to sing of objects, but their skill at doing so was achieved with outstanding naturalness and cannot be reached again. Their feelings are true, their flavor long-lasting, and their spirit abundant; they can be looked at next to the Three Hundred Poems almost without embarrassment, for they all attain the fundamental purpose of poets. After Pan [Yue] and Lu [Ji] poets solely planned to sing of objects. Their skill at carving and engraving increased daily, but the fundamental purpose of poets was entirely swept away.[2]

This analysis had already become the standard one by Zhang Jie's time and was to continue so over the centuries, resumed recently by Li Zhifang 李直方 as the opposition between the urge to "express one's intent" (*xie zhi* 寫志) typical of Han and Wei dynasty poetry and one to "embody objects" (*ti wu* 體物). The first phrase harks back to the earliest statements on the function of poetry (in the *Classic of History* and the Great Preface to the *Classic of Poetry*) as the expression of the poet's will or intent, which is assumed to represent in part a response to contemporary social and political conditions. The second type, Li asserts, begins with the landscape poetry of Xie Lingyun 謝靈運 (385–433) and degenerates into the facile descriptions of the palace-style poetry popular during the Qi and Liang dynasties.[3]

While these accounts of the origins and fate of description in the Chinese poetic tradition are debatable, their suggestion that the poetry of

[2] Zhang Jie, *Suihantang shihua, juan shang* 卷上, included in *Xu Lidai shihua*, I, 541.
[3] Li Zhifang, "Ruan Ji yong huai shi lun" 阮籍詠懷詩論, in *Han Wei liu chao shi lun gao* 漢魏六朝詩論稿 (Hong Kong: Longmen shudian, 1978), pp. 69–102.

the earlier period is not interested primarily in the mimetic representation of, for example, the natural world is certainly well-taken. Burton Watson has made much the same point in discussing the typically "generalized landscape" of Chinese nature poetry, which he attributes partly to

> the poetic division of labor between the *fu* [rhymeprose or exposition] and the *shih* [lyric poem], Whereas it was the function of the *fu* to give exhaustive lists of the trees, plants, fish, etc. that made up the scene being described, the aim of the *shih* was more often to evoke a mood or convey an emotion. Moreover, because the *shih* was usually relatively brief, it simply did not allow room for lengthy and detailed description.[4]

Again, Watson's assertion that the elaborate enumerations of objects and their details found so frequently in the exposition are intended to be truly descriptive is definitely subject to debate; certainly Qu Yuan's "Encountering Sorrow," traditionally acknowledged as the ancestor of the *fu*, can hardly be said to be bent on a literal depiction of the natural world, and the breathtaking catalogues of objects in later expositions seem more intent on incantation, persuasion, or demonstrations of power than mere description.

Nevertheless, his characterization of the type of lyric poem he is concerned with is well-founded. Indeed, although Li Zhifang restricts the scope of his discussion to Six Dynasties poetry and Watson to that of the Tang, anyone familiar with the *Classic of Poetry* and the *Songs of Chu* should have trouble arguing for the primacy of straight realistic description in those anthologies as well; despite their urge to contextualize the poems, traditional commentators certainly did not assume this to be the case.[5] The songs in the *Classic of Poetry* do, to be sure, contain details from the everyday life and surroundings of their authors, but with few exceptions their inclusion does not flesh out a coherent scene. Critics have found this use of juxtaposed, potentially symbolic imagery to be typical of anonymous folk poetry, but this does little to explain why Qu Yuan, writing within a much broader framework, should have been equally disinclined to focus his attention on the world around him. The non-mimetic

[4] Burton Watson, *Chinese Lyricism: Shih Poetry from the Second to the Twelfth Century, with Translations* (New York: Columbia University Press, 1971), p. 133.

[5] Given this situation, it is odd that Watson should choose to introduce his discussion of Ruan Ji by writing that the poet "is *no longer* interested in describing the natural world as it exists in reality, but only in extracting from it elements that will serve as symbols for his ideas and emotions" (p. 69; emphasis added). Granted, the composers of the songs in the *Classic of Poetry* may give more specific details about the objects they mention, but they were no more intent on describing the natural world than Ruan Ji.

force of cultural assumptions was powerful indeed. As we have seen, unlike the Western tradition, in which imagery's first and sole function was *enargia*—making the reader seem to see something—and was expanded only much later, the Chinese poetic image carried with it from the start a more important association or concept which was identified by the earliest commentators and then adopted as convention by later poets. And the earliest poetry by individual authors displays by and large a typical anonymity or universality in keeping with the generalizing tendencies of these conventionalized images.

This is true, for example, of the first group of poems written in the pentasyllabic meter which was to become the backbone of the tradition, the "Nineteen Ancient Poems" (*Gu shi shijiu shou* 古詩十九首) of the Han dynasty. They make their first appearance in the *Literary Anthology* (*Wen xuan* 文選) compiled under Xiao Tong 蕭統 (501–531), crown prince Zhaoming 昭明 of Liang; twelve of them are also included in slightly different order in the *New Songs from a Jade Terrace* (*Yu tai xin yong* 玉臺新詠), compiled by Xu Ling 徐陵 (507–583) around the year 545, under the patronage of Xiao Tong's younger brother Xiao Gang 綱 (503–551), who became emperor Jianwen 簡文 of Liang. Much critical controversy has centered on the authorship and hence dating of these poems. Xu Ling ascribed nine of them to Mei Cheng 枚乘 (d. 140 B.C.), an attribution doubted, among others, by both Liu Xie in his *Literary Mind* and Li Shan 李善 (d. 689), the well-known Tang commentator on the *Wen xuan*.[6] The Qing critic Chen Hang 陳沆 (1785–1826), on the other hand, endorses Xu Ling's assertion and consequent rearrangement (from the *Wen xuan*) of the order of the poems he annotates in his selection of poems, which, "when history is used to document the poems," he finds "far superior to the *Wen xuan*," for it follows more closely the chronology of Mei Cheng's biography as given in the Han history.[7] Jean-Pierre Diény surveys some of this debate in the "Conclusion" to his translation and commentary of the entire group, rejects the Mei Cheng attribution, and argues convincingly on various grounds that it was probably composed no earlier than the Eastern Han, sometime between A.D. 50–150.[8]

For all their disputes over these questions, traditional critics do concur with the connection first made by Zhong Hong when he wrote that "the

[6] See the *Wenxin diaolong zhu*, 2/p.66 and *Wen xuan*, 29/1a/p.535.

[7] Chen Hang, *Shi bi xing jian* 詩比興箋 (rpt. Peking: Zhonghua, 1965), 1/p.16.

[8] Jean-Pierre Diény, *Les Dix-neuf poèmes anciens*, in *Bulletin de la Maison Franco-Japonaise*, Nouvelle Série, VII.4 (Paris: Presses universitaires de France, 1963), pp. 176–87. Cf. also Sui Shusen 隋樹森, *Pinglun* 評論, 4/pp.1–9 (separately paginated) of his *Gu shi shijiu shou ji shi* 古詩十九首集釋 (rpt. Hong Kong: Zhonghua, 1975), for several remarks by traditional scholars pertaining to this issue.

style [of the "Nineteen Ancient Poems"] originated with the Airs of the States."[9] Most of their reasoning centers on their perception of the shared oblique and imagistic critical purposes of the two collections. Wang Shimou 王世懋 (1536–1588), for example, writes that, with the exception of the *song* 頌, hymns of praise written for temple sacrifices, the rest of the *Classic of Poetry* "generally relies on categorical comparisons stimulated by contact with objects, expressing human nature and sentiments that are vague, floating, and usually unfixed. Thus of those who have explicated the poems, each has made his own explanation." And "in later ages," he writes, "only the Nineteen Poems have retained the significance," so that they can be called the *"Classic of Poetry* in pentasyllabic meter."[10] Wang Fuzhi alludes to a previously cited passage from the *Analects* (XVII.9) when he states that in "stimulating, observing, harmonizing, and repining, poetry is fulfilled. After the three hundred works in the *Poetry* only the Nineteen Poems can accomplish this."[11] And Shen Deqian 沈德潛 (1673–1769) writes that

> The Nineteen Poems by and large [express] the emotions of exiled minister and abandoned wife, of friendships separated or cut off, of life and death, the new and the old. They include among them both veiled and overt language that lingers on and on, rising and falling inexhaustibly, so that the reader's mournful feelings have no end and can be amply savored. This is the legacy of the Airs of the States.[12]

The commentators' conviction as to the validity of this lineage is adequately attested to by the frequency with which the *fu bi xing* terminology appears in their exegeses, and references to various lines in the *Classic* abound in the "Nineteen Ancient Poems." Allusions to works in the *Songs of Chu* are equally numerous, of course, and the nineteen poems' obsessive brooding on transience and separation is certainly closer to the prevailing mood of the southern anthology, but, as we have seen, scholars had already seen fit to link the imagistic practices of the two early anthologies.

Traditional exegeses of the "Nineteen Ancient Poems" center on the slandered and exiled minister topos definitively established by Qu Yuan's "Encountering Sorrow." As in the earlier work, this theme is frequently couched in terms of a troubled love relationship. Consider, for example, the first of the group (following the sequence of the *Wen xuan*):

[9] Zhong Hong, *Shi pin*, in *Lidai shihua*, I, 6.

[10] Wang Shimou, *Yi pu xie yu* 藝圃擷餘, included in the *Lidai shihua*, II, 774.

[11] From his *Jiang zhai shihua* 薑齋詩話, cited in Sui Shusen, *Pinglun*, 4/p.5.

[12] Shen Deqian, *Gu shi yuan jian zhu* 古詩源箋註 (rpt. Taipei: Guting, 1970), 2/6a–b/ pp.117–18; also cited by Sui Shusen, *Pinglun*, 4/p.6.

Traveling on, on and on again—	行行重行行
Parted from you while still alive;	與君生別離
Gone from here a myriad miles or more,	相去萬餘里
Each at different borders of the sky.	各在天一涯
The road is both difficult and long—	道路阻且長
How to know when we shall meet again?	會面安可知
Barbarian horses cleave to northern winds;	胡馬依北風
Viet birds nest in southern branches.	越鳥巢南枝
Gone from here each day a greater distance,	相去日已遠
Robe and belt each day grow more slack.	衣帶日已緩
Floating clouds obscure the white sun;	浮雲蔽白日
The traveler looks not to return.	遊子不顧反
Longing for you makes one old.	思君令人老
Years and months suddenly grow late.	歲月忽已晚
Cast aside—let's not speak again:	棄捐勿復道
One should strive to eat a little more.[13]	努力加餐飯

This poem demonstrates stylistic features common to many in the series: the reduplicative compounds, frequent repetition and parallelism in couplets, images interspersed with strong symbolic overtones, and a mood of vague and ominous melancholy. Traditional scholars agree with the Tang dynasty *Wen xuan* commentator Zhang Xian 張銑 that "the meaning of this poem is that a loyal minister meets with the slander of deceitful men and is exiled" (29/1a/p.535). The Qing commentators Yao Nai 姚鼐 (1731–1815) and Zhang Qi 張琦 (1764–1833) echo this reading, which is amplified somewhat by Fang Tinggui 方廷珪: "This is a loyal person in exile or a virtuous wife who has been rejected, expressing a wish to return that cannot be forgotten."[14] Diény notes that modern critics have preferred the abandoned wife theme but argues quite sensibly that "neither of these two figures has the force to impose itself and eliminate the other" (p. 54). Indeed, as we have seen in the previous chapter, the categorical correspondence between wife and minister was a deeply rooted cultural assumption, so that any allusion to one would unavoidably implicate the other.

Critical interest has centered on the two key couplets employing natural imagery, lines 7–8 and 11–12. Commenting on the barbarian horses and

---

[13] Included in *Wen xuan*, 29/1a–b/p.535; Sui Shusen, *Gu shi shijiu shou ji shi*, 2/pp.1–2; Chen Hang, *Shi bi xing jian*, 1/p.18. All translations of poems in this chapter and the next are my own. Cf. trans. of Diény, *Les dix-neuf poèmes anciens*, p. 9; Watson, *Chinese Lyricism*, p. 20; Arthur Waley, *Translations from the Chinese* (New York: Vintage, 1971), pp. 37–38; and Charles Hartman, in *Sunflower Splendor: Three Thousand Years of Chinese Poetry*, ed. Irving Yu-cheng Lo and Wu-chi Liu (New York: Doubleday, 1975), pp. 30–31.

[14] All are given in Sui Shusen, 2/p.3.

Viet birds, Li Shan cites a similar couplet from the *Han shi wai zhuan* 韓詩外傳 and says that both "speak of the inability to forget one's roots"; the Tang commentator Li Zhouhan 李周翰 also writes that the animals are "both thinking of their native lands" (*Wen xuan*, 29/1b/p.535). It is unclear whether or not they construe these creatures as part of some actual scene, and neither commentator, moreover, expressly identifies the images as comparative ones, although their similarity to what had been labeled a "stimulus" (*xing*) in the *Classic of Poetry*—albeit migrated from the opening position—is striking. The analogical function of the "floating clouds," however, is clearly spelled out, although with some disagreement as to details. Li Shan writes that they "are used as a comparison (*yu* 喻) to treacherous deceivers who have slandered a loyal man, thus the wanderer on his travels cannot consider returning." Another Tang commentator, Liu Liang 劉良, on the other hand, believes that "the white sun is a comparison to the ruler, and the floating clouds refer to slanderous deceivers. This is saying that deceitful ministers obscure the ruler's brightness and cause a loyal minister to leave and not return" (*ibid.*). Interestingly, no Chinese critic claims that this image is simply a literal detail drawn from a putative scene viewed by the poet, as had been frequently done for poems in the *Classic*. Diény notes that some Japanese scholars have attempted to do just this and dismisses their arguments— "One does not, however, take from this text any purely descriptive utterance, any verse that does not possess a moral or affective meaning" (p. 56)—but also takes care to point out that the context is not necessarily a political one.

The argument for a political reference is certainly strained to a considerably greater degree in the second poem:

Green, green, the riverbank grass.	青青河畔草
Thick, thick, willows in the garden.	鬱鬱園中柳
Delicate and fair, the woman in the tower—	盈盈樓上女
Shimmering white before the lattice window.	皎皎當窗牖
Beautiful is her red face powder;	娥娥紅粉粧
Slender, slender, she puts out a pale hand.	纖纖出素手
Once she was a singing-house girl,	昔爲倡家女
Now she is a wanderer's wife.	今爲蕩子婦
The wanderer has gone without return—	蕩子行不歸
An empty bed is hard to keep alone.[15]	空床難獨守

---

[15] *Wen xuan*, 29/1b–2a/pp.535–36; Sui Shusen, 2/p.4; Chen Hang, 1/p.19. Cf. trans. by Diény, p. 11; Watson, p. 23; Waley, p. 38; and Dell R. Hales in *Sunflower Splendor*, p. 31.

Zhu Xi identifies the first line here and in the next poem as *xing* because, in keeping with his conception of the term, they are used simply as an opening: "The stimulus is used to start the words. One speaks of the evoked object and stimulates one's meaning. For example, 'Green, green, the cypresses on the mound' [first line of poem 3] and 'Green, green, the riverbank grass' are both poems starting with/evoking an object."[16] But the *Wen xuan* commentators, among others, are convinced of the comparative functions, not only of the line but of the entire situation presented. Li Shan notes that "the grass growing by the riverbank and the willows flourishing in the garden are used as comparisons to the beautiful person before the window" (29/2a/p.536). Zhang Xian takes the comparison one step farther: "This is a comparison to a person possessing abundant talents who serves a benighted lord and thus uses the situation of a wife serving her husband as words to which something is entrusted" (29/1b/p.535), and Lü Yanji 呂延濟, after providing a convoluted series of equivalences, continues: "A minister's serving the ruler is also like a woman's serving her husband, thus there is a comparison in the words" (29/2a/p.536). These interpretations are questionable, of course, for what is striking above all about this poem is the apparent lack of any conventional meaning attached to the elements of the scene. For all of the Qing annotator Chen Zuoming's 陳祚明 insistence that the image of "facing the window and putting a hand out is an obvious critique,"[17] what the first six lines of the poem do seem to display, on the contrary, is the poet's interest in presenting a scene (with at most emotional connotations of isolation) employing a gradually and logically narrowing focus. These images are grouped together rather than being interspersed among the next three narrative lines of the poem, which must then dangle limply from them, to be rescued by the disarming force of the last verse. The poet clearly has difficulties, but one senses the beginnings of a willingness to entrust images with significance in a more sustained way than by the mere injection of isolated lines.

Nevertheless, the traditional interpretations of the "Nineteen Ancient Poems" continue along avenues that should by now be quite predictable. The fifth poem, for example, which opens with the lines "In the northwest is a tall pavilion, / As high as the floating clouds above" 西北有高樓 / 上與浮雲齊, describes the melancholy strains produced by a widowed musician and concludes with a lament over the difficulty of finding sympathetic partners and the wish to fly away as a pair of cranes. Li Shan

[16] *Zhuzi yu lei*, VI, 81/1b/p.3,388.

[17] Chen Zuoming, *Caishutang gu shi xuan* 采菽堂古詩選, in Sui Shusen, 2/p.4.

125

writes that "this piece explains how a man of lofty talent fails to attain an official position and finds few understanding friends," to which Li Zhouhan adds: "This poem is a comparison to a benighted ruler who does not use the advice of a virtuous official. The northwest is the place on earth of [the first hexagram in the *Classic of Changes*] qian 乾, the position of the ruler. The tall pavilion speaks of his occupying a lofty position" (*Wen xuan*, 29/3b/p.536). The type of cosmic correspondence which this commentator draws upon here comes into play again in his note to a slightly later couplet describing the music ("A clear *shang*[18] mode emerges with the wind, / Halfway through the song it lingers, hesitant" 清商隨風發 / 中曲正徘徊): "The clear *shang* is the sound of autumn, and in autumn things are all in decline. This is a comparison to the ruler's virtue in decline. What follows the wind, rising and hesitating, is a will that is not stable." And to the penultimate couplet another Tang commentator, Lü Xiang 呂向, supplies this explanation: "'One does not regret the singer's pain' 不惜歌者苦 says that the minister does not regret the pain of making loyal criticisms but only grieves that the ruler does not know him" (29/4a/p.537).

In their readings of poem 8, the commentators exercise surprising self-restraint and do not insist on a political context. The opening of the poem is clearly reminiscent of the evocative stimulus in the *Classic of Poetry*, although no one labels it as such:

Supple, supple, the lone-growing bamboo.	冉冉孤生竹
Binding its roots to the slope of Mt. Tai.	結根泰山阿
With you, sir, I have newly married:	與君爲新婚
Dodder clinging to the moss.[19]	兔絲附女蘿

Li Shan writes that "The bamboo binding its roots to the mountain slope is a comparison to a wife's entrusting herself to her lord," and Li Zhouhan expatiates at somewhat greater length: "This is a comparison of a wife's chastity to bamboo. 'Binding roots to Mt. Tai' says that entrusting one's heart to a husband is like bamboo growing deep into Mt. Tai.... Mt. Tai is venerated among all mountains; a husband is what a wife venerates, hence the comparison" (*Wen xuan*, 29/5b/p.537). But in the case of poem 10, they are considerably less circumspect:

---

[18] Second of the five pentatonic modes; music in this mode was felt to possess the characteristics Li Zhouhan refers to, all centering on autumn. Other such seasonal correspondences figure prominently in the seventh poem of the collection.

[19] There is some dispute as to whether the two plants mentioned here (*tusi* 兔絲 and *nüluo* 女蘿) are actually one and the same. Sui Shusen (2/p.12) gives the major arguments and concludes that they are indeed different: the former a kind of parasitic vine and the latter a fine-stemmed ground-hugging creeper.

Far, far, the Herdboy star,   迢迢牽牛星
Shimmering white, the Han River maid.   皎皎河漢女
Slender, slender, she lifts a pale hand,   纖纖擢素手
Click, clack, she plies the loom's shuttle. 札札弄機杼
In one whole day not finishing a piece,   終日不成章
Tears flowing down like rain.   泣涕零如雨
The River Han is clear and shallow—   河漢清且淺
How far apart can they be?   相去復幾許
Trilling onward, the water between;   盈盈一水間
Looking, looking, but finding no words.[20] 脉脉不得語

This is probably the earliest and best-known poetic account of the Herdboy and Weaving Maid, legendary star-crossed lovers who became constellations themselves, separated by the Milky Way (the "River Han") on all but the seventh day of the seventh lunar month, when magpies formed a bridge allowing them to meet. Commentators are surprisingly of one mind in insisting on the political import of the poem. Lü Yanji explains that "the Herdboy and Weaving Maid stars [embody] the way of husband and wife. Blocked most of the time by the River Han they are unable to get close to each other. This is using the husband as a comparison to a ruler and the wife to a minister. It speaks of a minister with talent and ability who is unable to serve his ruler but is separated from him by slanderers." Zhang Xian further notes that "'Slender, slender, she raises a pale hand' is a comparison to possessing decorum and modesty; 'Click, clack, she plies the loom's shuttle' is a comparison to accomplished virtue and learning" (*Wen xuan*, 29/6b/p.538). Later critics like Fang Tinggui and Yao Nai also subscribe to this reading (Sui, 2/pp.15–16). And similar convictions motivate the various exegeses of the remaining poems in the group.

What concerns me, of course, is not the persuasiveness of such traditional interpretations—my guess is that most modern readers would reject a large majority of them out of hand and grant the rest but a grudging plausibility—but rather an examination of the impulses and stylistic features that might have motivated and encouraged them. I have discussed the former at some length in earlier chapters, and it seems to me that a consideration of the latter must necessarily focus on the nature and usage of the imagery in the "Nineteen Ancient Poems." Jean-Pierre Diény insists at several points in his study of the collection on the symbolic, formulaic, generalizing, and non-representational quality of its images. About the first poem, for example, he writes that it

[20] *Wen xuan*, 29/6a–b/p.538; Sui Shusen, 2/pp.15–16. Cf. trans. by Diény, p. 27; Watson, p. 28; Waley, p. 43; Hales in *Sunflower Splendor*, p. 32.

does not narrate a story but is a complaint about separation. Its force lies in its generality. It matters little whether the separated one is man or woman, traveler or sedentary; the only thing that counts is his/her state of mind, and anyone can lend him/her a visage as one wishes. Of course the landscape counts no more than the physiognomy of the characters.... Our text replaces concrete details with a pure notion of distance.... Rather than a story or even a spontaneous confession, this is a skillful combination of formulas, proverbs, and sanctified images. Each of its elements keeping a relative autonomy, their conjunction does not comprise an anecdote but an atmosphere. (pp. 58–59)

Similarly, he argues in a comment on the ninth poem that it presents "one of the fundamental literary principles of the collection: the object is nothing, only the feeling counts. The landscape, the 'accessories' (flower, piece of fabric, letter) have no value of their own. They are signs" (p. 104). And his Conclusion resumes these and other scattered remarks about the "Nineteen Ancient Poems":

The fact, no matter how picturesque, is only an index of feeling and only merits a schematic presentation.... Just like narration, description is not an end in itself.... Sometimes it substitutes for direct expression of emotions *attitudes* that manifest them conventionally.... Sometimes the poem opens with a semi-symbolic scene, decor that is as much spiritual as material: the landscape of autumn or winter, the solitary bedroom by the light of the moon, the cemetery. This type of preamble, part descriptive 賦 and part symbolic 興, derives from the *Classic of Poetry*. It is a mode of expression common to all the world's poetry, but which has developed particularly in China, the sole survivor of the famous prologues of the *Classic of Poetry*.... It is clear that description tends to congeal into formulas. It is in the greatest generality that these poems evoke the sentiments of common humanity. (pp. 166–67)

These "formulas," of course, are the numerous images in both the *Classic of Poetry* and the *Songs of Chu* that commentators thought conveyed certain categorical, cosmic correspondences, a conviction sustained by an overpowering culturally shared assumption of organic correlations in the universe. Diény's ascription of the primary responsibility for the ongoing usefulness of these images to the prefaces above all, i.e., the critical literature rather than the poems themselves, is particularly telling and supports a point I have been developing myself. I would prefer, however, to temper somewhat his insistence on the radically more coherent structure of the

"Nineteen Ancient Poems," their logical development of theme as compared with the merely rhythmic unity of the *Poetry*, the prolixity of the *Songs of Chu*, and the anarchy of the Han *yuefu* or anonymous Music Bureau ballads (p. 169). There is no doubt, of course, that the not necessarily incremental repetition and often mystifying juxtaposition of images in the songs in the *Shi jing* do not usually contribute to a rigorously logical development of theme or situation. Nor, despite its larger scope and its generally autobiographical framework, does "Encountering Sorrow" develop a consistently linear progression of events. It is equally true that, by contrast, many of the "Nineteen Ancient Poems" do present the outlines of a coherent narrative, as I mentioned in my discussion of the second poem. Nevertheless, these accounts are almost always either set off by a distinctly separate opening image and/or truncated along the way by others, as is the case with the first poem. These interruptions of a narrative by images that cannot apparently be naturalized as elements belonging to an empirically observed scene are precisely what reinforce their conventional, formulaic character. A consideration of their probable emblematic function thus becomes paramount, particularly since the lack of the refrain and repetition pattern typical of the *Classic of Poetry* discounts the likelihood of selection for the purposes of rhyme.

Diény's praise of these formulaic and generalizing qualities of images in the "Nineteen Ancient Poems" is clearly addressed to some contemporary readers' frequent impatience with the annoying vagueness and thematic narrowness and repetitiveness of the collection. As Diény himself notes, traditional Chinese critics encountered no such difficulties with the poems' characteristic ambiguity of reference, lauding them, on the contrary, for their much-prized ability to "contain implicit meaning" (*han xu* 含蓄):

> It appears, therefore, that the Nineteen Poems feign an insistence on what counts for little—things—and only indirectly touch upon what is essential—feeling. This paradox has greatly contributed to their glory. It lies at the source, in fact, of the qualities that Chinese critics celebrate with the greatest enthusiasm: the true meaning lies unexpressed and the poem goes on even as it ends; if everything had been said "to the limit" then there would remain nothing else to think about, but in explicating itself by an indirect route, by means of an object or a situation, the feeling cannot be exhausted. (p. 167)

According to Chen Zuoming, for example, the ninth poem ("There is a strange tree in the garden" 庭中有奇樹 [*Wen xuan*, 29/6a/p.538; Sui, 2/p.14]) demonstrates "the excellence of the Ancient Poems, which rests entirely in their containing implicit meaning." The poem speaks of sending a branch of the tree as a token of affection to a loved one far away, suggesting but not mentioning directly, writes Chen, the fact that the separation is in fact permanent, that the speaker has been rejected. "Because it does not speak exhaustively of feelings, the feelings are thereby prolonged; this is the legacy of the Airs' and Elegances' 'mildness and sincerity' (*wen rou dun hou* 溫柔敦厚).[21] To apprehend words and only upon reflection probe to their basic meaning is what is called repinement without anger. Easily understood exhaustive language is insipid and lacks lingering flavor" (Sui, 2/p.15). Similarly, he writes of poem 13, "I press my carriage through Upper East Gate" 驅車上東門 (*Wen xuan*, 29/8a–b/ p.539; Sui, 2/p.20) that "its painful emotion and agitation are extreme, yet throughout the entire piece there is not one word that discloses the true meaning.... Its marvelousness lies wholly in not letting the true meaning emerge [directly], hence its excellence" (Sui, 2/p.21). Several other commentators cited in the Sui edition echo this esteem for what they view as the remarkable restraint of the poem, whereas poem 16, "Biting cold, the year draws to a close" 凜凜歲云暮 (*Wen xuan*, 29/9b–10a/ p.539–40; Sui, 2/pp.23–24), they agree, suffers by contrast for expressing its lament over abandonment too directly (Sui, 2/p.25).

While it is quite true, however, that "containing implicit meaning" or evoking endless significance were two of the most prized qualities in classical Chinese poetics, Diény's willingness to equate them in the case of the "Nineteen Ancient Poems" with terms like ambiguity and generality is, I feel, somewhat hasty. The traditional commentators were not attributing to these poems, and Chinese poetry as a whole, a concern primarily with the suggestion of universal themes, for which they have somewhat ironically drawn the praise of Diény and other modern Western critics. Rather, it becomes clear upon reading their scattered remarks that they assumed that each poem did indeed have a specific reference and represented a response to some particular situation in the poet's experience—generally political, to be sure—and not an attempt to discourse on some abstract theme like separation or mortality. What impressed them, therefore, was the poet's reticence at speaking directly of the motivation for the poem. For all the interruptive quality of the images in the poems—which enhances their emblematic value—they were convinced that an historically true story was nevertheless being told. Certainly, Chen Hang's insistence on reading the nine Ancient Poems he includes as chronicles of his putative author Mei Cheng's experiences with his ruler provides a good illustration of their conviction that all references in a poem, no matter how

---

[21] This phrase appears in the *Li ji* 禮記, *Jing jie pian* 經解篇. For a discussion of the concept, see Zhu Ziqing, *Shi yan zhi bian*, esp. pp. 107–14.

skillfully veiled, were ultimately specific ones. This is not to say, of course, that their presuppositions were necessarily correct, but Diény's suggestion that they admired vagueness per se should not go unquestioned.

II.

We can find further support for the claim that the Chinese critics' notion of implicit meaning in the case of Han and Wei poetry denoted the suppression of overt discussion of a specific reference rather than any lack of one in the critical literature on Ruan Ji. Commentators over the centuries have taken for granted the integral relationship between his series of 82 "Poems Singing My Thoughts" (*Yong huai shi* 詠懷詩) and his problematic attitudes to and experiences in connection with the shift in power from the Cao 曹 family rulers of the Wei dynasty and the gradual usurpation of their power during the mid-third century by the Sima 司馬 clan, who went on to establish the Jin dynasty; links between the two have been ably chronicled by Donald Holzman.[22] To be sure, there is a large measure of perplexity on the part of some critics at the poems' resistance to an indisputably biographical and political interpretation. Thus the earliest commentator on the collection, Yan Yanzhi 顏延之 (384–456), cited in the prefatory remarks to the selection of seventeen poems included in the *Wen xuan*, first situates them within an historical context: "It is said that Ruan Ji during the era of Jin Wen 文 [Sima Zhao 昭, r. 211–265] lived in constant anxiety over catastrophe, thus he produced these songs."[23] But his comment following the first poem already questions his ability to establish the putative links between poetry and politics to anyone's satisfaction. Ruan Ji, he writes,

> personally served a dynasty in disorder and was in constant fear of being slandered and meeting disaster. That is why he expressed himself in song, and that is why each time he sighs, lamenting his life, although his aim is to criticize and reprimand, his style is full of obscurities. Many generations later, it is difficult to fathom his true intentions. Therefore I have explained the main ideas in these verses in a general way and touched on their hidden meanings.[24]

[22] In his *Poetry and Politics: The Life and Works of Juan Chi (A.D. 210–263)* (Cambridge: Cambridge University Press, 1976).

[23] *Wen xuan*, 23/1a/p.417; cf. trans. by Holzman, p. 7.

[24] Trans. Holzman, ibid.; *Wen xuan*, 23/1b/p.417. The Six Ministers edition of the *Wen xuan* and Huang Jie 黃節, *Ruan Bubing yong huai shi zhu* 阮步兵詠懷詩註 (Peking: Renmin, 1957), among others, both attribute the longer statement to Li Shan, as do the *Wei Jin*

Zhong Hong also calls attention to the recalcitrance of Ruan's poetry. After placing him in the venerable tradition of both the Lesser Elegances and the Airs of the States of the *Classic of Poetry* and praising the loftiness and power of his emotions, he writes that Ruan's "thoughts are profound and unrestrained and their ultimate meaning difficult to seek out," finally alluding to the comments of Yan Yanzhi just cited.[25] Liu Xie agrees that "Ruan's thoughts are deep and far-reaching,"[26] and Shen Deqian warns against an overzealous search for precise referents:

> Mister Ruan's inspired thoughts are vacillating and fragmentary; there is no logic to what is stimulated and entrusted (*xing ji* 興寄). Genial contentment and grievous lament are mixed together within them. Good readers will not seek out their ultimate meaning: this is how to deal with Mister Ruan's poems. If one insists on seeking out time and event to substantiate them, this will be forced.[27]

Shen's position, however, though perhaps congenial to Western readers, is somewhat anomalous among the traditional Chinese, and there is no shortage of commentators heedless of his advice, most notable among them Gu Zhi 古直[28] and the indefatigable Chen Hang. In the introduction to his selection of Ruan's poems the latter first cites the statements of Yan Yanzhi given above and, after mentioning some of the Cao and Sima family members who most engaged the poet's attention, begs to differ with Yan's overly general assessment of the thrust of his writing:

> For the ardor of a humane person and determined man exerts itself there [in the poetry]. How could it merely be sighs "lamenting his life"? In particular, his entrusting [words with meaning] is extremely profound, and there is structure in his establishment of words. Comparison and stimulus (*bi xing*) are more numerous than exposition

---

nan bei chao wenxue shi cankao ziliao 魏晉南北朝文學史參考資料 (Peking, 1961; rpt. Hong Kong: Hongzhi, n.d.), p. 175, and Zhang Zhiyue 張志岳, "Lue lun Ruan Ji ji qi yong huai shi" 略論阮籍及其詠懷詩, in *Wei Jin liu chao shi yanjiu lunwen ji* 魏晉六朝詩研究論文集, *Zhongguo gudian wenxue yanjiu lun zhi ji hui bian* 中國古典文學研究論之集滙編, 2 (1969), p. 78. Holzman argues, however, that this is probably an error (pp. 248–9n2), and Li Zhifang, "Ruan Ji yong huai shi lun," p. 81, agrees.

[25] Zhong Hong, *Shi pin*, in *Lidai shihua*, I, 8. Zhong Hong's summary judgment of Ruan is translated in full by Holzman, p. 233.

[26] *Wenxin diaolong zhu*, 2/p.67.

[27] Shen Deqian, *Gu shi yuan jian zhu*, 2/27b/p.160. Also cited in Li Zhifang, "Ruan Ji yong huai shi lun," p. 81.

[28] In his *Ruan Sizong yong huai shi jian ding ben* 阮嗣宗詠懷詩箋定本; cited by Holzman, p. 286.

and hymn, but when their subtleties are investigated then one can reach his boundless thoughts. Because of his use of comparison and stimulus, sound and feeling linger on at length and his words seem immeasurable. When one investigates their subtleties then one can comprehend what is abstruse and the hearer will be without fault....[29]

Chen concludes that after making a comparative classification of the 38 poems he has chosen and drawing out their meaning he has divided them into three groups, the first mourning "the imminent demise of his honored state [of Wei]," the second "criticizing powerful schemers," and the third "speaking his own mind."[30]

Modern critics have pointed out that these statements represent two schools of interpreting Ruan Ji's poetry—one arguing that the historical reference and satirical meaning of the poems are too veiled to be nailed down, and the other insisting on this very possibility.[31] What is important to note, however, is that neither camp—with the possible exception of Shen Deqian—denies the presence of such elements: they disagree only on the extent to which they can be retrieved. Yet the fact remains that many critics do yield to the elusiveness of reference in the poetry, and what in the "Nineteen Ancient Poems" had been a praiseworthy containment of implicit—yet ultimately graspable—meaning becomes in Ruan's case mystifyingly difficult. Whence the difference in attitude?

Scholars who concentrated on writing commentaries to Ruan's "Poems Singing My Thoughts" were, to be sure, much less wary of pinning down their meaning than the critics with more general theoretical interests cited above. Their explications of the first ten poems, for example (in Huang Jie's edition; the *Wen xuan* order is different), betray no hesitation in identifying the comparative dimensions and referents of the imagery. Because Holzman includes a wider spectrum of their comments in his study than I have consulted, I shall not recapitulate them here, focusing instead on but a few. The first poem is probably the best known:

Midnight and I cannot sleep:	夜中不能寐
I sit up and pluck my singing zither.	起坐彈鳴琴
Through the thin curtain the bright moon shines,	薄帷鑒明月
And a cool wind blows my lapels.	清風吹我襟
A lone wild goose cries beyond the wilds,	孤鴻號野外

[29] Chen Hang, *Shi bi xing jian*, 2/p.40.
[30] *Ibid.*, 2/pp.41,45,48.
[31] Chen Yanjie 陳延傑, ed., *Shi pin zhu* 詩品注 (Hong Kong, 1959); cited by Holzman, p. 245, and Li Zhifang, p. 81.

Soaring birds sing in northern woods. 翔鳥鳴北林

I pace to and fro: what shall I see? 徘徊將何見

Mournful thoughts alone wound my heart.[32] 憂思獨傷心

The Five Ministers' notes to this poem in their edition of the *Wen xuan* are quite direct and predictable. Lü Yanji writes that "'Midnight' is a comparison to dark disorder; 'I cannot sleep' speaks of sadness; in 'plucking his zither' he wishes to console his heart." Lü Xiang explains the famous bird imagery of the third couplet: "The 'lone wild goose' is a comparison to virtuous officials left out [of court] alone; a 'cry' is a sound of pain. 'Soaring birds' are birds of prey that like to fly in circles; they are used as comparisons to powerful officials near [the throne]—thus referring to Wen of Jin [Sima Zhao]."[33]

There is much critical disagreement as to whether or not this poem should be viewed as a kind of summary statement for the collection as a whole, because of its position, but scholars do concur with Fang Dongshu's 方東樹 (1772–1851) assessment of its skill: "Feeling and scene are fused together, the implicit meaning contained is endless, and the flavor of its significance is inexhaustible." No matter how familiar it has become through later imitations, Ruan's "stimulative imagery (*xing xiang* 興象) is always fresh and will never be spoiled in the least."[34] Yet, as Holzman points out, this poem's theme is not new at all, situated firmly in a well-established "insomniac tradition" of troubled, sleepless poets arising to play their zithers (pp. 229–30). What is different, of course, is that Ruan Ji does not mention the source of his agitation, such as the traveling, separation, and concern over mortality that obsessed the authors of the "Nineteen Ancient Poems." There is no initial summarizing couplet to orient the reader and, in particular, to help explain the significance of the bird images. Although it is plausible that Ruan is simply recalling his auditory perceptions, the level of generality maintained by the poem as a whole encourages a symbolic reading. But of what? Lü Xiang rises to the occasion, followed by several later commentators, but Chen Hang, strangely daunted, is unable to fit the poem within his framework and does not even include it in his selection. In short, there seem to be as many skeptics regarding the certain political relevance of the poem (cf. He Zhuo 何焯 [1661–1720]: "Ruan's mournful thoughts speak of being overbur-

---

[32] Huang Jie, *Ruan Bubing*, pp. 1–2; *Wen xuan*, 23/1b/p.417; cf. trans. of Holzman, p. 229.

[33] *Wen xuan*, 23/1b/p.417; cf. Holzman, p. 231.

[34] Fang Dongshu 方東樹, *Zhaomei zhan yan* 昭昧詹言, ed. Wang Shaoying 汪紹楹 (rpt. Peking: Renmin, 1961), p. 83.

dened by life: how can the commentators adequately understand him?")[35] as there are believers.

This is much less true of other poems in the group. The second poem, for example, relates the legend of Zheng Jiaofu 鄭交甫, who encountered two nymphs and received their girdle gems as love tokens, but after parting from them realized that women and jewels had both vanished.[36] Two more allusions to beautiful women are followed by references to separation and then a concluding statement: "Why do relations [as strong as] metal or stone / In one day change to the pain of parting?" 如何金石交 / 一旦更離傷？[37] Zhang Xian feels that there is a similarity in the poem to the behavior of Sima Zhao (Wen xuan, 23/2a/p.417), and the Yuan commentator Liu Lü 劉履 (1317–1379) agrees that Ruan Ji is here "employing gentle words to criticize" Sima Zhao for using the important position to which he had been entrusted by the Wei rulers in order to gain power for himself.[38] Other poems in which Ruan Ji employs familiar stories—e.g., poem 6, which tells of the marquis of Dongling 東陵侯, who became a commoner after the fall of the Qin dynasty but then made a good living raising fine melons in a patch outside the Chang'an city wall[39]—are similarly given political contexts.

The third poem, more than the first, typifies Ruan's techniques:

Fine trees form their paths beneath—	嘉樹下成蹊
Under the east garden's peach and plum.	東園桃與李
The autumn wind blows flying beans:	秋風吹飛藋
This is where decline begins.	零落從此始
Brilliant flowers all turn sere;	繁華有憔悴
Above the wall grow brambles and thorns.	堂上生荊杞
I press my horse to leave this place,	驅馬舍之去
Go up to the foot of Western Mountain.	去上西山趾
One's own life cannot be preserved—	一身不自保
How much less love for wife and child?	何況戀妻子
Hard frost covers grass in the wilds,	凝霜被野草
And the year's dusk nears its end.[40]	歲暮亦云已

[35] He Zhuo 何焯, Yi men du shu ji 義門讀書記, cited in Huang Jie, p. 2; cf. Holzman, p. 231.

[36] The anecdote appears in the Lie xian zhuan 列仙傳, trans. Max Kaltenmark, Le Lie-sien tchouan (Peking, 1953), pp. 96–101; cited by Holzman, p. 120.

[37] Huang, p. 3; Wen xuan, 23/1b–2a/p.417; cf. Holzman, p. 120.

[38] Liu Lü, Xuan shi bu zhu 選詩補注, cited by Huang Jie, p. 4.

[39] The story is given in the Shi ji, 53/p.777; also cited by Huang, pp. 8–9, and Holzman, p. 116.

[40] Huang, p. 4; Wen xuan, 23/2b–3a/pp.417–18; cf. trans. Holzman, p. 155.

As Holzman points out (p. 155), the two well-known allusions here seem to validate a political reading:

> The Western Mountain is another name for Mt. Shouyang, where Po I and Shu Ch'i found refuge so as not to serve the usurping Chou dynasty [*Shi ji*, 61/pp.825–26]. The first two lines, moreover, seem clearly to refer to an often-quoted metaphor which compares good officials to peach and plum trees: "The peach and plum do not talk, yet a path forms under them," made by people coming to see their flowers and gather their fruits. [*Han shu*, 54/p.2,469 (Peking: Zhong-hua, 1975)]

Most commentators agree, therefore, that this poem speaks of the imminent demise of the Wei dynasty; as Fang Dongshu puts it, "this uses peach and plum as comparisons to Cao Shuang 曹爽 [appointed co-regent by Cao Rui 叡, emperor Ming 明 of the Wei in 240, along with Sima Yi 懿, who in 249 had him captured and executed]. It says that his glory will not last long, to be extinguished soon by the Sima clan."[41] Fang explicates the fifth, sixth, eighth, and tenth poems as equally critical, for various reasons, of Cao Shuang (pp. 85–86). Whatever the case, the poem characteristically interweaves familiar allusions, conventional imagery drawn from nature, and a brief but helpful suggestion of Ruan's real concern—no matter what the context—in the fifth couplet. Most of the collection proceeds along these lines, with the notable exception of the first poem—hence the widespread perplexity.

In terms of method, then, Ruan's "Poems Singing My Thoughts" are very similar to the "Nineteen Ancient Poems." Both collections employ the stock, emblematic, and structurally isolated imagery that for many critics represents the *bi xing* tradition derived from the *Classic of Poetry* and directed toward the veiled criticism of contemporary society and/or politics. Both are heavily allusive, and generally to legends or texts that had already been given a moral or political gloss. Both also treat of general, if not universal, problems like separation, betrayal, and the passage of time, although much of the exegetical tradition in each case has attempted to supply specific historical causes for their concerns.

Donald Holzman, echoing Burton Watson in *Chinese Lyricism* (p. 69), has claimed, however, that the "universal" qualities of Ruan's poetry were unprecedented:

> Poets before Juan Chi spoke almost exclusively of themselves, of their own lives. Their poetry was close to the story-telling verse of the folk poets who originated the pentameter form. When they wrote about

[41] *Zhaomei zhan yan*, p. 84.

136

women (the abandoned or lonely wife was a favorite theme), the woman usually symbolized their own separation from their sovereign, or, if one refuses to accept this traditional interpretation, these women represented the poets themselves, or an actual abandoned woman, not "solitude," not anything approaching a universal or abstract or philosophical point of view. When such points of view are found in the verse, they are usually tags on the shortness of life or the sadness of separation, nuggets of wisdom that are not really the subject of the poem, do not show the poet struggling with what is at once a personal and universal problem. (pp. 228–29)

And his discussion of the first poem, therefore, concludes:

However you interpret it, Juan Chi's poem remains abstract; his point of view, general and philosophical. If the birds he hears symbolize those who are in and out of the graces of the court, the last two lines remain obstinately abstract: his melancholy may be inspired by current political conditions, or simply by the avian night noises that accompany his insomnia, but it remains an abstract *Weltschmerz*, not the limited, distinctly personal and contingent homesickness or disappointment that inspired his predecessors. (p. 232)

A number of responses to these somewhat extravagant claims for the novelty of Ruan Ji's poetry suggest themselves immediately. In the first place, the group of poets before Ruan Ji that Holzman must be using as a basis for comparison is quite small but should certainly, at the least, include the authors of the 'Nineteen Ancient Poems." Jean-Pierre Diény would, I suspect, beg to differ with Holzman's claim that Ruan Ji was the first to treat such problems as separation or mortality from a "universal" perspective; these themes certainly do represent more than mere "tags" or tangential "nuggets" in several of the earlier poems. For that matter, the same is true of Qu Yuan's concern with transience in "Encountering Sorrow." More important, however, is the question raised earlier in connection with the "Nineteen Ancient Poems"—the degree to which one should in fact regard them—and Ruan's poetry as well—as wrestling with issues on a purely "abstract" level. Certainly, as I argued above, no traditional commentator would have considered such a possibility, and while that by no means proves that the poets could not have proceeded otherwise, it does nonetheless suggest the prevalence of a cultural attitude that would predictably have influenced their creative activity. Furthermore, Holzman's claim that Ruan's poetry presents an "abstract *Weltschmerz*" is ultimately difficult, if not impossible, to substantiate, and he himself anticipates the problems with such a formulation when he grants, for example, that the poet's "melancholy may be inspired by current political conditions." To consider *any* issue at a totally abstract level would have been highly unlikely within the Chinese philosophical and cultural context, where thinking—and certainly poetry—began and often remained within the bounds of the concrete and the specific. And there is no way in which we can legitimately discount the possibility that any or all of Ruan's works were not speaking of—no matter how veiled—intensely personal situations. Indeed, Zhu Ziqing argues that Ruan was the first poet to "shed the [anonymous] *yuefu* style and use the pentasyllabic poem to sing of himself," and no matter how general or political his poems may be, "they all come from the successes and failures of his own life."[42] As Holzman himself suggests, it would be less arguable, if less startling, to say simply that Ruan was "struggling with what is at once a personal and universal problem," but this is true of any good poet, several of Ruan's predecessors included.

Nevertheless, in Holzman's defense I should mention again the definite differences in traditional critical attitudes toward the "Nineteen Ancient Poems" as opposed to the "Poems Singing My Thoughts." Whereas scholars praised the obliquity and suggestiveness of the former collection, apparently confident of their ability to retrieve the words' "implicit meaning," they were notably less sanguine about such possibilities in the case of Ruan's poems. Nowhere, however, do we find the problem construed as a difference in the level at which the poet has approached his theme—it is simply a question of its presentation and apprehension. The two groups of poems are actually quite similar in terms of theme and imagery. One suspects that the main problem the critics had was the fact that they knew the identity of the later collection's author and hence harbored greater expectations as to their ability to tie the poetry to biographical and historical data. Ruan's poems did not, however, offer even the helpful guideline of specific titles. Frustrated, the critics concluded that they were therefore more obscure.

In any event, the two collections together established an important precedent for later Chinese poetry that would in emulation employ the same titles or similar ones: "Imitating the Ancients" (*ni gu* 擬古), "Miscellaneous Poems" (*za shi* 雜詩), "Responses to What I Have Encountered" (*gan yu* 感遇), "Ancient Airs" (*gu feng*), or the like. In addition to the vagueness of title, such poems share a certain distance from—but not elimination of—explicitly mentioned personal concerns of the poet and hence the impression of a greater level of generality, a high moral purpose, and a distinctive use of imagery. Images in them were not plausible

[42]Zhu Ziqing, *Shi yan zhi bian*, p. 35.

elements of the poet's perceptual field, integrated into a naturalistic scene, but rather selected for their emblematic functions. Holzman remarks on the hoary and conventional nature of Ruan Ji's images, and Burton Watson notes that "birds play a role of particular importance as symbols of freedom and longed-for escape, being mentioned 56 times."[43] Watson's point that the apparently high level of generality goes hand in hand with a characteristic type of imagery (p. 69) is also well taken: not only do the images evoke stock cultural associations, fulfilling the *bi xing* functions attributed to the *Classic of Poetry*, but they are also typically isolated within the narrative or expository framework of a poem—placed at the beginning or else set apart along the way by discursive statements. Any combination of these features—and they are usually all present—would alert the reader and validate a reading that assumed politically or morally remonstrative aims.

III.

These poems, then, fall squarely within the tradition of "expressing one's intent," one that dominated poetry during the Han and Wei dynasties and remained alive for centuries afterward as well. In the work of Tao Qian, however, one can discern revisions of the way in which the will can be expressed. Tao did, of course, write several poems in the mode of the "Nineteen Ancient Poems" and Ruan Ji, and they are the ones included in the *Wen xuan*'s limited selection, for instance, and favored by Chen Hang as amenable to his *bi xing* analysis. Typical examples include his twelve untitled "Miscellaneous Poems," seven poems "Singing of Impoverished Men" (*Yong pin shi* 詠貧士), and eight poems "Imitating the Ancients," of which I shall give the first:

Lush, lush, the orchids before the window,	榮榮牕下蘭
Dense, dense, willows in front of the hall.	密密堂前柳
When at first I parted from you,	初與君別時
No one said the journey should last so long.	不謂行當久
Out of the door—a traveler for a myriad miles	出門萬里客
On his way meets a good friend.	中道逢嘉友
Without a word their hearts are drunk,	未言心相醉
And not from taking a cup of wine.	不在接杯酒
Orchids wither and willows also fade,	蘭枯柳亦衰
And so you have betrayed your words.	遂令此言負
I much regret all those young in years	多謝諸少年

[43] Holzman, pp. 234–35; Watson, *Chinese Lyricism*, p. 70.

With friendships neither loyal nor deep.	相知不忠厚
Ardor for which one would give one's life:	意氣傾人命
What remains of it after separation?[44]	離隔復何有

As James Robert Hightower points out (pp. 169–71), this poem is very much in the tradition I have been discussing: untitled, referentially vague, and employing familiar emblematic imagery. The traveling topos and re-duplicatives in the opening couplet are particularly reminiscent of the "Nineteen Ancient Poems." Several commentators, therefore, are quick to read this as a veiled critique of contemporary politics. The Yuan editor Liu Lü explains, for example, that "All of Jingjie's 靖節 (Tao's) poems written after his retirement seem to be full of words that lament for the state, grieve for the times, and are entrusted with criticism. Yet he did not wish to upbraid openly, so he used 'Imitating the Ancients,' 'Miscellaneous Poems,' and the like as titles."[45] The Qing editor Wen Runeng 溫如能 (eighteenth century) adds that the imitations in particular "as a whole confront changes in dynasties and respond to the many alterations in affairs of the world."[46] Liu Lü specifies the change here as the decline of the Jin dynasty, with the addresses (jun 君) in line 3 identified as the ruler (Hui bian, II, 222). Chen Hang agrees, linking the poem to venerable precedents: "When the Songs of Chu speak of the ruler, they usually borrow friendship as a 'lodging' (yu 寓) for the state. This poem is also a 'Lament for Ying' of a Jin official scholar."[47] And Wu Rulun 吳汝綸 (1840–1903) provides precise political equivalents for the various elements of the poem:

> Orchids and willows are soft and weak in quality and are used as comparisons to the Jin ruler and all those loyal to his house. "All those young in years" are those attached to the house of Song. "When at first parting from orchids and willows" speaks of being sent in service to distant posts. "Good friend" refers to the Song ruler. The two lines beginning with "I much regret" present the proper,

[44] Yang Yong 楊勇, ed., Tao Yuanming ji jiao jian 陶淵明集校箋 (Hong Kong: Wuxingji shuju, 1971), p. 186. Cf. trans. by James Robert Hightower, The Poetry of T'ao Ch'ien (Oxford; Clarendon, 1971), pp. 169–70.

[45] Liu Lü, Xuan shi bu zhu, 5; cited in Tao Yuanming yanjiu ziliao hui bian 陶淵明研究資料彙編, ed., Beijing Daxue Beijing Shifan Daxue Zhongwen xi jiaoshi tong-xue 北京大學北京師範大學中文系教師同學 (Peking: Zhonghua, 1962, 2 vols. in 1), II, 220. This edition will be cited hereafter as Hui bian.

[46] Tao shi hui ping 陶詩彙評, 4; cited in Hui bian, II, 221.

[47] Chen Hang is referring to the poem entitled Ai Ying 哀郢, the third of the Nine Declarations in the Songs of Chu, which mourns the demise of the state of Chu (see Hong Xingzu, Chu ci bu zhu, 4/10b–14a/pp.220–27; trans. Hawkes, Ch'u Tz'u, pp. 65–67). Chen Hang, Shi bi xing jian, 2/p.66; also cited in Hui bian, II, 224.

literal meaning. The last two lines take the role of "all those young in years" in order to respond—saying that the Song ruler has been generous to them and they regard the departing Jin as cast-off sandals.[48]

Tao Zhu 陶澍 (1778–1839), perhaps the best-known Qing editor of Tao Qian's works, also focuses on the imagery, writing that the poem "entrusts orchids and willows with evoking the stimulus (qi xing 起興), and the 'lord' [jun in line 3] refers to orchids and willows,"[49] but he refrains from placing it in a political context. Other commentators are equally reluctant to do so. Wu Zhantai 吳瞻泰 of the Qing, for example, argues that

> the word jun is vaguely referential and should not be tied to the Jin ruler. This sighs over a person who alters his principles along the way, makes empty boasts of a devoted ardor yet is vacillating and inconstant. It uses orchid and willow as comparison and stimulus intermittently and in succession, which is truly the regulating pulse of the Nineteen Poems.[50]

Despite their reservations, however, it is clear that the poem elicits—by virtue of its thematic, imagistic, and formal features—this general type of interpretation. The case is true of other poems in the series as well.

Poems like Tao's "Imitating the Ancients," for all their familiarity to his contemporaries, are not the works which caught and held the attention of later readers. As Stephen Owen has discussed, interest in other poems—the ones for which he has gained the admiration of modern readers as well—first burgeoned during the Tang dynasty, when poets like Wang Wei 王維 (701–61), Chu Guangxi 儲光羲 (707–59), Meng Haoran 孟浩然 (689–740), and Wei Yingwu 韋應物 (773–828) seized upon them as a welcome contrast to the stultified court modes in which they had been trained.[51] Critical attention became increasingly appreciative from the Song dynasty onward, revealing an admiration for one quality above all, "naturalness" (ziran 自然). Thus Zhu Xi writes that "in Tao Yuanming's 淵明 poetry, the 'even and bland' (pingdan 平淡)[52] quality

---

[48] From his Gu shi chao 古詩鈔, cited in Hui bian, II, 225.

[49] Tao Zhu 陶澍, Jingjie xiansheng ji 靖節先生集, 4; cited in Hui bian, II, 224.

[50] Wu Zhantai 吳瞻泰, Tao shi hui zhu 陶詩彙註, 4; cited in Hui bian, II, 223.

[51] Stephen Owen, The Great Age of Chinese Poetry: The High T'ang (New Haven: Yale University Press, 1981), pp. 6–7 and passim.

[52] This had become vaunted as a positive aesthetic characteristic during the late Tang and Song dynasties, used in reference to poetry that was felt to be simple, sincere, and understated. For a discussion of the term, see Jonathan Chaves, Mei Yao-ch'en and the Development of Early Sung Poetry (New York: Columbia University Press, 1976), esp. pp. 114–25.

comes from its naturalness. Men afterwards imitated his even blandness yet were far off the mark."[53] Another citation notes that

> what makes Yuanming's poetry lofty is precisely that it has not been handled in a systematic way. What is within his breast flows out with naturalness. [Su] Dongpo 東坡 [Su Shi 蘇軾 (1037–1101)] emulated him piece for piece and verse for verse, following his rhymes and harmonizing with them. Although [Su's] lofty talent does not appear to have wasted any effort, he nevertheless lost the intrigue of [Tao's] naturalness.[54]

Yang Guishan 楊龜山 offers similar praise: "What is unapproachable in Yuanming's poetry is its unassuming placidity (*chongdan* 沖澹) and profound purity, which come from naturalness. If one has ever exerted effort to imitate it, then one learns that Yuanming's poetry is not something that can be accomplished by applied effort."[55] In his *Canglang's Remarks on Poetry* (*Canglang shihua* 滄浪詩話) Yan Yu 嚴羽 (fl. 1180–1235) compares a verse of Tao's with one of Xie Lingyun's and concludes that "the reason Xie does not attain the level of Tao is that Kangle's [Xie's] poetry is quintessentially skillful and Yuanming's poetry's character is one of naturalness,"[56] although Wang Shizhen 王世眞 (1526–1590) later cautions that "Yuanming entrusts meaning to unassuming placidity, but his syntax and diction involve extreme skill. After undergoing great thought their composition leaves no traces of it. If later poets concentrate all their forces to seek his likeness and call that naturalness, they are grossly mistaken."[57]

Finally, Fang Dongshu is impressed by the "true" or "real" (*zhen* 眞) qualities of Tao's poetry. The Yuan commentator Liu Lü had written of Tao's second poem on "Returning To Live on the Farm" (*Gui yuantian ju* 歸園田居), which describes a placid life as a farmer concerned only about his crops, that its concluding couplet—"I often fear that freezing sleet will come / To wither both the plants and the weeds" 常恐霜霰至 / 零落同草莽 —speaks of "catastrophes about to endanger the current ruling house."[58] In response to this and other readings that attribute a com-

---

[53] From *Zhuzi yu lu*, cited in Tao Zhu, ed., *Zhu jia ping Tao hui ji* 諸家評陶彙集 (hereafter cited as *Hui ji*), a separately paginated section of his *Tao Jingjie ji* 陶靖節集 (rpt. Taipei: Shangwu, 1967), p. 1.

[54] From his *Wen ji* 文集; cited in Tao Zhu, *Hui ji*, p. 10.

[55] From his *Yu lu* 語錄; cited in *Hui ji*, p. 1.

[56] Yan Yu 嚴羽, *Canglang shihua jiao shi* 滄浪詩話校釋, ed. Guo Shaoyu (Peking: Renmin, 1961), *Shi ping* 詩評 10, p. 138. Also cited in *Hui ji*, p. 6.

[57] Wang Shizhen, *Yi yuan zhi yan* 藝苑卮言, included in *Xu Lidai shihua*, II,3/p.1,152. Also cited in *Hui ji*, p. 7.

[58] Liu Lü, *Xuan shi bu zhu*, 5; cited in *Hui bian*, II, 54. The poem is given in Yang Yong, p. 59; cf. trans. Hightower, p. 51.

parative function to the image, Fang insists that its "true meaning in fact lies with rural concerns, it is not a likeness for [the poet's] own self."[59] About the third poem in the series, "I planted beans beneath the Southern Mountains" 種豆南山下, he writes that, like the second poem, it creates a "real scene, real flavor, and real meaning, just as the transforming skill of the primal force set forth in all naturalness the suspended images [of sun, moon, and stars]" (*Zhaomei zhan yan*, p. 107; also cited *Hui bian*, II, 57). More generally, Fang remarks that "in reading Mister Tao's poetry, one can grasp the reality of a situation: the situation is real, the scene is real, feelings are real, and thoughts are real. Without the bother of revision and deletion they come together by themselves. Xie [Lingyun] and Bao [Zhao 鮑照 (d. 466)] revise and delete situations and events, and their fine points lie in using revision and deletion to produce the real" (*Zhaomei zhan yan*, p. 89).

Such appreciative notices derive, of course, from a longstanding admiration for the poetic skill that manages to conceal its traces, the artfulness of apparent artlessness, but what was it about Tao Qian's poetry that drew them forth in such profusion? Certainly, the fact that he provides, in titles and prefaces, a fairly extensive chronology of his poems helps to tie the poems more closely to the life and give the impression of verisimilitude that Fang so esteems. But Tao was not the first to do so, for many poets from before Ruan Ji's time, during the Jian'an reign period of the Han dynasty and afterward, had been known for establishing explicit links between poem and both individual biography and the larger historical situation. There is nothing new in Tao's providing personal contexts for his works—what is different is the scope of those contexts. Whereas earlier poets like Cao Zhi had written on a grand scale—of specific concerns with government, war, mortality, or immortality—and generally on rather formal occasions, Tao in his most distinctive poems confines himself to the level of the individual—his retirement, farm, and family—and in the most casual of circumstances. Goethe once wrote that all of his poetry was occasional,[60] a statement that expresses in a nutshell the assumption guiding most exegetes of Chinese poetry as well, but Tao Qian changes the expected dimensions of the occasion, leaving the commentators consequently often at a loss to extend them, for example, to the realm of politics.

Nothing could make this clearer than the contrast between Tao's prefaces to his two four-poem series on "Hovering Clouds" (*Ting yun* 停雲) and "The Seasons Pass By" (*Shi yun* 時運) and those written to elucidate

---

[59] Fang Dongshu, *Zhaomei zhan yan*, p. 106; also cited *Hui bian*, II, 55.
[60] Included in Eckermann's *Gespräche mit Goethe*, ed. H. H. Houben (Leipzig, 1948), I, Sept. 18, 1823. Cited by René Wellek in *A History of Modern Criticism*, I, 207.

songs in the *Classic of Poetry*. As Zhang Yugu 張玉穀 of the Qing pointed out, Tao's tetrasyllabic meter and derivation of the titles from the first verse of the first poem in each case are clearly intended to hark back to the classical anthology, as are the prefaces.[61] The preface to "The Seasons Pass By," however, tells us that it has to do with "a stroll in late spring. The spring clothes having been made, all things in nature are in harmony. With my shadow as companion, I stroll alone, pleasure and melancholy mingled in my heart."[62] Not only is the preface written by the author himself, rather than some latter-day exegete, but it also does not claim that the poems are aiming for more than a limited, personal reference. It is in large measure for such reasons that critics concluded that Tao's poetry possessed qualities of "naturalness" and "realism," that it meant what it said without veiled references to other situations. Needless to say, his characteristic simplicity of diction, vocabulary, and syntax were instrumental as well.

Another especially important factor contributing to this effect is Tao's use of imagery. In line with poets both before and after him, Tao relied heavily on natural images fraught with hoary associations, like the pine which appears as a frequent emblem for constancy amid change. Other images, however, while rooted in texts and traditions of the culture, did not until Tao establish themselves as poetic conventions; the white clouds suggestive of distant purity, the bird returning to its true home after venturing out into the world, and the chrysanthemum associated with longevity, for example, take on, by virtue of their recurrence in his work, conventional meanings upon which later poets could draw. Two other features of his imagistic practice are particularly distinctive as harbingers of new directions in the tradition. One can be seen in the first of Tao's poems on "Returning To Live on the Farm":

From youth out of tune with the common run,	少無適俗韻
My nature has always loved the hills and mountains.	性本愛丘山
By mistake I fell into the dusty net—	誤落塵網中
Gone at once for thirteen years.	一去三十年
The fettered bird cherishes its old forest;	羈鳥戀舊林
Fish in a pond long for former deeps.	池魚思故淵
Clearing wastes at the south wilds' edge,	開荒南野際
I hold to the simple, returning to the farm.	守拙歸園田
My plot is one-odd acre square,	方宅十餘畝
A thatched hut eight or nine measures large.	草屋八九間
Elms and willows shade the back eaves;	榆柳蔭後簷

---

[61] Zhang Yugu, *Gu shi shang xi* 古詩賞析, preface dated 1772, cited in *Wei Jin nan bei chao wenxue shi cankao ziliao*, p. 393.

[62] Yang Yong, p. 6; cf. trans. Hightower, p. 16.

Peach and plum spread in front of the hall.	桃李羅堂前
Wreathed in clouds is a distant town,	曖曖遠人村
Lingering thickly, the village's smoke.	依依墟里煙
A dog barks deep within the lane,	狗吠深巷中
Cocks crow atop mulberry trees.	雞鳴桑樹顛
My door and courtyard lack dusty chaos—	戶庭無塵雜
In empty rooms there is peace to spare.	虛室有餘閒
So long confined within a cage,	久在樊籠裏
I've come back again to naturalness.[63]	復得返自然

After acquainting us briefly with his life's course and inclinations, Tao employs two images in lines 5 and 6 that encapsulate his view of his past—presumably as an official—an experience akin to that of the animal captured and wrenched away from its natural habitat, for which it longs in anguish. The Ming commentator He Mengchun 何孟春 (fl. 1510) points out the similarity between this couplet and, among others, that of the barbarian horses and Viet birds in the first of the "Nineteen Ancient Poems,"[64] and, predictably, Qiu Jiasui 邱嘉穗 of the Qing identifies it as a "stimulus with comparison" (*xing er bi* 興而比).[65] Although, like their immediate predecessor, the images distinguish themselves from those opening the *Shi jing* poems by virtue of their location, they do all interrupt the narrative and descriptive flow and thus call attention to their emblematic function.

Lines 15 and 16, by contrast, suggest their meaning in a much less obtrusive way, despite the fact that they are even more derivative. The Yuan critic Wu Shidao 吳師道 (*jin shi* 進士 1321–1324) identified them as lifted almost verbatim from a Han *yuefu*, and he was seconded by Li Guangdi 李光地 (1642–1718).[66] An even earlier source may be a passage in the *Dao de jing* 道德經 which speaks of a peaceful isolation so pervasive and powerful that, though communities may adjoin each other so closely that dogs barking and cocks crowing can be heard from one to the next, no contact takes place between them.[67] Yet the impact of this cou-

---

[63] Yang Yong, pp. 55–56; cf. trans. Hightower, p. 50.

[64] He Mengchun, *Tao Jingjie shi* 陶靖節詩, 2; cited in *Hui bian*, II, 51.

[65] Qiu Jiasui, *Dong shan cao tang Tao shi jian* 東山草堂陶詩箋, 2; cited in *Hui bian*, II, 52.

[66] Wu Shidao, *Wu Libu shihua* 吳禮部詩話; cited in *Hui bian*, II, 50.

[67] Section 80 of the text urges the ruler to take various measures to ensure a peaceful, sedentary, and simple life for the populace and concludes: "Though adjoining states are within sight of one another, and the sound of dogs barking and cocks crowing in one state can be heard in another, yet the people of one state will grow old and die without having had any dealings with those of another." Trans. D. C. Lau, *Tao Te Ching* (Harmondsworth: Penguin, 1963), p. 142. The images are used for similar purposes in other philosophical texts as well.

plet differs markedly from that of the one earlier in the poem, such that
Wu Rulun feels impelled to deny any relevance of the literary allusion at
all: "Yao [Peiqian 姚培謙 (fl. 1730)] says that the 'dog barks' couplet
imitates an ancient Music Bureau song, but the evoked images are completely different, and one should not suspect the words of being the
same."[68] Despite the fact that the images clearly possess conventional
associations, they are naturalized by the reader as part of a hypothetically
perceived scene because of their location in the poem, surrounded by
other descriptive details. The couplet's effect and significance would have
been quite different had it been isolated in some way and thus apparently
not empirically observed, as was the earlier one. This ability to let imagery
developed within the context of a scene fulfill multiple functions reaches
its peak during the Tang dynasty and finds important precedents in Tao
Qian's poetry.

Perhaps the best-known example of this technique is the fifth of his
twenty poems on "Drinking Wine" (*Yin jiu* 飲酒):

I built my hut in the world of men,	結廬在人境
Yet there is no din of carriage and horse.	而無車馬喧
You ask me how this could be so:	問君何能爾
With a distant heart, one's place is remote.	心遠地自偏
I pluck chrysanthemums beneath the eastern hedge	採菊東籬下
And glimpse faraway Southern Mountain.	悠然見南山
The mountain air at sunset is fine;	山氣日夕佳
Flying birds return with one another.	飛鳥相與還
Within this there is true meaning—	此中有眞意
About to discuss it, I've already forgotten words.[69]	欲辨已忘言

Noteworthy first about this poem is the contrast it presents to the four
preceding it in the series, which are all highly allusive, discursive, more
abstract and tendentious; the fourth is purely symbolic. Here, however,
the burden of expression is vested in images that both construct a brief if
plausible tableau and simultaneously carry a rich cargo of associations.
The first couplet situates the poet and presents a paradox that reflection
reveals to be only an apparent one: the "din of carriage and horse," which
suggests in particular the life of an official, may be present, yet Tao's
point is that he is oblivious to it—the space he is concerned with is not
physical but mental, and his state of mind is more important than his
actual location. After spelling this out in the question and answer of the
next two lines, he places himself within the scene.

[68] Wu Rulun, *Gu shi chao* 古詩鈔; cited in *Hui bian*, II, 53. Yao Peiqian edited the *Tao Xie shi ji* 陶謝詩集.

[69] Yang, p. 138; cf. trans. Hightower, p. 124.

The poem's third couplet has elicited countless critical appreciations and explanations, although the Qing editor Ma Pu 馬璞 insists that they are misguided. These two verses, he writes,

> continue the one above about a "distant heart." Generations have sighed over the marvelousness of these lines: some speak of their naturalness, others of their fusing scene and meaning, but none succeeds in elucidating them. Because he is plucking chrysanthemums, faraway Southern Mountain appears: this is a stimulus. A stimulus uses one thing to lead to another without being partial to one or the other. The meaning is not one-sided, so there is nothing untouched: this is the meaning of "not swerving" (*Analects* II.2), it is the source of government, and those since the Three Hundred [songs in the *Classic of Poetry*] who have known this are rare indeed. The means by which Jingjie reveals his true nature and feelings can therefore not be adequately explained in only one way.[70]

Ma's opinion remains in a distinct minority, however, for most commentators are convinced that the suggestiveness of these lines moves in other directions, centered on the various cultural associations of chrysanthemums and Southern Mountain; Hightower recapitulates some of the most salient ironies and complexities of their analyses (pp. 131–32). Again what is striking, though, is the manner in which Tao integrates a charged image into a visualizable scene. Qu Yuan, after all, also busied himself with flowers—he wove them into garlands and garments and even ate chrysanthemum petals—but for all his involvement it is the qualities of persistence and longevity associated with the flowers that remain paramount for the reader. Tao is also obviously evoking those implications, but a telling difference between the two poets is that for later generations the mention of chrysanthemums would call to mind Tao the poet sooner than longevity tonics. And the primary reason for this is his ability to attach images like the flowers and the mountain to both person and scene instead of setting them apart in an obviously emblematic way.

The much discussed final couplet no doubt alludes to passages in the *Zhuangzi* concerning the dispensability of language, but it also says something about Tao's method throughout the poem. "There is true meaning," he suggests, "within this"—the scene he has evoked, for which he has "already forgotten" the discursive language with which he could otherwise analyze it. Images, however, which are conveyed in words but outlast them, have been given and remain to communicate their meaning, just as promised by the passage from the Great Commentary to the *Classic of*

---

[70] Ma Pu, *Tao shi ben yi* 陶詩本義, 3; cited in *Hui bian*, II, 173.

Changes assuaging a disciple's worries about the inadequacy of words (cited in Chapter One). Ma Pu's protestations notwithstanding, this is the "fusion of scene and meaning" in the poem celebrated by its readers from Su Shi onward,[71] an example of what Wang Guowei 王國維 (1877–1927) called "a world without a self" (*wu wo zhi jing* 無我之境).[72] Tao's poetry as a whole is more likely to separate scene and self, image and comment, but this poem serves as an important harbinger for later trends.

IV

Commentators have difficulty applying the *bi xing* terminology deriving from the *Classic of Poetry* to Tao Qian's works; for examples of poems in which images can be claimed to carry fixed, conventional, and generally political associations they must look to Tao's poems in the Han/Wei tradition—those tied neither to title nor to an overtly specific and personal experience. The task is even more difficult in the case of Xie Lingyun; telling evidence of this can be found in Chen Hang's failure to include any of Xie's poems in his *Shi bi xing jian* and in the similar paucity of political exegeses on the part of the Tang *Wen xuan* commentators. Some modern scholars have insisted on the religious symbolism of his works, but even this claim has been disputed.

What seems clear, rather, is a sense shared by many critics that Xie's poetry embodies an imagistic practice distinctively different from that of his predecessors. As I mentioned at the beginning of this chapter, Li Zhifang credits Xie with initiating the method of "embodying objects," as opposed to the earlier trend of "expressing one's intent." More specifically, critics seem inclined to agree with the modern editor Ye Xiaoxue 葉笑雪 that Xie Lingyun represents a new development of landscape as the most important, if not sole, content of poetry.[73]

Three interrelated questions arise in connection with this view, the first concerning Xie's place within this process. J. D. Frodsham surveys the prevailing traditional Chinese critical opinion, first adumbrated in Liu Xie's statement that "Zhuangzi and Laozi retreated and then landscape flourished,"[74] and exemplified in statements by Wang Shizhen 王士禎

---

[71] Su Shi, *Dongpo ti ba* 東坡題跋, 2: "Ti Yuanming yin jiu shi hou" 題淵明飲酒詩後; cited in *Hui bian*, II, 167.

[72] Wang Guowei, *Ren jian cihua* 人間詞話 (rpt. Taipei: Kaiming, 1975), *juan shang*/p.1; also cited in Yang Yong, p. 146.

[73] See his introduction to *Xie Lingyun shixuan* 謝靈運詩選 (Hong Kong: Hanwen chubanshe, n.d.), pp. 1–22.

[74] *Wenxin diaolong zhu*, 2/p.67.

(1634–1711) and Shen Deqian to the effect that Xie was "the first to write verse depicting landscape,"[75] and then contends that

> Chinese literary criticism has long been guilty of a gross over-simplification in seeing Nature poetry as springing in "celestial panoplie all armed" from Ling-yün's ingenious imagination, for his verse represents but the culminating point of a movement which had begun centuries before.... We see in fact that the essential characteristics of Nature poetry existed within the corpus of the earlier Taoist Hsüan-yen 玄言 verse.[76]

A second question, however, immediately comes to mind: were those critics being corrected by Frodsham assuming with him that "Nature poetry is defined ... as verse inspired by a mystic philosophy which sees all natural phenomena as symbols charged with a mysterious and cathartic power"? (p. 72.) And, finally, to what extent does Xie's poetry actually focus on landscape, whether as description or as "symbol" of something ineffable? It is with these latter two questions that I shall primarily be concerned.

Even more than was the case with Tao Qian, the poems for which Xie is best known are replete with details of time and place, especially in their titles, a fact which has enabled commentators to place them within the chronology of his life and which helps to militate against a purely general political or philosophical reading of them. At the same time, Xie is clearly interested in providing more than a descriptive travelogue of various scenic locales. "Emerging Late from West Archery Hall" (*Wan chu xi she tang* 晚出西射堂) reveals both significant similarities and differences between Xie's work and earlier traditions:

Walking out of the western citywall gate,	步出西城門
I gaze in the distance at peaks west of the wall.	遙望城西岑
Range upon range of towering crags,	連障疊巇崿
Their green-blue hues sunk in murky depths.	青翠杳深沈
Dawn frosts turn maple leaves cinnabar red;	曉霜楓葉丹
In dusk glow mountain mists are dark.	夕曛嵐氣陰
The season passes and sorrow is not slight.	節往感不淺
Feelings come, memories already profound.	感來念已深

[75] See Wang Shizhen, *Daijingtang shihua* 帶經堂詩話 (rpt. Peking: Renming, 1982; 2 vols.), I,5/p.115.

[76] J. D. Frodsham, "The Origins of Chinese Nature Poetry," *Asia Major*, 8 (1960), p. 73. Cf. also *The Murmuring Stream: The Life and Works of the Chinese Nature Poet Hsieh Ling-yün (385–433), Duke of K'ang-lo* (abbreviated hereafter as *MS*) (Kuala Lumpur: University of Malaya Press, 1967; 2 vols.), I, 86–100.

The stray widow-bird longs for her mate of old;   羈雌戀舊侶
Lost birds cherish their former woods.   迷鳥懷故林
Bearing emotions they suffer yet from their love—   含情尚勞愛
How much more I, apart from those dear to my heart?   如何離賞心
I polish the mirror: silver flecks my temples;   撫鏡華緇鬢
I cinch my belt around a loose-hanging shirt.   攬帶緩促衿
"At peace with things" are merely empty words: 安排徒空言
In deep solitude, I trust to my singing zither.[77]   幽獨賴鳴琴

As Francis A. Westbrook pointed out, this poem is rife with stock phrases and topoi, formulae—such as the repetition in the first couplet and the sadness conventionally evoked by autumn—commonly seen in earlier *yuefu* and lyric poetry alike.[78] The first line recalls the opening of the ninth of Ruan Ji's "Poems Singing My Thoughts"—"I walk out of Upper East Gate" 步出上東門 —which in turn echoes no. 13 of the "Nineteen Ancient Poems": "I press my carriage through Upper East Gate" 驅車上東門.[79] What follows each opening, however, reveals a crucial difference between Xie and his predecessors. The anonymous author on leaving the gate spies in the distance the graves traditionally located north of the city wall, and the poem consequently launches into a general lament on human mortality. Ruan Ji, for his part, leaves the gate to spy Mt. Shouyang in the distance, which, since Bo Yi and Shu Qi retreated there to eat ferns and die of starvation rather than partake of the grain of the usurping Zhou dynasty, immediately suggests a political critique; the poem is typically vague on the reasons behind the poet's expressed grief, but traditional commentators by and large agree that they center on the poet's criticism of the Sima usurpers. Xie, by contrast, leaves the gate to view a mountain scene devoid of any such conventional associations; this fact, coupled with the identifiable place name in the title, not only enables scholars to situate the poem (late autumn or early winter of 422 in Yong-jia 永嘉, according to Frodsham [*MS*, II, 121]), but also prepares the reader for a narrative whose references are largely personal.

The rest of the poem fulfills this expectations. After a transition in lines 7–8 from scene to self which is based on the associations mentioned earlier, Xie employs two images to introduce the discussion of his own feel-

[77] Ye Xiaoxue, *Xie Lingyun shixuan*, p. 32; Huang Jie, *Xie Kangle shi zhu* 謝康樂詩註 (Peking: Renming, 1958), p. 34. Cf. trans. of Frodsham, *MS*, I, 120 and Francis A. Westbrook, "Landscape Description in the Lyric Poetry and 'Fuh on Dwelling in the Mountains' of Shieh Ling-yunn," Ph.D. Diss. Yale University, 1972, pp. 27–28.

[78] Westbrook, "Landscape Description," p. 29.

[79] Ruan Ji's poem is included in Huang Jie, *Ruan Bubing*, p. 12, and the other in Sui Shusen, *Gu shi shijiu shou*, 2/p.20. Holzman cites several other precedents as well in *Poetry and Politics*, p. 252n64.

ings that closely resemble the paired animals employed as comparisons in poems we have seen before. As was the case with the first of Tao Qian's "Returning To Live on the Farm," the contrast in ontological status of these birds—as opposed, for example, to the mountains and maples earlier in the poem—is striking: we read the latter as empirically observed, the former as unavoidably emblematic. Xie does, however, integrate them more closely into his narrative, comparing himself directly to them and then alluding to the reasons for his sorrow.

Although the lament over separation is a theme encountered in countless earlier poems, here it elicits nothing in critics' minds beyond the assumption of a limited autobiographical reference. Lü Xiang writes of the zither in the last line simply that "Lingyun uses this to relieve his [pain]" (*Wen xuan*, 22/11b/p.405), a kind of purely personal annotation unlikely in a Ruan Ji poem; contrast, for example, the readings of the first of the "Poems Singing My Thoughts," which also had a "singing zither." Instrumental, of course, are the identification of author and biography, the specificity of the title, and the presentation of scenic details that are read as literally observed, even if they do provoke stock responses. At the same time, the relatively limited attention Xie pays to them is noteworthy in a poet praised for his interest in landscape.

Indeed, there is very little indication in Xie's poetry that elements of nature should be dwelled on at great length and for their own sake, for the space he devotes to them is relatively quite small. "Climbing the Pondside Tower" (*Deng chi shang lou* 登池上樓),[80] for example, begins with two images drawn from the *Classic of Changes*—the submerged dragon embodying a successful retreat and the flying wild goose whose far-sounding echo suggests worldly success—to introduce, by contrast, Xie's consideration of his own failures, one which continues for the next six lines. As Westbrook observes, this first section serves primarily to deflate an established tradition of viewing scenes from on high as an index and source of personal and poetic power, and he remarks further that "Language imbued with symbolic force, not visual imagery, dominates the first eight lines, where the poet's view is so introspective that he cannot appreciate the landscape."[81] It is important to note, however, that Xie's treatment of the allusions does not recognize what Western readers might construe as an ontological gap between abstract symbol and concrete scene, for the dragons and geese could almost at first glance be read as part of the perceived landscape.

[80] Ye Xiaoxue, p. 33; Huang Jie, p. 35; cf. trans. Frodsham, *MS*, I, 121.

[81] Westbrook, "Landscape Transformation in the Poetry of Hsieh Ling-yün," *Journal of the American Oriental Society*, 100.3 (July–Oct. 1980), p. 242.

To what extent, moreover, does Xie actually emerge from this "intro-spection" to overturn the negative connotations of this opening and achieve what Westbrook claims is a "harmony with Nature and its sea-son" (p. 243)? The poet looks out, hears waves breaking and sees craggy peaks, tells us that the winds have changed as the spring force of *yang* replaces winter's *yin*, and then sums up this transformation in what is undoubtedly his most frequently cited couplet: "The pond's banks grow spring grasses; / Garden willows have changed the cries of birds" 池塘生春草 / 園柳變鳴禽 .[82] But Xie immediately follows this striking foray into description by two allusions to the *Classic of Poetry* and *Songs of Chu*, and a discussion of his own reconciliation to retirement. Those six lines out of a total of 22 do not argue convincingly for an interest in purely scenic description on Xie's part; they mark a turning point in the poem and inspire, at best, the poet's reassessment of his attitude to retreat.

Xie's relative inattention to details of nature for its own sake, as opposed to how it impinges on, reflects, affects, or contrasts with his own state of mind, is equally apparent in several other poems in his collection. Consider, for example, "Visiting White Banks Pavilion" (*Guo bai an ting* 過白岸亭):

Brushing my clothes I follow the sandy dike,	拂衣遵沙渚
Slacken my pace to enter my grass-thatched house.	緩步入蓬屋
A nearby stream trickles on densely packed rocks;	近澗涓密石
Against distant mountains scattered trees stand out.	遠山映疏木
The empty azure is hard to force into a name,	空翠難強名
Though the fisherman can easily make a tune.	漁釣易爲曲
Clutching moss I listen on greenish banks:	援蘿聆青崖
Spring and my heart together of themselves.	春心自相屬
"*Jiao-jiao*," the yellow ones perched on oaks;	交交止栩黃
"*You-you*," deer feeding on artemisia.	呦呦食苹鹿

[82] Without wishing to fuel an ongoing debate over inversion in classical Chinese poetry, I would hazard the opinion that the sheer amount of critical attention over the centuries to these lines suggests the likelihood of a reading that would not naturalize this particular couplet, at least, into inverted lines beginning with locative phrases, i.e., "On the pond's banks grow spring grasses; /In garden willows change the cries of birds." Indeed, comments by two Song dynasty critics, Luo Dajing 羅大經 and Ye Mengde 葉夢得 (1077–1148) bear this out. In his *Shi lin shihua* 石林詩話, for example, Ye Mengde cites the couplet and says that "its skill lies in its being totally unintentional; [the poet] suddenly came upon a scene which he borrowed to complete his piece without availing himself of rules and revisions. Thus this is not something that ordinary feelings can arrive at" (included in *Lidai shihua*, I, 426). In a similar vein, Luo Dajing praises the first line as an example of an apparently "clumsy verse" (*zhuo ju* 拙句) that in its total naturalness is actually the most difficult thing to achieve in poetry. See his *He lin yu lu* 鶴林玉露, *Congshu jicheng* ed. (Shanghai: Shang-wu, 1939), 3/pp.27–28. These observations would suggest that these scholars assumed a more unconventional reading of the lines.

I grieve for those men of a hundred sorrows,	傷彼人百哀
Delight in the joy of those favored with baskets of gifts.	嘉爾承筐樂
Bounty and want come and go after each other.	榮悴迭去來
Success and failure turn to sorrow and joy.	窮通成休慼
There is nothing like a long and distant retreat;	未若長疎散
Of the myriad things I'll constantly harbor the simple.[83]	萬事恆抱朴

Although some scholars believe that the opening phrase is simply a means of getting started,[84] the association of "brushing one's clothes off" and going into retirement was already established by Xie's time and is certainly appropriate for the poem as a whole. After three brief lines of description, Xie shifts into a more discursive mode, commenting on his inability to put the scene into language, as opposed to the fisherman's ease of self-expression. The baldness of the statement in line 8 is striking: nothing has prepared us for this assertion of harmony with nature—certainly not the sparse scenic details just provided, and to which Xie does not return.

The remaining half of the poem seems to bear little connection with this statement nor, for that matter, with the particular scene; it does, however, confirm the implication of the opening phrase. Lines 9–10 may, of course, register sensory perceptions; more likely, however, is their function as allusions to songs in the *Classic of Poetry*. "The yellow ones" refers most clearly to poem 131 (discussed in Chapter Two), which documents the sacrifices of three men at the burial of their lord and "probably hints," as Frodsham suggests in *The Murmuring Stream* (II, 128), at the political misfortunes of some of Xie's closest friends. The feeding deer, by contrast, recalls poem 161 in the anthology, traditionally interpreted as a song "feasting the gathered officials as honored guests" (*Zheng yi*, 9B/1a/p.765) and anticipates the blessings of those in line 12. Given such wide fluctuations in fortunes, Xie concludes for the expediency of life in retirement.

Xie's corpus includes surprisingly few works in which the relative proportion of imagery to discursive statement increases markedly in comparison with those just cited. The following poem is distinctive for this reason.

Written on the Lake, Returning from Stone Cliff
   Retreat (*Shi bi jingshe huan hu zhong zuo* 石壁精舍
   還湖中作)

From dusk to dawn the weather always changes.	昏旦變氣候
Mountains and rivers retain a lucid glow.	山水含清暉

83 Ye Xiaoxue, p. 47; Huang Jie, p. 41; cf. trans. Frodsham, *MS*, I, 125.
84 See the notes to this poem in the *Wei Jin nan bei chao wenxue shi cankao ziliao*, p. 471.

The lucid glow can give one so much pleasure	清暉能娛人
That the traveler at peace forgets about return.	遊子憺忘歸
When I leave the valley, day has just begun;	出谷日尚早
I board my boat when the light is already dim.	入舟陽已微
Forested gorges harbor somber colors;	林壑斂暝色
Rose-tinged clouds gather in evening haze.	雲霞收夕霏
Water chestnut and lotus by turns are bright and thick;	芰荷迭映蔚
Rushes and reeds press upon each other.	蒲稗相因依
I sweep them aside to take to the southern path,	披拂趨南逕
So happy to rest at my cottage in the east.	愉悅偃東扉
When thoughts have stilled things naturally seem unimportant;	慮澹物自輕
The mind content will never leave the truth.	意愜理無違
I send these words to all who would nurture their lives—	寄言攝生客
Try using this Way to learn.[85]	試用此道推

Ye Xiaoxue notes that this poem inaugurates a "beautifully refined style" of poetry new to the southern dynasties (p. 73), but it is significant for other reasons as well. Here fully three-quarters of the poem details Xie's perceptions of and reactions to an apparently observed scene, with the last four lines conveying the message he derives from his experience. Also striking here is the emotional equanimity pervasive throughout, and in particular the lack of any remarks about the poet's loneliness. As Ye Xiaoxue notes, the word "return" (*huan* 還) in the title serves as the key to this attitude, suggesting as it does the peace of going back to what is basic in one's nature.[86] The same theme is central to Tao Qian's poetry as well, but the two poets' differing treatment of their material should be noted. Whereas Xie provides many more precise details of the scene and his involvement in it, he seems less willing than Tao to let those imagistic elements carry the burden of his meaning and consequently must rely on a more explicit statement summing it up for his readers.

This is also true of another poem whose overall structure is much the same, "Climbing Stone Gate's Highest Peak" (*Deng Shimen zui gao ding* 登石門最高頂).[87] Once again there is a noticeable bifurcation in the poem between the first half (twelve of the poem's twenty lines) chronicling the poet's activities and observations along winding paths through craggy

[85] Ye Xiaoxue, p. 72; Huang Jie, p. 63; cf. trans. Frodsham, *MS*, I, 138.
[86] This same pont was made earlier by Fang Dongshu, *Zhaomei zhan yan*, p. 152. Fang was also struck by the fact that "the inspired imagery (*xing xiang* 興象) of this poem fully attains the meaning of parting; afterwards only Mister Du [Fu] had it."
[87] Ye Xiaoxue, p. 87; Huang Jie, p. 72; cf. trans. Frodsham, *MS*, I, 144.

peaks and the long conclusion discussing the mental peace and harmony with nature exemplified by his experience. Although the break between the two sections is somewhat jarring, Xie's procedure here represents an important change in the tradition's treatment of imagery and meaning. Whereas earlier poetry seemed to start with some general statement, often given explicitly at the beginning, and then selected a few illustrative images from a stockpile of cultural conventions, Xie appears to sense that carefully selected, empirically observed imagery from nature can indeed convey meaning, even if he still lacks the confidence necessary to avoid spelling it out at the end. He resists this urge most successfully in this last poem to be considered, "Following Jinzhu Torrent I Cross the Peaks and Journey by Stream" (*Cong Jinzhu jian yue ling xi xing* 從斤竹澗越嶺溪行):

When gibbons cry, I truly know it's dawn.	猿鳴誠知曙
In the valley's darkness light has not yet appeared.	谷幽光未顯
Beneath the cliffs clouds begin to gather;	巖下雲方合
Upon the flowers dew still sparkles brightly.	花上露猶泫
Winding round by curving coves and bays,	逶迤傍隈隩
I climb far up the passes in the hills.	迢遞陟陘峴
To cross the stream I lift my gown above the current,	過澗既厲急
Climb wooden planks that take me ever higher.	登棧亦陵緬
By river islets, one bend after another,	川渚屢逕復
I follow the flow, enjoying its twists and turns.	乘流翫迴轉
Duckweed floats upon the murky deeps;	蘋萍泛沈深
Zizania and rushes cover its clear shallows.	菰蒲冒清淺
I clamber up a rock to cup the water's fall,	企石挹飛泉
Pull down a branch to pluck its budding leaves.	攀林摘葉卷
I think I see someone in the mountain's fold—	想見山阿人
Fig leaves and rabbit floss seem before my eyes.	薜羅若在眼
A handful of orchids I toil in vain to twine;	握蘭勤徒結
Pluck hemp though my heart can bare itself to none.	折麻心莫展
Feelings treat what's appreciated as beauty:	情用賞爲美
These things are obscure—who discusses them after all?	事昧竟誰辨
I contemplate this and cast off worldly thoughts:	觀此遺物慮
Once enlightened I gain what has been abandoned.[88]	一悟得所遣

As in the last two works just discussed, more than half of this poem details the poet's excursion, beginning at the darkness of dawn along a stream winding high over a mountain peak. And, as in so many other poems, literary allusions occupy a pivotal position in the overall structure,

[88] Ye Xiaoxue, pp. 92–93; Huang Jie, p. 133; cf. trans. Frodsham, *MS*, I, 142.

signaling an important transition in Xie's mode of presentation and bridging the passage from scene to self, external concerns to internal ones. Lines 15–18 here draw on various passages from the *Songs of Chu*, the first to the opening lines of "The Mountain Spirit" (*Shan gui* 山鬼), ninth of the *Nine Songs*: "There seems to be some one in the fold of the mountain / In a coat of fig-leaves with a rabbit-floss girdle." (*Chu ci bu zhu*, 2/20/p.135; trans. Hawkes, p. 43) Ye Xiaoxue notes that rabbit floss was used as a symbol for the attire of a recluse, suggesting the kind of person with whom Xie would like to share his pleasure. Orchids, of course, are used throughout the Chu anthology as emblems of purity; Li Shan provides one possible source that does not, however, correspond with any exactitude to Xie's wording here (*Wen xuan*, 22/18b/p.409). And, finally, line 18 alludes to a couplet from the fifth of the *Nine Songs*, the "Greater Master of Fate" (*Da si ming* 大司命): "I have plucked the glistening flower of the Holy Hemp / To give to one who lives far away" (*Chu ci bu zhu*, 2/13b/p.122; trans. Hawkes, p. 40). All of these references evoke the emotional tenor and themes of the *Chu ci* poets to introduce the problem to which Xie then addresses himself—the absence of a sympathetic friend. It is a testament to the power of the commentaries on the earlier works that some of Xie's readers are led by these allusions to suspect political references at play here. Lü Yanji writes that "orchid and hemp are both fragrant plants that can be bestowed on someone. This says that in serving the ruler he has toiled laboriously but joined in vain with someone of a mutually understanding heart, so he has no one to express himself to" (*Wen xuan*, 22/18b/p.409). Liu Tanzhi 劉坦之 then argues that this refers obliquely to the loss of Xie's friend Liu Yizhen 劉義眞, the prince of Luling 廬陵 (407–24), in a power struggle with Xu Xianzhi 徐羨之 (364–426) (cited in Huang, *Xie Kangle*, p. 78). Whatever the case, Xie has successfully integrated the literary allusions into the narrative of his poem; they follow so unobtrusively upon the preceding description that one is almost inclined to take them at face value, and they lead quite smoothly into the ensuing statement of Xie's plight.

This concluding couplet suggests the greater likelihood of philosophical or even religious, rather than political, implications for the poem, although they are not unrelated. The verb "contemplate" (*guan* 觀) implies the attainment of a meditative insight that can discern the illusory from the real, and "enlightened" of course confirms this reading. As Li Shan notes, the last line refers to a Guo Xiang 郭象 (d. 312) commentary on the *Zhuangzi*:

If [two things] are greatly not of a kind, nothing serves so well as to be mindless. When one abandons distinctions, and abandons that which has been abandoned, and abandons this in order to arrive at a state of there being no abandonment—only then is there nothing that has not been abandoned so that distinctions can vanish.[89]

In other words, Xie is employing a paradox familiar to both Taoist and Buddhist thinking by virtue of which distinctions can be simultaneously transcended and embraced. Thus contemplation of the mountain scene not only releases Xie from all concerns about the material world, including the very beauties of nature he is observing, it also effects a realization of the ultimate meaninglessness of all such distinctions as that between the worldly and the supramundane and hence enables him to recover his attachment to scene.

Traditional critics declined the invitation offered by these concluding connotations to read "Following Jinzhu Torrent ..." as a religious allegory, with the steep and winding ascent paralleling the laborious process preceding the sudden attainment of an enlightened view of reality. This speaks for nothing so much as the pull of the concrete, which either takes natural images literally or reads them as emblems of the equally concrete political world. Modern Western commentators, by contrast, have argued for the quintessentially "symbolic" qualities of imagery in Xie Lingyun's poetry. Richard B. Mather, for example, has proposed that there is more to his mountain scenery than meets the eye: "Since Reality for the Buddhist is often described in terms of emptiness or quiescence, landscape makes a very fitting symbol of that Reality, a symbol that in some respects surpasses the cult images of the temples themselves."[90] To which J. D. Frodsham responds in *The Murmuring Stream*:

> we may put the matter much more exactly. Landscape was not just a *symbol* for the Tao—the term was at this period as much a Buddhist as a Taoist expression—it is the Tao itself. This is brought out very clearly by a passage in Sun Ch'o's "Fu of My Wanderings on Mount T'ien T'ai":
>> When [the Tao] dissolves it becomes rivers;
>> When it coagulates it becomes mountains.
> So the contemplation of landscape is the contemplation of Reality itself. (I, 100)

To which Burton Watson in turn objects:

> What Hsieh must have known, however, is that both Taoism and Buddhism, while on a practical level approving the freedom from

[89]Trans. Westbrook, "Landscape Description," pp. 147–48.

[90]Richard B. Mather, "The Landscape Buddhism of the Fifth-Century Poet Hsieh Lingyün," *Journal of Asian Studies*, XVIII.1 (Nov. 1958), p. 76.

human distraction that a mountain retreat customarily affords, on a philosophical level condemned any attachment to place that would see the landscape of the far-off hills as intrinsically more beautiful or valuable than the landscape near the city, or that would see beauty or value at all in the landscape. (*Chinese Lyricism*, p. 82)

And Paul Demiéville, for his part, argues that "the role of Buddhism in the formation of landscape art in China" has been "much exaggerated,"[91] and that

Buddhism never enters into [Xie's] poetry, at least on the surface. Although Western and even Chinese historians claim this willingly, I do not think that Buddhism, even sinicized in the manner of the Dhyāna [Chan or Zen] school, played any role in the literary and artistic revolution of the fourth and fifth centuries than that of catalyst of new tendencies within an essentially Chinese movement.[92]

Demiéville's point is well taken, even if one acknowledges the presence of overtly Buddhist poems in Xie's corpus and the possibility of covert allusions in others. For one thing, the poetry gives us few indications, such as repetitions of key words or patterns, of any hidden symbolic overtones to the descriptions of landscape. A case might be made for Xie's frequent accounts of arduous mountain ascents as an analogue to the gradual effort toward enlightenment, but the fact that Xie was a known exponent of the opposing theory of sudden or instantaneous enlightenment (*dun wu* 頓悟) seriously undermines this attempt. The numerous allusions in his works are, as Demiéville also notes, preponderantly classical or Taoist, and, with precious few exceptions, the poet does not present himself as having achieved or even striving for a typically Buddhist equanimity or detachment from the world, but rather as someone obsessed with the lack of a like-minded friend with whom to share his appreciation of the natural beauties surrounding him. Most important, however, is the fact that descriptions of landscape simply do not comprise a portion of most poems significant enough to warrant such symbolic interpretations nor, furthermore, are the connections in many cases between those sections and the discursive conclusions more than tenuous. In some instances, to be sure, Xie attributes a certain stimulative efficacy to his mountain experiences, but in many others the necessity of any such links is difficult to discern.

---

[91] Paul Demiéville, "Présentation d'un poète" (review of Frodsham, *The Murmuring Stream*), *T'oung Pao*, LXV.4–5 (1970), p. 256.

[92] Paul Demiéville, "La Montagne dans l'art littéraire chinois," included in *Choix d'études sinologiques*, ed. Yves Hervouet et al. (Leiden: E. J. Brill, 1973), p. 377; originally published in *France-Asie*, CLXXXIII (Paris, 1965), pp. 7–32.

Francis Westbrook has argued for a somewhat different sort of symbolism: "there evolves in the lyric poetry an allegorical journey through the mountain landscape which results in the poet's loss of awareness of self as well as of other distinctions, and in his acquiring a new transcendental perception. Thus through careful manipulation of strikingly realistic descriptive details, the landscape and the state of mind which envisions it are transformed."[93] Although perhaps less arguable than a strictly Buddhist interpretation, this view still encounters problems mentioned above: that Xie's poetry does not generally devote enough space to landscape description to justify the epithet "allegory" (not to speak, of course, of the difficulty of applying this term to Chinese poetry of all), and that it is rare to find Xie enjoying a truly "transcendental perception." Earlier Taoist- and Buddhist-influenced poets may indeed, as Westbrook argues elsewhere, have concentrated "on elaborately symbolic descriptions of mountain landscapes,"[94] but I find it difficult to place Xie squarely within this tradition.

"Symbolic" would, in any case, be a rather infelicitous term for a poet whose world-view would likely reject the ontological distinction between concretion and abstraction implied by the term. One could well argue, with Westbrook, that the mountain experiences in some poems mirror or provoke internal processes or trains of thought within the poet himself, but this is not symbolism. This epithet might be more convincingly applied to the work of earlier poets like Sun Chuo 孫綽 (?320–?380), who, while devoting much attention to images of nature, were primarily interested in alluding to the ineffable Tao presumably embodied in them, although even in such cases there is no assumption of a fundamental dichotomy between the sensible and the supra-sensible. And, finally, no matter how limited the actual scope of Xie's landscape descriptions, they certainly suggest that he was more interested in literal accuracy than conventional associations, in marked contrast to the tradition. Yet, in the end, perhaps uncertain of the ability of concrete images to convey other kinds of meaning, he found it necessary to entrust that task to the discursive sections following them.

V.

Xie Lingyun's emphasis, however limited, on the details of a natural scene reflects a broader burgeoning of interest in description evident in Six

---

[93] Westbrook, "Landscape Description," p. 5.
[94] Westbrook, "Landscape Transformation," p. 252.

Dynasties theoretical texts as well. It is during this period that the tradition first concerns itself with fidelity to the image as perceived object in a lyric poem; at the same time, however, it never loses sight of imagery as embodiment of a larger concept—a notion central to the *fu bi xing* rhetoric as formulated by early exegetes of the *Classic of Poetry*. Moreover, a second development introduces new conceptions of that classical terminology that not only reject this older didactic function of imagery in favor of more exclusively affective purposes, but also ultimately undermine any further emphasis on mimetic representation for its own sake. Indeed, the Chinese tradition provides arid ground for a poetics of description that would contemplate a full and accurate rendering of the thing in itself; interest in objects centers rather on their potential evocation of a network of intellectual and/or emotional associations.

Lu Ji's *Exposition on Literature* is the first text to call critical attention to the importance of description:

Genres differ in myriad ways;	體有萬殊
Objects lack one single measure.	物無一量
Countless, confused, scattered, and fleeting,	紛紜揮霍
Forms are hard to describe.	形難爲狀
Words display talent and show one's skill;	辭程才以效伎
Ideas control them inventively.	意司契而爲匠
Facing being and non-being one struggles and strives;	在有無而僶俛
Before the shallow and deep one does not yield.	當淺深而不讓
Though leaving the square and discarding the compass,	雖離方而遯員
One hopes to probe all shapes and exhaust appearance.[95]	期窮形而盡相

In this passage discussing the many challenges faced by the writer, the last line in particular addresses the issue of description. Guo Shaoyu, following Li Shan's annotation, suggests that the "square" and "compass" refer to formal rules,[96] which is certainly the case in later texts. Wang Yuanhua

[95] *Wen xuan*, 17/5a–b/p.309; cf. trans. by Fang, p. 535, and Chen, pp. 207–8.
[96] Guo Shaoyu, ed., *Zhongguo lidai wenlun xuan* 中國歷代文論選 (Hong Kong: Dawen she, 1978), p. 146.

王元化 argues that Lu Ji is advocating an indirect and evocative method of presentation, as opposed to one that would name an object directly.[97] Given what follows the terms here, however, it seems more likely that Lu Ji means by them the depiction of things according to abstract, ideal, conventional formulae, which his writer should reject in favor of a complete and faithful presentation of their external appearance. To what extent this is actually possible, of course, is a much larger question that has been discussed extensively by Western theorists, and with particular lucidity by Sir Ernst Gombrich,[98] but what is important here is the choice Lu Ji makes between two hypothetical possibilities.

Interest in fidelity to the object surfaces in other texts as well. Shen Yue 沈約 (441–512), for example, in a Postface to his biography of Xie Lingyun, outlines the course of literary development from the *Classic of Poetry* onward and singles out three significant changes that occurred during the four hundred years from the Han through the Wei dynasties, the first of which was Sima Xiangru's 司馬相如 (179–117 B.C.) "skill at formal likeness (*xing si* 形似) in words."[99] Sima Xiangru, of course, was a renowned writer of the *fu* or exposition, for which the necessity for keen descriptive powers was traditionally assumed, but Shen Yue does not make a point of restricting this skill to that one genre in particular. Similarly, although the same concept comes up in a chapter of Liu Xie's *The Literary Mind* whose title, "The Forms of Phenomena" (*Wu se* 物色), is associated most closely with a section of expositions in the *Wen xuan* (*juan* 13), the examples the critic cites are drawn from other genres as well. As Jiang Zuyi 蔣祖怡 suggests, Liu Xie is concerned with providing a systematic account of landscape literature in general.[100]

Liu Xie opens this chapter with a discussion of notions touched on ear-

[97] Wang Yuanhua, "Shi 'Bi xing pian' 'Ni rong qu xin' shuo" 釋比興篇擬容取心說, *Wenxue pinglun*, 1 (1978), p. 69.

[98] E. H. Gombrich, *Art and Illusion: A Study in the Psychology of Pictorial Representation*, Bollingen Series XXXV.5 (Princeton: Princeton University Press, 1960).

[99] This passage (as part of Shen Yue's biography) is included in *Song shu* 宋書, 67 and the *Wen xuan*, 50/16a/p.943. Cited in Zhu Zhiqing, *Shi yan zhi bian*, p. 32, and also trans. Richard W. Bodman, "Poetics and Prosody in Early Mediaeval China: A Study and Translation of Kūkai's *Bunkyō Hifuron*," Ph.D. Diss. Cornell University, 1978, p. 484.

[100] Jiang Zuyi, "'Wenxin diaolong: Wu se pian' shi shi" 文心雕龍物色篇試釋, *Wenxue yichan* 文學遺產, 2 (1982), p. 31.

Li Shan notes that the category of *wu se* includes "the forms of phenomena observed during the four seasons that have been written about in expositions," e.g., wind, autumn, moon, and snow. He further explains that "what has matter (*wu*) and pattern (*wen*) is called form (*se*); although the wind does not have a proper form, it does nevertheless have sound" (*Wen xuan*, 13/1a/p.244).

lier in this study, tracing the source of literature to be stimuli provided by the external world. As seasons and phenomena change, he writes, so also do human responses to them, and no one is immune to these resonances:

> Thus poets in responding to things associate endless categorical cor-respondences with them. They abandon themselves to the realm of the myriad images, absorbed deep within the frontiers of sight and sound. In describing atmospheres and sketching appearances, they just follow along with fluctuations in phenomena; their visual and tonal correspondences also tally with waverings of the heart.[101]

He then provides a long list of reduplicatives and other bisyllabic com-pounds that, he feels, "exhaust the form and use few [words] to sum up many, so that [no aspects of] emotion nor of appearance are omitted" (Fan, 10/p.694; cf. Shih, p. 349). Among other things this passage re-veals the persistent strength of the assumption that inner feeling and external scene mutually correspond.

After noting the unfortunate development of elaborate and formulaic descriptive epithets, which encourage nothing but prolixity, Liu Xie re-minds the writer how important it is to depict details of season and place accurately. Such concerns have come to the fore of late:

> From recent years onward, literature has valued formal likeness, peering through to the feeling beyond a scene and penetrating within the appearances of plants and trees. What emerges in these songs is a meaning that is purely profound and far-reaching. To embody ob-jects marvelously, one must be skilled at matching them closely. Thus ingenious words that suit the shape are like a seal to its paste: without additional carving and paring they intricately describe the minutest detail. Therefore, one can read the words and see the appearance, and know the season from the words. (Fan, 10/p.694; cf. Shih, pp. 350–51)

Even more important, however, is something that transcends description, for Liu Xie writes near the close of the chapter that "when the appearance of objects has been exhausted yet feeling lingers on, then one's under-standing [of the art of writing] is complete" (Fan, 10/p.694; cf. Shih, p. 352).

Throughout this discussion, then, it is clear that Liu Xie is not primarily concerned with the literal representation of the external contours of an object for its own sake. In addition to assuming that a depiction should

---

[101] *Wenxin diaolong zhu*, 10/p.693; cf. trans. Shih, p. 349.

evoke a network of associations, he also consistently places his advocacy of accurate physical description within a larger perspective—the need to ensure that external imagery correlate with the emotional situation of the poet and also resonate in the mind of the reader.[102] This interest in the affective powers of imagery also greatly influenced conceptions of the terminology inherited by Six Dynasties critics as the rhetorical legacy of the *Classic of Poetry*. The earliest evidence of this shift from the didactic emphases of most of the classical commentators appears in a fragmentary essay, "Discourse on the Different Traditions in Literature" (*Wen zhang liu bie lun* 文章流別論) by the Jin dynasty scholar Zhi Yu 摯虞 (d. 311), whose similarly titled anthology of literary genres has unfortunately been lost.

Zhi Yu opens with cosmic claims for the function of literature, provides a brief chronology of the development of specific genres, and then turns to the Six Principles of the *Shi jing*:

> Literature is that by which one makes known images above and below, clarifies the principles of human relationships, probes meaning thoroughly, and exhausts all of human nature, so as to examine the proper order of the myriad phenomena. When the goodness of kings flowed, then the *Poetry* was composed. When accomplishments reached their utmost, then hymns began. When virtue and merit were established, then they were made known in inscriptions (*ming* 銘). When admirable men died, then dirges (*lei* 誄) were collected. Sacrificial priests presented words, and officials criticized the oversights of kings.
>
> According to the *Rituals of Zhou* the Grand Master takes charge of the Six Song-Methods, called *feng, fu, bi, xing, ya,* and *song*. What speaks of the affairs of one state and is bound up with what is basic to an individual is called an air. What speaks of the affairs of all under heaven and gives form to the customs of the four quarters [of the earth] is called an elegance. A hymn praises the outward manifestation of abundant virtue. An exposition is a statement that sets something forth. A comparison is a word that compares by cate-

---

[102] According to Kiyohiko Munakata, much the same case holds with Zong Bing's 宗炳 (375–443) view of the concept of *lei* 類, as expressed in his famous "Preface to Landscape Painting" (*Hua shan shui xu* 畫山水序). Although Zong's use of the term in the essay is generally translated as "verisimilitude" or "resemblance" and taken as evidence of his commitment to naturalistic representation, Munakata argues that it not only should be defined more accurately as "the nature of the kind"—i.e., similar to my translation, "categorical correspondence"—but also, in the compound *gan lei* 感類, lies at the heart of Zong Bing's conception of the sympathetic response between two beings or objects as a kind of "karmic interaction." See his "Concepts of *Lei* and *Kan-lei*," esp. pp. 116–28.

gorical correspondence (*lei*). A stimulus is a word in which there is response.[103]

Needless to say, Zhi Yu does not rule out the possibility that this last-mentioned "response" might be exclusively political, and his preceding chronology certainly enhances such a likelihood, but his reticence is nevertheless quite striking. Two centuries later, Zhong Hong resumed this discussion and took his definitions in directions only vaguely hinted at by Zhi Yu. The notion of response is central to his conception of poetry as outlined in a preface to his *Classification of Poetry*, and whereas for Zhi Yu it could have meant that of either poet or reader, Zhong Hong focuses on the latter:

> Among literary forms the pentasyllabic meter is very important; it is the one composition of the lot that has flavor, and therefore it is said to suit the current taste. How could it not be most precise and appropriate for indicating events, creating forms, examining emotions, and describing objects? Thus there are three principles in poetry: one is called stimulus, the second is comparison, and the third is exposition. When the words come to an end but meaning lingers on, that is a stimulus. Relying on an object as a comparison to one's intent/will is a comparison. Writing about a situation directly and lodging descriptions of objects in words is exposition. By extending these three principles and using them carefully, giving them body by means of inspired vigor and adorning them with colorful embellishment, one can give endless pleasure to those who savor them and move the hearts of those who listen: this is the utmost in poetry. If one solely uses comparison and stimulus, the meaning may suffer from being overly profound; if meaning is overly profound, then the words will not flow smoothly. If one only uses the method of exposition, the meaning may suffer from being too shallow; if meaning is too shallow, then the language will not cohere. If in sport one drifts and rambles [among these methods], then one's writing will lack moorage and will suffer from diffuseness.[104]

[103] *Yi wen lei ju* 藝文類聚, 56 and *Quan Jin wen* 全晉文, 77; included in Guo Shaoyu, ed., *Zhongguo lidai wenlun xuan*, p. 156. For recent translations and discussions of Zhi Yu, see Joseph Roe Allen III, "Chih Yü's *Discussions of Different Types of Literature*: A Translation and Brief Comment," in *Parerga*, 3: *Two Studies in Chinese Literary Criticism* (Seattle: Institute for Comparative and Foreign Area Studies, 1976), pp. 1–36, and Siu-kit Wong, *Early Chinese Literary Criticism*, pp. 61–68.

[104] *Lidai shihua*, I, 3. Much of this passage has also been translated by Chia-ying Yeh Chao and Jan W. Walls in "Theory, Standards, and Practice of Criticizing Poetry in Chung Hung's *Shih-p'in*," in Ronald C. Miao, ed., *Studies in Chinese Poetry and Poetics*, Vol. I

This discussion is noteworthy for several reasons. For one thing, it is much more extensive than anything before it; also, picking up on Wang Yi's example with the *Songs of Chu*, it applies the three rhetorical terms to non-canonical poems in pentayllabic meter for the first time. Furthermore, it fails to place them within an explicitly moralistic framework, calling attention instead to Zhong Hong's greater concern with the aesthetic powers or "flavor" of poetry by reversing the traditional order of the three tropes and placing the stimulus first. This presumably also lies behind his grouping the comparison and stimulus together as more suggestive—perhaps because more indirect—methods than the exposition, although it is important to note that he insists that they all are necessary to good poetry.

This special link between two of the three methods became common practice in later writings. Liu Xie, for example, also links *bi* and *xing* together, devoting an entire chapter of his *Literary Mind* to a discussion of the terms. At the same time, however, he also attempts to distinguish the two, a task that was to exercise countless later critics as well. While discussing them in connection with all sorts of non-canonical poems, he does resuscitate the Han commentators' politically didactic dimension, drawing on the definitions of both Zheng Zhong[105] and Zheng Xuan.[106]

Liu Xie opens the chapter by pointing out that the Mao editors of the *Classic of Poetry* had paid particular attention to the stimulus because it was obscure, whereas the comparison was straightforward—one of the most frequently repeated distinctions to appear in subsequent literature—and continues:

> Therefore, *bi* means to match, and *xing* means to arouse. What matches a meaning uses close categorical correspondence in order to indicate a situation. What arouses emotions relies on the subtle to formulate conceptions. Arouse emotions, and forms of the stimulus will be established. Match a meaning, and examples of comparisons will be produced. A comparison stores up indignation to castigate with words; a stimulus links analogies to record criticisms. (Fan, 8/p.601; cf. Shih, p. 276)

Like Zheng Xuan, Liu Xie believes that the comparison and stimulus function as political critique, although he notes another difference: a com-

(San Francisco: Chinese Materials Center, 1978), pp. 52–53, and by John Timothy Wixted in "The Nature of Evaluation in the *Shih-p'in* (*Gradings of Poets*) by Chung Hung (A.D. 469–518)," in Bush and Murck, eds., *Theories of the Arts in China*, pp. 238–39.

[105] As pointed out by Huang Kan 黃侃 in *Wenxin diaolong zhu*, p. 604n3.
[106] As pointed out by Fan Wenlan, *ibid.*

parison is concerned with specifying the logically reasoned, previously established connection between a situation and the object being compared to it, whereas the stimulus is more affective, though providing an intellectual appeal through its failure to make an explicit connection between the two. He then cites the passage discussed in Chapter One from the Great Commentary to the *Classic of Changes* to emphasize the suggestive qualities of the stimulus: "Looking at the way the stimulus criticizes indirectly, it is subtle yet becomes clear. 'The names given [to objects] are insignificant, but the categorical correspondences that they take hold of are great'" (*ibid.*). Somewhat later he alludes to the importance of the critical function when he writes that, from the Han onward, "the way of remonstrance was lost, so the principle of the stimulus died out."[107]

Most of the rest of the chapter, however, focuses on the comparison alone, a fact that has exasperated many later critics. Huang Kan tries to provide an explanation for it:

> Although the title says "Comparison and Stimulus," [Liu Xie] actually only discusses the comparison. This is because the principle of the stimulus was seldom employed, thus it was difficult to grasp and multifaceted in application. From the beginning the use of the stimulus lay in contacting an object in order to arouse a feeling, selecting it in order to invest it with meaning. Thus there were instances when the object was identical yet responses differed, and also when the situations were different yet the feelings the same.

Huang then cites as the first of many such examples the "cypress boat" (*bo zhou* 柏舟), which is labeled a stimulus in two different Airs of the States (poems 26 and 45), yet in the one is believed to evoke a virtuous man out of favor and in the other a faithful yet deserted wife. His inference thus seems to be that in Liu Xie's view the categorical correspondences upon which the comparison draws are more fixed, limited, and hence predictable than those for the stimulus (Fan, 8/p.603n1).

In any event, Liu Xie continues by first attempting to further elucidate the meaning of the term: "Now what do we mean by a comparison? It is what describes objects in order to match a meaning, a rush of words apposite to a situation" (Fan, 8/p.601; cf. Shih, p. 277). There are, however, two ways in which this can be accomplished. The first, which is said to "fit the image" (*qie xiang* 切象) and 'compare the meaning" (*bi yi* 比義), involves a true substitution of a concrete object for a concept which it is presumed to embody, and Liu Xie provides a number of such exam-

---

[107] *Wenxin diaolong zhu*, 8/602; cf. Shih, pp. 277–78. I am reading *feng* 諷 for *shi* 詩, as suggested by Fan Wenlan, p. 608n8.

ples (gold and pewter for illustrious virtue, washing clothes for sadness of heart, etc.). The second, however, seems to consist of merely descriptive similes (e.g., "The hemp robe is like snow") and is therefore merely "in the category of comparisons" (*bi lei zhe* 比類者).[108] One could note in passing that Liu Xie's insistence here on some truly substitutive operation as the essence of the comparison—something that comes closest to the Western notion of metaphor—prevailed over Kong Yingda's attempt, mentioned earlier, to include all explicit similes (those using the words "like" or "as") under the rubric as well. However, Liu Xie himself goes on to list a number of other examples of the usage, many of which are clearly mere descriptive similes. Whatever the case, he does assert, in apparent agreement with Zhong Hong, the superiority of the stimulus over the comparison, for he notes in his concluding *zan* 贊 to the chapter that as writers "used the comparison day by day, / Month by month they forgot the stimulus. / They practiced the small and neglected the great / So that their writing was inferior to that of the people of the Zhou dynasty" (Fan,8/p.602; cf. Shih, p. 278).

Had the stimulus, however, truly been forgotten? As Liu Xie himself suggests in his brief definition of the term, and as is clearly evident in Zhong Hong's discussion, it seems rather to have undergone an important transformation over the course of the Six Dynasties as its application was extended beyond the domain of the *Classic of Poetry*. For one thing, concern with distinguishing it from the comparison gradually yielded, on the part of many critics, to the sense that the shared properties of the two—in contrast to the method of exposition—were perhaps greater than their dissimilarities. Moreover, the very notion of what their function was had begun to change. Some Tang dynasty writers would continue to emphasize the moral and political purposes of the terms, though in a manner somewhat different from that of the Han scholiasts. Other critics, however, would, with Zhong Hong, abandon such concerns for a new focus on the emotionally suggestive openendedness of the image. Such an emphasis would have the concomitant effect of qualifying the only recently cultivated interest in description, for no sooner would one critic speak of fidelity to the external object than another would counter with the call to go beyond appearances and transcend the image. All of these developments begin to take shape in the poetry and criticism of the Tang dynasty.

---

[108]*Wenxin diaolong zhu*, 8/p.601; cf. Shih, p. 277. As Fan Wenlan notes (p. 606n6), Liu Xie seems to be distinguishing those focusing on mere outward form (*xing zhuang* 形狀) from comparisons of a more profound nature.

CHAPTER FIVE

The Tang Dynasty

and Beyond

I.

T HE *Classic of Poetry* and its commentary literature, as we have seen, left a legacy of two important assumptions about imagery that were developed and refined in subsequent centuries of poetic practice and criticism. One focused on the analogical, meaning-conveying properties of the images and assumed, as had been the case with theories deriving from the *Classic of Changes*, that concrete phenomena could, by virtue of cosmic categorical correspondences, embody and evoke a larger significance. This presumption of meaning as pre-established, of course, differentiates the Chinese attitude from Western conceptions of metaphor as the creative artifice of the poet. The other centered on the belief that the poem as a whole constituted an historical or autobiographical document, and that its images were drawn from the author's lived experience, actually perceived and literally represented, although not necessarily in a systematic or coherent manner. This presupposition characterizes the Little Prefaces to the songs in the first anthology in particular and distinguishes those readings from Western allegorical interpretations, based as the latter are on the notion of fictionality. While these two assumptions about the conventional and the empirical origins of images were frequently mutually compatible and share a presumption about the non-fictional origins of imagery, the possibilities for developments in contrary directions should be evident as well: insistence on oblique referentiality on the one hand and direct referentiality on the other did not always lead to identical conclusions.

Both notions did share, however, an orientation toward the concrete realm of social and political experience, a belief that poetry was stimulated by and responded to that world, and a faith that whatever meaning might be drawn from a text was in fact what the author had "put into" it.

Western critical theory has of course questioned this identification, emphasizing instead the disjunction between the two. Paul Ricoeur argues, for example, that whereas in spoken discourse

> it is the same thing to understand what the speaker means and what his discourse means ..., [w]ith written discourse, the author's meaning and the meaning of the text cease to coincide. This dissociation of the verbal meaning of the text and the mental intention is what is really at stake in the inscription of discourse. Not that we can conceive of a text without an author; the tie between the speaker and the discourse is not abolished, but distended and complicated. The dissociation of the meaning and the intention is still an adventure of the reference of discourse to the speaking subject. But the text's career escapes the finite horizon of its author. What the text says now matters more than what the author meant to say, and every exegesis unfolds its procedures within the circumference that has broken its moorings to the psychology of its author.[1]

The Chinese reader, however, would never entertain the possibility of such a dissociation. Language itself might not be fully commensurate with meaning, which lay "beyond words," but the assumptions remained that imagery was and, moreover, that whatever the reader drew from the text—however incompletely conveyed—did indeed coincide with the original "message" entrusted by the poet to the words.

Of the two possible imagistic tendencies noted above, it was the first that played a greater role in the *Songs of Chu* and poetry of the Han and Wei dynasties, as well as in later criticism of it. These works developed the use of objects, generally drawn from the natural world, as emblems of various moral qualities established by cultural convention. The lexicon was a large one: the pine tree, for example, embodied moral fortitude, the bamboo integrity, cypresses human mortality because of their traditional planting by gravesites, a tumbleweed the traveler's plight, etc., and it was expandable by analogy. Objects employed in this way would be set off, frequently in pairs, from the rest of the poem—either at the beginning or somewhere in the middle, surrounded by narrative or discursive comment. Or, in a poetic subgenre first exemplified by the "Hymn to the Orange" in the *Songs of Chu* and developed into poems "singing of objects" (*yong wu* 詠物) during the Six Dynasties, one object alone, with all of its associated qualities, would serve as the focus of the poem and vehicle of some unnamed subject. Poems employing isolated emblematic im-

[1] Paul Ricoeur, "The Model of the Text: Meaningful Action Considered as a Text," *New Literary History*, V.1 (Autumn 1973), p. 95.

ages were commoner by far, but in both types the objects were not to be naturalized as belonging to some scene empirically observed by the poet. In either case, moreover, their presence, as well as the rather vague titles of the works in which they appeared, generally signaled a poet's concern with some moral or political problem. Traditional Chinese commentators by and large assumed that such poems represented veiled critiques of specific historical situations, whereas Western criticis like Diény and Holzman have preferred to read them as examinations of more abstract, general issues. Yet despite attempts by such scholars as Stephen Owen to distinguish between topical and general "allegory," what seems clear, at least from the brief sample I have examined, is that most such poems do not allow one to rule out one or the other possibility, thus vitiating the value of the distinction.[2]

The second assumption mentioned above—that a poem's images were plausible elements from an actually perceived scene—is certainly justified by a number of poems in the *Classic of Poetry*, although not argued actively by commentators until the Song dynasty. In non-canonical poetry we have seen significant developments of this tendency in the works of Tao Qian and Xie Lingyun, both of whom, to a limited degree, bring together images from an ostensibly observed natural scene and integrate them into a coherent tableau. The scenic elements are striking not only for their vivid detail but, more important, for the fact that they are not single images functioning purely in a one-to-one relationship as vehicles for some conventionally coded abstract quality but are combined into an integral whole. Pre-established cultural associations play an essential role, of course, in generating their evocative powers, but the illusion of verisimilitude is crucial as well.

The poetry of the Tang dynasty continues and modifies both of these tendencies, but it was the second in particular that has been recognized by both Chinese and Western critics as its primary achievement. Nevertheless, the first assumption governing imagistic practice and interpretation remained central to the tradition, valorized as it was by the fact that most of the poems linked to it demonstrated and affirmed more obviously than others the Confucian notion of poetry as fulfilling a crucial function of moral, social, and political critique. Thus in this chapter we shall be considering the primary exponents and exemplars of both.

The poet most clearly associated with a renewed emphasis on the imagistic practices and functions of Chu, Han, and Wei dynasty poetry is the

[2] Stephen Owen, *The Poetry of the Early T'ang* (New Haven: Yale University Press, 1977), pp. 169–70 and *passim*. Owen himself states that the distinction is by no means absolute.

170

early Tang figure Chen Ziang 陳子昂 (661–702). His affinities with the earlier mode may first have been recognized within a century of his death, for the poet-monk Jiaoran 皎然 (734?–799) traced the source of Chen's 38 poems entitled "Responses to What I Have Encountered" (*Gan yu* 感遇) to Ruan Ji's "Poems Singing My Thoughts."[3] The Ming critic Hu Yinglin reaffirms this connection, writing that "Ziang's *Gan yu* completely eliminate all shallow frivolity. With one stroke ancient elegance was revived at the beginning of the Tang dynasty with the appearance of this eminent man. From the Wei and Jin dynasties onward, only he still retained the lingering rhymes of Bubing [Ruan Ji]."[4]

Like Ruan's poems, Chen's "Responses" have provoked considerable debate as to the specificity of their referentiality. The Qing scholar Chen Hang acknowledges the difficulty of providing precise topical referents for their images but rises undaunted to the task nonetheless, whereas Stephen Owen usually prefers a moral general reading.[5] Certainly, a look at almost any work in the series might help to explain this quandary; the moon-sun *yin-yang* imagery dominating the first poem, for example, may be calling upon a cosmic symbolism to comment on universal processes of change or to allude to the empress Wu Zetian's 武則天 (r. 684–705) position at court, and neither possibility can be definitively eliminated. Whatever the case, the most important point for our purposes is that Chen employs conventional emblems of moral qualities, sometimes extended, as in the *Songs of Chu*, throughout an entire poem, as in the second in the group:

Orchid and ginger grow in spring and summer—	蘭若生春夏
Profuse and dense, how luxuriant!	芊蔚何青青
Secluded deep in the beauty of empty forests,	幽獨空林色
Vermilion petals droop over purple stems.	朱蕤冒紫莖
Lingering slowly the white sun dusks;	遲遲白日晚
Rustling gently autumn winds arise.	嫋嫋秋風生
When the year's florescence all flutters and falls,	歲華盡搖落
How can their fragrant intentions be fulfilled?[6]	芳意竟何成

[3] In the *Shiwan juan lou congshu* 十萬卷樓叢書 ed. of his *Shi shi* 詩式, 3.1a–b. Cited in Holzman, *Poetry and Politics*, p. 284n29 and Li Zhifang, "Ruan Ji yong huai shi lun," p. 92. As Stephen Owen points out, however, the citation only appears in the five-fascicle edition of the work and not in the one-*juan* version more firmly attributed to Jiaoran, thus its authenticity is questionable. See *The Poetry of the Early T'ang*, p. 433n15.

[4] Hu Yinglin, *Shi sou, nei bian* 內編 (rpt. Taipei: Wenxing chubanshe, 1973), 2/p.35. Also cited in Holzman, *ibid.*, and Li Zhifang, *ibid.*

[5] See Chen Hang, *Shi bi xing jian*, 3/pp.97–113 and Owen, *Early T'ang*, pp. 184–223.

[6] Included in *Quan Tang shi* 全唐詩 (rpt. Taipei: Minglun, 1971), 83/p.890; Gao Buying 高步瀛, ed., *Xin jiao Tang Song shi juyao* 新校唐宋詩舉要 (rpt. Taipei: Shijie, 1968; 2 vols.), I,1/p.3; and Chen Hang, 3/p.112. Cf. trans. by Owen, *Early T'ang*, p. 218.

The imagistic mode of this poem, if not evident at first glance, becomes clear once one recognizes the numerous allusions to works in the *Songs of Chu*. Orchids, of course, flower throughout the southern anthology as images of moral virtue, and just as they grow in deep seclusion here, so they "bloom unseen and waft their scents in loneliness" in "Grieving at the Eddying Wind" (*Bei hui feng* 悲回風), the fifth of the *Nine Declarations*.[7] Wang Yi provides a hint at Chen Ziang's likely purposes here when he comments that this "is used to say that although the virtuous man lives deep in the mountains he does not abandon his loyal and upright conduct." The phrases for "luxuriant" (1. 2) and "purple stems" (1. 4) appear in a couplet from one of the *Nine Songs*, the "Lesser Master of Fate" (*Shao si ming* 少司命): "The autumn orchids bloom luxuriant, / With leaves of green and purple stems."[8] The white sun at evening can be found in the *Nine Arguments* (*Jiu bian* 九辯)—"The white sun reddens towards his setting"[9]—and again Wang Yi offers an important guideline for the reading of Chen's poem when he notes that "the season is about to end and talents and energy have weakened." Chen Ziang's sixth line appears almost verbatim in "The Lady of the Xiang": "Gently the wind of autumn whispers,"[10] and the reference of dying foliage in the *Nine Arguments*: "flower and leaf fluttering fall and turn to decay."[11] Given the tradition of *Chu ci* exegesis, with which Chen would have been thoroughly familiar, it should come as no surprise that readers of his poem would write that "this laments his not encountering a brilliant era"[12] and "sighs over a failure to fulfill his intention to serve."[13] And indeed there is little reason to question this interpretation.

That Chen Ziang placed his own imagistic practice within the tradition deriving from commentaries on the *Classic of Poetry* can be seen in passages from prefaces to two poems in his corpus. He makes one brief reference to the methods of *bi* and *xing* in the preface to a poem entitled "A Drunken Song of Joy at Meeting Administrator Ma" (*Xi Ma canjun xiang yu zui ge* 喜馬參軍相遇醉歌): "Poetry can be used for comparison and stimulus."[14] A slightly longer discussion, albeit employing a different term, occurs at the beginning of the preface to "A Composition on Slender

[7]Hong Xingzu, ed., *Chu ci bu zhu*, 4/31a/p.259; trans. Hawkes, *Ch'u Tz'u*, p. 78.
[8]Hong, 2/25a/p.125; trans. Hawkes, p. 41.
[9]Hong, 8/10a/p.317; trans. Hawkes, p. 97.
[10]Hong, 2/9b/p.114; trans. Hawkes, p. 38.
[11]Hong, 8/1b/p.300; trans. Hawkes, p. 92.
[12]Wu Zhifu 吳摯甫, cited in Gao Buying, *Xin jiao Tang Song shi juyao*, I, 1/3.
[13]Chen Hang, 3/p.112.
[14]*Quan Tang shi*, 83/p.903. Cited in Wang Yunxi 王運熙, "Tan Zhongguo gudai wenlun zhong de bi xing shuo" 談中國古代文論中的比興說, *Wenyi luncong* 文藝論叢, 4 (Shanghai: Wenyi chubanshe, 1978), p. 49.

Bamboos for Annalist Dongfang Qiu" (*Yu Dongfang zuoshi Qiu xiu zhu bian* 與東方左史虬修竹編):

> The way of letters has been in decline for five hundred years. Of the wind and bones (moral force and structure) of the Han and Wei dynasties, nothing was transmitted during the Jin and Song, yet there is still evidence [of those qualities] in their writings. During my leisure time I have looked at the poetry of the Qi and Liang periods, where embellishment and beauty vie in abundance yet stimulating and entrusting have both utterly vanished, and each time I sigh deeply. When I think of the ancients I always fear that their way has become lost and that Airs and Elegances are no longer being composed, which upsets me greatly.[15]

What I have translated as "stimulating and entrusting" (*xing ji* 興寄) is clearly, as Wang Yunxi observes, equivalent to entrusting one's meaning to comparative and evocative images (*bi xing*), and, indeed, the poem which follows develops at length the traditional association of bamboos with integrity and steadfastness as an image for the poet himself. It is also clear that Chen agrees with such Confucian commentators as Zheng Xuan that this type of imagery functions primarily as political critique, and he is even less concerned than the earlier scholars with distinguishing between the various tropes. Indeed, one can discern an incipient sense that the imagery per se is less important than its ultimate purpose. Morever, the chronology of decline Chen traces from the Han and Wei through the Jin and Song and finally the Qi and Liang dynasties was to become a commonplace among later advocates of a "return to antiquity" (*fu gu* 復古) and "ancient-style prose" (*gu wen* 古文) in particular and of the critical tradition in general.

Yin Fan 殷璠 expresses similar opinions in the preface to his anthology compiled in 753, the *Collection of Eminent Men of Our Rivers and Peaks* (*He yue ying ling ji* 河嶽英靈集). After remarking on the difficulties the anthologist encounters when faced with a multitude of literary works, he distinguishes between two major poetic styles of the past:

> Now literature comes from spirit, from energy, and from feelings; it has elegant, rustic, humble, and vulgar forms. An editor can examine these various forms, carefully investigate their origins, and can then decide between the good and the bad and discuss [his reasons for]

---

[15] *Quan Tang shi*, 83/pp.895–96. Cited, *inter alia*, by Wang Yunxi, *ibid.*, and Mei Yunsheng 梅運生, "Shi lun Bo Juyi de 'mei ci xing bi' shuo" 試論白居易的美刺興比說, in *Gudai wenxue lilun yanjiu* 古代文學理論研究, 1 (Shanghai: Guji chubanshe, 1979), p. 253. Cf. trans. by Owen, *Early T'ang*, p. 166.

selection and rejection. As for Cao [Zhi] and Liu [Zheng], their poetry contains much straightfoward language and few antithetical couplets. At times they have five deflected-tone words in a row or ten words all of which are level tone, yet in the end they retain value to spare. However, those of limited experience and superficial knowledge upbraid the ancients for not distinguishing between [the notes] *gong* and *shang* and for language that is simple and plain; they are ashamed to study them as models. Therefore they attack all heterodoxy and offer foolishly far-fetched interpretations. Thus their ideas are insufficient yet their words are often excessive, completely lacking in comparison and stimulus and only valuing a trivial beauty. Though they fill up portfolios, of what use will they be?[16]

Yin Fan entertains much the same view of literary history as does Chen Ziang, castigating the poets of the Qi and Liang dynasties for their preoccupation with tones and formal rules at the expense of substance. Like Chen he also associates the methods of comparison and stimulus (*bi xing*, which in the *Wen jing mifu lun* edition of the text reads *xing xiang* 興象, "evocative imagery," implying among other things the gradual identification being made between *bi xing* and suggestive imagery in general) with purposes beyond the merely aesthetic.

Of the poets whom Yin Fan chooses to include in his anthology, however, the ones he singles out in the preface are Wang Wei, Wang Changling 王昌齡 (?698–756), and Chu Guangxi, none of whom is closely associated with the imagistic practices characteristic of the tradition embraced by Chen Ziang. More likely to be placed in this line were the fifty-nine "Ancient Airs" of Li Bo, of which the first presents the orthodox views we have seen:

Great Elegances have long not been composed.	大雅久不作
With my decline, who can present them now?	吾衰竟誰陳
The Kingly Airs were abandoned to creepers and grass,	王風委蔓草
The Warring States all full of brambles and thorns.	戰國多荊榛
Dragons and tigers devoured one another;	龍虎相啖食
Swords and spears reached the lawless Qin.	兵戈逮狂秦
How did orthodox sounds fade and vanish?	正聲何微茫
In sad complaint arose the *sao* poet.	哀怨起騷人
Yang and Sima stirred the ebbing waves,	揚馬激頹波
Opening up a wild, unbounded flow.	開流蕩無垠

[16]Included in *Quan Tang wen*, 436; Kūkai 空海 (774–835), ed., *Wen jing mifu lun* 文鏡秘府論, ed. Zhou Weide 周維德 (Peking: Renmin, 1975), pp. 160–61; and Guo Shaoyu, ed., *Zhongguo lidai wenlun xuan*, pp. 393–94. Cf. trans. by Bodman, "Poetics and Prosody," pp. 450–51.

Although rising and falling countless times,	廢興雖萬變
Poetry's principles also were engulfed.	憲章亦已淪
Ever since the Jian'an period,	自從建安來
Fine beauty has not been worth treasuring.	綺麗不足珍
Our sagely era has returned to primordial antiquity;	聖代復元古
With hanging robes it values the pure and true.	垂衣貴清眞
Gathered talents surround the ruling brilliance,	羣才屬休明
Take advantage of fate, all leaping dragons.	乘運共躍鱗
Pattern and substance illuminate one another:	文質相炳煥
A host of stars displayed in the autumn sky.	衆星羅秋旻
My purpose lies in editing and transmitting,	我志在刪述
To hand down glories to dazzle a thousand springs.	垂輝映千春
If an aspiring sage could be established,	希聖如有立
I would stop my pen when the unicorn was caught.[17]	絕筆於獲麟

Li Bo's "Ancient Airs" are perhaps less accessible than some of his better-known poetry but link him for that very reason with the tradition I have been discussing. Several later critics recognized this affinity. Wang Shizhen of the Qing, for example, remarked that Li's poems "can be traced back to Sizong's [Ruan Ji's] 'Singing My Thoughts,'" and Hu Zhenheng 胡震亨 (fl. 1600) wrote that "Taibo's 'Ancient Airs' are richer than Ziang's 'Responses to What I Have Encountered' but slighter than Sizong's 'Singing My Thoughts.' In their unburdening of his native sensibility and investment with remonstrance, they are certainly in accord with that original tradition."[18] Like the earlier works, this poem relies heavily on historical narrative and predominantly discursive language, interspersed sparingly with a few substitutive images. The title alerts us to the archaism of the poem's views, rife with classical allusions and a conviction as to the downward path of literature from the age of the *Classic of Poetry*, which includes, of course, the "Great Elegances" and "Kingly Airs." References to Confucius play key roles here: "my decline" in line 2 may allude to *Analects* VII.5, in which the sage laments that his degeneracy is evident in his no longer dreaming of the duke of Zhou. The necessary mutuality of "pattern" and "substance" (*wen* 文 and *zhi* 質) in line 19 refers to *Analects* VI.18, and Li Bo's expression of his own "purpose" recalls Confucius' description of himself as "transmitting and not creating" in *Analects* VII.I and the commonly accepted belief that he had

---

[17] Included in *Li Taibo quanji* 李太白全集, ed. Wang Qi 王琦 (1696–1774) (1758; rpt. Taipei: Heluo, n.d.), 2/p.43, and Gao Buying, I,1/p.25. Cf. trans. by Joseph J. Lee in *Sunflower Splendor*, pp. 113–14.

[18] Wang Shizhen, introduction to *Gu shi xuan* 古詩選, and Hu Zhenheng cited in Wang Qi, *Li Taibo quanji*, 3/p.77. Both citations also in Li Zhifang, pp. 93–94.

edited the Classics. And the last line refers to the final entry in the *Spring and Autumn Annals*, the capture of a unicorn in the spring of the fourteenth year of Duke Ai's 哀 reign, with which, as the commentator Du Yu 杜預 (222–84) noted, Confucius too "stopped his pen."[19]

The literary history Li Bo presents should also be a familiar one: the disappearance of orthodoxy with the demise of the Zhou and its anthology; important revivals—but of a second order—by the *sao* poet Qu Yuan and the *fu* writers Yang Xiong and Sima Xiangru; a renewed strength evident in the work of Cao Zhi and other poets of the Jian'an reign period, followed by a gradual decline into the trivial prettiness of Qi and Liang poetry. Li Bo finally proclaims a return to the values of "primordial antiquity" during his own Tang dynasty, which embraces the governing principles of the legendary sages like the Yellow Emperor, Yao, and Shun, whose robes hung loosely because they ruled by moral example rather than direct action,[20] and allows literary talents to emerge and distinguish themselves. Typically, but unlike earlier writers of this type of poem, Li Bo does not distance himself from his topic at all but places himself right at its center.

This is the kind of poem which many critics regarded as an example of "investing" or "entrusting" (*ji tuo* 寄托) images (*bi xing*) with meaning. A passage in Meng Qi's 孟棨 *Original Incidents of Poems* (*Ben shi shi* 本事詩; preface dated the twelfth month of 886) associates Li Bo in a more general way with this method:

> [Li] Bo's talent was outstanding and his force lofty, equal in fame to Reminder Chen [Ziang], former and latter both united in virtue. Discussing poetry he said: "Since the Liang and Chen dynasties, beauty has become superficial to an extreme, with Shen Xiuwen 修文 [Yue] valuing total rules above all. To return to ancient ways—if not I, then who?" Thus in the two collections of Chen and Li regulated verse is quite rare. It has been said that entrusting to a stimulus (*ji xing* 寄興) is profound and subtle; pentasyllabic verse is less well suited than tetrasyllabic, with heptasyllabic even more prolix: how much less would he have allowed himself to be bound by the game of tonal harmonies?[21]

[19] *Chun qiu Zuo zhuan zheng yi* 春秋左傳正義, in *Shisan jing zhushu*, II,59/470b/ p.2,172.

[20] *Zhou yi zheng yi*, in *Shisan jing zhushu*, I,7/75a/p.87; cf. trans. Wilhelm/Baynes, p. 332.

[21] Meng Qi, *Ben shi shi*, *Gao yi* 高逸, included in *Xu Lidai shihua* I, 24. Cited by Wang Yunxi, "Tan Zhongguo gudai wenlun zhong de bi xing shuo," p. 49 and Wang Qi, *Li Taibo quanji*, 2/p.43.

Yet Li Bo's actual failure to rely significantly on imagery in this "Ancient Air"—even of the conventional type found in Chen Ziang—should be evident. The development of an attitude during the Tang which deemphasized the original connections of those rhetorical terms to concrete imagery for the sake of a focus purely on their function as political critique alone can be seen most clearly in the writings of Bo Juyi. It is above all in his well-known letter to his friend Yuan Zhen 元稹 (779–831) that he expatiates on the subject, opening with an obligatory discourse on *wen* (culture, civilization, pattern, embellishment, scholarship, writing) that goes back to commentaries on the *Classic of Changes* by way of Liu Xie[22] and brings him to assert the pre-eminence of poetry:

> Now *wen* is hoary, and each of the Three Talents (heaven, earth, and man) has its pattern. Of the patterns of heaven, the Three Luminaries (sun, moon, and stars) are principal. Of the patterns of earth, the Five Agents (metal, wood, water, fire, earth) are principal. Of the patterns of men, the Six Classics (Poetry, History, Changes, Music, Ritual, Spring and Autumn) are principal. When we come to speak of the Six Classics, then the *Classic of Poetry* is principal. Why is this so? The sages responded to the hearts and minds of men, and all under heaven was at peace. For responding to the hearts and minds of men, nothing comes before feeling, nothing starts earlier than words, nothing is more fitting than sound, and nothing more profound than meaning. Poetry has its roots in feeling, its sprouts in words, its flowers in sound, and its fruits in meaning. From sages and worthies on high down to simpletons and fools, from small creatures like suckling pigs and fish to the profound mysteries of ghosts and spirits—they are all distinct yet share the same senses, their forms are different yet their emotions are one, so that no sound enters without being answered, no feeling communicated without a response.
>
> The sages, knowing this was so, went to the basis of words and ordered them with the Six Principles; they went to the source of sounds and organized them with the five tones (*gong* 宮, *shang* 商, *jiao* 角, *zhi* 徵, *yu* 羽). The tones have rhymes, and the principles have categories. When rhymes are harmonious, then words will be chanted smoothly; when words are chanted smoothly, then sounds will enter more easily; when categorical correspondences are drawn, then emotions will be manifest; and when emotions are manifest then responses will be easily communicated.[23]

[22] See *Wenxin diaolong zhu*, 1/pp.1ff.
[23] *Yu Yuan Jiu shu*, in *Bo Juyi xuanji*, ed. Wang Rubi, pp. 345–46; subsequent page references to this edition to be given in the text. Wang's annotations are generally quite

Shortly afterward, Bo launches into a brief history of Chinese poetry from the point of view of the Six Principles:

> By the fall of the Zhou and rise of the Qin, the office in charge of collecting and selecting songs [of the people] had disappeared, so that those above did not use poetry to correct and examine the current government, and those below did not use songs to reveal and point out their human emotions. Thus it happened that a style of baseless flattery arose, and the way of correcting failings was lacking. At this time the Six Principles began to be diminished.

> The "Airs of the States" changed to become the *Songs of Chu*, and the pentasyllabic meter began with Su Wu and Li Ling. Su Wu, Li Ling, and the *Li sao* poet [Qu Yuan] were all unfortunate men; each followed out his intent and expressed it in writing. Thus, the verse about the bridge over the river[24] remains a lament over parting, and the song on the marsh's edge[25] returns to repinement and longing. Fretful and despondent, they never said anything else. Yet since they were not far removed in time from the *Classic of Poetry*, they still retained its general principles. Thus to stimulate (*xing*) parting one introduced the pair of wild ducks and lone wild goose as analogies,[26] and to remonstrate with the ruler and inferior men one introduced fragrant plants and noxious birds as comparisons.[27] Although the Six Principles were not all employed, still these poets attained about twenty to thirty percent of what the authors of the *Poetry* did. At this time the Six Principles began to break down.

---

helpful. This letter has also been summarized and partially translated by Arthur Waley in *The Life and Times of Po Chü-i* (London: Allen and Unwin, 1949), pp. 107–14.

[24] This is an allusion to the third of three poems "To Su Wu" (*Yu Su Wu* 與蘇武), which begins: "Holding hands we climbed the bridge over the river" 攜手上河梁 (*Wen xuan*, 29/12b/p.541). Wang Rubi erroneously reverses the putative author and recipient (p.350n40).

[25] An allusion to "The Fisherman" (*Yu fu* 漁夫), which begins:
When Ch'ü Yüan was banished,
He wandered along the river's banks, or walked at the marsh's edge, singing as he went,... *Chu ci bu zhu*, 7/1a/p.295; trans. Hawkes, p. 90.

[26] Upon leaving Li Ling to return to China from his captivity in Xiongnu territory in 81 B.C., Su Wu is said to have written a poem, not included in the *Wen xuan*, containing the following lines: "Two wild ducks flew north together; /A lone wild goose soars south alone" 雙鳧俱北飛 / 一雁獨南翔. Cited by Wang Rubi, p. 350n43. However, the authorship of this poem (as of all works attributed to Su Wu and Li Ling) is subject to dispute. See *Liang Han wenxue shi cankao ziliao* 兩漢文學史參考資料 (rpt. Hong Kong: Hongzhi, n.d.), pp. 603–04.

[27] Cf. Wang Yi's discussion of the use of the stimulus in "Encountering Sorrow" in Chapter Two above.

From the Jin and Song dynasties on down, those who were able to attain them grew fewer. Kangle [Xie Lingyun], for all his broad and abstruse learning, was much weakened by his fondness for landscape; Yuanming [Tao Qian], for all his lofty archaism, let himself go excessively in the pastoral. Jiang [Yan 江淹 (444–505)] and Bao [Zhao] and those like them suffered from the same limitations. Of exemplary poems like Liang Hong's 梁鴻 (Eastern Han) "Five Sighs" (*Wu yi* 五噫),[28] there were but one or two out of a hundred. At this time, the Six Principles gradually became more feeble. (p. 346)

Bo then goes on to distinguish the use of natural imagery in the *Classic of Poetry*, which he, agreeing with the earlier Confucian commentators, sees as performing an analogical and critical function, from the burgeoning interest in aspects of nature in Six Dynasties poetry:

They [the Six Principles] were further weakened through the middle of the Liang and Chen dynasties, during which time most poetry but sported with wind and snow and toyed with flowers and plants. Alas! Natural objects such as wind, snow, flowers, and plants—how could the Three Hundred Poems [of the *Classic of Poetry*] do without them? But consider how they are employed there. For example, "How cold is the north wind"[29] borrows the wind to criticize oppressive government; "Rain and snow fall thickly"[30] uses the snow to express sympathy for [those suffering from the hardships of] military travels. "The flowers of the *changdi*"[31] responds to the flowers in order to admonish elder and younger brothers. "We gather the plantain"[32] praises the plant to take joy in having children. In all of these, the stimulus comes from there [the object], but the meaning comes back here [criticism of the human situation]. Can one really go contrary to this?! This being so, lines like "The last rosy clouds disperse like meshed silk; / The limpid river is as clear as if bleached,"[33] and "Leaving blossoms are first to drop, bedewed; / Departing leaves

[28] A poem criticizing the intolerable sufferings of the common people in Luoyang; Wang Rubi, pp. 350–51n52.

[29] Poem 41, *Mao shi zheng yi*, 2C/6b/p.252.

[30] Poem 167, *Zheng yi*, 9C/9b/p.810.

[31] Poem 164, *Zheng yi*, 9B/8a/p.779. Bo Juyi gives the name of the plant as *tangdi* 棠棣, following the Han 韓 text (Wang Rubi, p. 351n60).

[32] Poem 8, *Zheng yi*, 1C/2b/p.98.

[33] From Xie Tiao 謝朓 (464–99), "Climbing the Three Mountains in the Evening and Turning Back to Gaze at the Capital" (*Wan deng san shan huan wang jingyi* 晚登三山還望京邑), in *Wen xuan*, 27/8b/p.503.

fall early, windblown"[34] are, granted, quite beautiful, but I don't know what they are admonishing. Therefore, as I said, they just sported with wind and snow and toyed with flowers and plants. At this time the Six Principles had utterly vanished. (pp. 346–47)

Finally, Bo turns to the poetry of his own dynasty:

The Tang arose two centuries ago, and has produced countless poets during that time. Among those to be singled out are Chen Ziang and his twenty [sic] poems, "Responses to What I have Encountered" and Bao Fang 鮑防 (fl. 750) and his fifteen "Responses to What Has Stirred Me" (Gan xing 感興).[35] And there are the greatest talents of poetry, among whom our age has praised Li Bo and Du Fu. Li's compositions are talented and marvelous, to be sure, and no one else could match them, but when one searches for examples of feng, ya, bi, and xing, there is not a one to be found. Du's poems are most numerous, and more than a thousand are worth transmitting. When it comes to the concatenation of recent- or ancient-style verses or the complexities of formal rules, his are totally skillful and excellent, and superior to Li's. Yet when one takes up poems like "Xin'an Official" (Xin'an li 新安吏),[36] "Shihao Official" (Shihao li 石壕吏 / Yinde 3/11), "Tongguan Official" (Tongguan li 潼關吏 / Yinde 3/10), "Defending Luzi Pass" (Sai Luzi 塞蘆子 / Yinde 3/18), and "Remaining at Huamen" (Liu Huamen 留花門 / Yinde 3/17), or verses like "The vermilion gate reeks of wine and meat; / On the road lie frozen bones of the dead"[37]—they comprise no more than a small fraction of his corpus. And if such is the case with Du Fu, how much more will it be so with those who are inferior to him! (p. 347)

The letter goes on to discuss Bo's own life and poetic career at some length, and somewhat later mentions his own efforts to rehabilitate the Six Principles in connection with his discussion of how he arranged his total collection:

[34] From Bao Zhao, "Enjoying the Moon at My West City Gate Office" (Wan yue cheng xi men xie zhong 翫月城西門廨中), Wen xuan, 30/13b/p.563.

[35] Bao Fang was a native of Xiangyang 襄陽, passed the jinshi examination in 753, and held office under the Tang emperor Daizong 代宗 (r. 763–80); his poems are no longer extant (Wang Rubi, p. 351n67).

[36] Du shi yinde 杜詩引得, Harvard-Yenching Institute Sinological Index Series, Supp. No. 14 (rpt. Taipei; Chinese Materials and Research Aids, 1966), 3/9. Subsequent references to this concordance will be given in the text.

[37] From his poem, "On Going from the Capital to Fengxian County: Singing My Thoughts in Five Hundred Words" (Zi jing fu Fengxian xian yong huai wu bai zi 自京赴奉先縣詠懷五百字), Yinde, 2/16/67–68.

Since I became Reminder [in 808], all poems recording experiences and responses and involving praise, blame, and *xing* and *bi*, as well as poems with topics based on events occurring between the Wude 武德 reign period (618–627) and the Yuanhe 元和 reign period (806–21) (i.e., from the beginning of the Tang to the present), I have titled the *New Yuefu* (*Xin yuefu* 新樂府)—150 poems in all—and I call them poems of remonstrance (*fengyu shi* 諷諭詩). (p. 359)

The other three categories he creates are "poems written at leisure" (*xian shi shi* 閑適詩), of which there are one hundred; "poems responding to grief" (*gan shang shi* 感傷詩)—another hundred; and four hundred-odd "miscellaneous regulated verse" (*za lü shi* 雜律詩). One might note in passing that despite Bo's vaunted reputation for espousing a Confucian view of literature's pragmatic purpose, his explicitly critical *New Yuefu* do not comprise an impressive proportion of his formidable output (actually 172 out of approximately 800 at the time this letter was written, although the total was eventually to hit some 2,800 in all). What is more interesting, however, is the treatment accorded to the terms *xing* and *bi*. As contemporary scholars have pointed out, in Bo's hands the words no longer refer to rhetorical devices—of whatever purpose, didactic or aesthetic—but simply have become equated with *mei ci* 美刺 or praising and blaming; they denote a content or function, rather than a formal method. Mei Yunsheng 梅運生 supports this contention by noting that the majority of Bo's *New Yuefu* employ straightforward exposition or *fu*, rather than the imagistic comparisons or juxtapositions of *bi* and *xing*, while his poems that are not critiques of social or political conditions frequently do employ those devices.[38] This is also true, for that matter, of many of the poems of Du Fu which Bo singles out as examples of those methods. Conversely, of course, one could find scores of other poems in Du Fu's corpus, as well as in those of the poets whom Bo dismisses, which most readers would agree demonstrated the use of comparative and evocative imagery. In other words, for Bo, *bi xing* no longer designate aesthetic methods, using natural imagery that could presumably be directed toward any number of purposes, but rather only a strictly defined critical, moralistic function.

II.

Wang Yunxi has argued that this transformation of the definition of *bi xing* in the hands of writers like Bo Juyi—into a single undifferentiated

---

[38] Mei Yunsheng, "Shi lun Bo Juyi," p. 250; the same point has been made by Wang Yunxi as well, in "Tan Zhongguo gudai," p. 51.

term referring to the politically critical content and function of an entire poem rather than its use of imagery—persisted not only into the Tang dynasty but for centuries afterward as well.[39] In many ways this view is a corollary to one pronounced long before by Liu Xie, who, as cited earlier, had written in his *Literary Mind* that even by his time the stimulus had "gradually died out." Zhu Ziqing also maintained that in fact few poets actually employed the imagistic methods identified with the *Classic of Poetry*, that the direct exposition of objects and events includes the comparison and stimulus, and that it therefore represents the core of the poetic tradition, which did not necessarily concern itself with political critique.[40] Two questions call for further investigation here: first, whether or not Bo Juyi's collapse of the two terms into one and lack of interest in imagery was indeed characteristic of Tang poetic theory, and, second, whether or not the indirect methods of presentation did in fact "die out."

Although pronouncements on the meaning of *bi* and *xing* during the Tang are both rare and brief—as indeed is the theoretical literature of the time as a whole—Bo Juyi's formulations by no means reflect a unanimity of critical opinion. Three other texts, for example, include discussions of the terms that both attempt to distinguish them and also view them as ways of using natural imagery. One is a collection of remarks by Jiaoran, the *Shi shi* 詩式 (*Forms of Poetry*), which defines *bi* and *xing* in a section titled "Using Allusions" (*Yong shi* 用事):

> Poets all think taking evidence from antiquity is using allusions, but this is not necessarily always the case. Now of the Six Principles, I shall briefly discuss the comparison and stimulus. Taking the image is called a comparison, and taking the meaning is called a stimulus. The meaning is the significance beneath the image. All animals, fish, plants and trees, people, and objects with different names—any of the myriad phenomena whose meaning-categories are the same can be used as comparison and stimulus. The *Guan ju* illustrates this principle.[41]

The *Guan ju* is the first poem in the Mao edition of the *Classic of Poetry*, discussed at length in Chapter Two. Jiaoran does not analyze that poem here, going on instead to give examples of images in various Six Dynasties poems that he thinks have been mistakenly read as historical allusions instead of comparisons, and vice versa. Yet however brief his definition, it is clear that his primary concern is not with any political function but

[39] "Tan Zhongguo gudai," pp. 52–53.
[40] Zhu Ziqing, *Shi yan zhi bian*, pp. 104–05.
[41] Jiaoran, *Shi shi*, in *Lidai shihua*, I, 31.

rather with imagistic practice per se. He is harking back to discussions like that of Wang Bi in his essay on "Elucidating the Image" (of the *Classic of Changes*; see Chapter One), which delineated a definite hierarchy among three elements: language exists for the sake of the image, and the image for the sake of meaning. In Jiaoran's view, therefore, the comparison would be inferior to the stimulus. And, like Wang Bi and other early scholars, Jiaoran also calls upon the notion of categorical correspondences (*lei*), according to which natural objects are felt to embody some kind of already determined meaning shared by other objects or situations belonging to some pre-existing and non-mutually-exclusive class.

Jiaoran's definitions of these tropes are recorded somewhat differently in the *Bunkyō hifuron* or *Wen jing mifu lun* 文鏡秘府論, a collection of various utterances, largely on poetic technique, compiled by the Japanese monk Kūkai 空海 (774–835). In a chapter entitled "The Six Principles," we find definitions of each term attributed to "Wang" and "Jiao," who are presumably Wang Changling and Jiaoran.[42] These remarks on the comparison and stimulus are particularly noteworthy not only because, like Zhong Hong's, they expand the scope of these devices beyond the *Classic of Poetry*, but also because they reveal the difficulty in distinguishing the two. About the comparison, for example, Jiaoran is quoted as saying that "A comparison involves completely taking an external image in order to evoke something, as in the line, 'In the northwest there is a floating cloud,'"[43] and Wang says, "A comparison involves a straightforward comparison with the self, what is called a comparative example, something like '*Guan guan* cry the ospreys.'" About the stimulus, however, Jiaoran says: "A stimulus involves placing an image first and using a human situation afterwards in comparison, as in '*Guan guan* cry the ospreys,'" while Wang is cited to the effect that "Indicating an object and comparing it to the self to explain it is what makes a stimulus. Thus relying on comparison is called a stimulus."[44] In other words, since *bi* by definition means comparison and *xing* in the hands of Confucian commentators seems to mean the same thing, how do they differ?

A similar fundamental confusion, belied by a superficial clarity of distinctions, is created by the discussion of these terms in the *Profound Meaning of the Two Souths* (*Er nan mi zhi* 二南密旨), attributed to the poet Jia Dao 賈島 (779–834). Unlike the two texts just mentioned, this work does share Bo Juyi's conviction of the politically commentative role

---

[42] Richard Bodman has discussed the authorship of this chapter in "Poetics and Prosody," p. 55.

[43] This is the first line of a "Miscellaneous Poem" by Cao Pi 曹丕 (187–226), included in the *Wen xuan*, 29/20a/p.545.

[44] *Wen jing mifu lun*, p. 56.

of poetry. At the same time, however, it does not simply equate *bi* and *xing* with this function per se but starts out by attempting to differentiate them as two separate techniques. After opening with some brief definitions of each of the Six Principles—for example, "To set forth meaning is called exposition, to draw forth a categorical correspondence is called comparison, and to respond to objects is called stimulus"[45]—Jia Dao elaborates on each term in a manner that unquestionably affirms the links between poetry and politics established by the Han commentators:

> Exposition means to develop and set forth, to indicate a situation and present it, and to expose the differing appearances of good and bad. Externally it develops the substance proper to its topic, and internally it sets forth the emotions basic to criticism and remonstrance.
>
> A comparison is a categorical correspondence, the principle that beautiful and ugly correspond to and mutually expose each other. If the ruler is confused and the minister fawning, then images of objects can compare with and criticize them. If the ruler is virtuous and minister bright, then one can also choose objects in comparison as images for them.
>
> A stimulus is feeling, meaning that externally one responds to objects and internally one is moved by feelings. Feelings cannot be blocked, thus they are said to be stimulated. One responds to the rise and fall of the ruler's and ministers' virtuous government and gives them form in words.[46]

Unlike earlier adherents of these views, however, Jia Dao goes on to provide elaborate illustrations of how this criticism is effected, thus affirming, unlike Bo Juyi, the difference between a purpose and the means to achieve it. Much of the work thus consists of lists detailing the ways in which poem titles and images can refer obliquely to meritorious or reprehensible situations and personages. For example, works entitled "Poems on Wandering Immortals" (*you xian shi* 游仙詩) are said to "criticize the obstruction of the ruler's and minister's way," and images of yellow, falling or withered leaves are said to be analogies for petty men.[47] Despite having taken the trouble to delineate the Six Principles from each other, Jia Dao does not mention explicitly which trope these lists exemplify,

---

[45] Jia Dao, *Er nan mi zhi* (*Xue hai lei bian* 學海類編 ed., compiled by Cao Rong 曹溶 [1613–1685], printed in 1831), *Congshu jicheng* (Changsha: Shangwu, 1939), p. 1. I am indebted to Professor Charles Hartman for sharing with me his unpublished translation and discussion of this text, *The Profound Sense of the "Two Souths": A T'ang Primer of Metaphor*.

[46] *Er nan mi zhi, ibid.*

[47] *Ibid.*, p. 7.

although it is clear that the images are all seen to be pre-established, substitutive comparisons of some kind, and the words *bi* or *yu* 喻 appear in almost every instance.

This text clearly addresses itself to the kind of poetry discussed earlier in this chapter, in which images—appearing either in isolation or as the subject of an entire poem—draw upon and develop conventional associations in a fixed one-to-one relationship. For that kind of poem, which identifies itself to us by title, by a focus on one object, or by the insertion into the narrative of images that are not plausible elements of an empirically observed scene, its assumptions and mode of composition and analysis are no doubt appropriate. But this is only one type of poetry in the Chinese tradition. Indeed, any consideration of the works of the major figures in the Tang dynasty would lead one to the conclusion that their achievement lay in a very different direction. As Stephen Owen has pointed out, poets like Chen Ziang were "successful in creating a powerful poetry using abstract ideas, but the real future of T'ang poetry lay precisely in the identification of the world of things and the world of ideas,"[48] uniting the goals of "expressing one's intent" and "embodying objects" by allowing sensuous imagery to embody meaning, without discursive explanation. This transformation led to significant reformulations in theoretical conceptions and terminology as well.

There are two passages in a text entitled "Precepts of Poetry" (*Shi ge* 詩格), attributed to Wang Changling,[49] that suggest some of the key attitudes underlying the best of Tang poetry. The first discusses briefly the way a poem comes into being, a problem that particularly preoccupied Wang Changling:

> Poetry has three precepts. The first is called letting thoughts arise. When one has employed the most subtle thinking for a long time without joining idea and image, so that one's energy is spent and wisdom exhausted, then one stills this profound thinking so that the mind can spontaneously reflect the world, which will suddenly come into being. The second is called responding with thoughts. One seeks out the flavor of words that have come before, hums and chants ancient models, and thoughts will arise in response. The third is called selecting thoughts. One examines images, the mind enters the world, and the spirit unites with objects, which are then attained by the mind.[50]

[48] Owen, *Early T'ang*, p. 223.

[49] For a discussion of the bibliographic and textual problems associated with this work, see Bodman, "Poetics and Prosody," pp. 50ff.

[50] Included in Gu Longzhen 顧龍振, ed., *Shi xue zhi nan* 詩學指南 (1759; rpt. Taipei: Guangwen, 1970), 3/7b/p.86. Cf. partial trans. by Bodman, p. 375n5.

This passage suggests that, as important as conscious effort and laborious study may be to the writing of a poem, equally or even more valuable is the poet's ability to adopt a more passive attitude and allow himself to be affected by and reflect spontaneously the world around him. This view can be traced back, of course, to some of the earliest Taoist, and then Buddhist, notions of ideal modes of behavior and cognition, ideas which were basic to critical texts both before and after the Tang.[51] What is most important for our purposes here, however, is Wang Changling's focus on the image, which is both external and internal, sensuous and intellectual, a fusion of mind and world.

These issues are discussed in slightly different terms in the passage immediately preceding this one in the text:

> Poetry has three worlds (*jing* 境). The first is called the world of objects. When one wishes to write a landscape poem, then one sets forth a world of streams and rocks, clouds and peaks—the utmost in beauty and elegance. As the spirit is in the mind, when one situates one's body in the world one sees the world in the mind, as if shimmering in one's palm. Only afterward does one use one's thinking to fully comprehend the world's images and thereby attain a formal likeness. The second is called the world of feelings. Pleasure and joy, grief and resentment are all set forth in one's ideas and situated in one's body. Then one presses one's thinking forward to deeply get to those feelings. The third is called the world of ideas, which also involves setting things forth in one's ideas and contemplating them in one's mind, so that the truth will be attained.[52]

Although Wang's reference to a "landscape poem" at the beginning suggests the likelihood that he is attempting to delineate three distinct types of poetry,[53] the ensuing remarks—which do not mention two other subgenres by name—do not rule out the possibility that he might also be speaking of different aspects of the same poem. In that case, Wang would be advocating an ideal poetry that arose from contact with the external world and succeeded in presenting objects from that world that were not only sensuously vivid but also imbued with emotional and intellectual content. Such a description would accurately characterize much of the poetry of the high Tang.

[51] For a brief discussion of some of these theories, see my book, *The Poetry of Wang Wei: New Translations and Commentary* (Bloomington: Indiana University Press, 1980), pp. 5–22.

[52] In *Shi xue zhi nan*, 3/7a/p.85. Cf. partial trans. by Bodman, p. 375n6.

[53] For such an analysis, see Bodman, pp. 78ff.

186

The aptness of this characterization hardly needs to be illustrated, for it encapsulates the very qualities that have come to be taken for granted in Tang poetry: its concentrated vision and form; its precise yet evocative imagery; its preference for the concise and concrete as opposed to the discursive and abstract; its mode of presentation which places as much value, if not more, on what is implied as on what is stated directly.[54] My aim is not to belabor these points yet one more time but rather to suggest how this style finds a place in a long and evolving tradition of poetic practice and commentary. Nevertheless, a few examples seem warranted, and I have limited myself to some very familiar ones.

III.

Of the three major high Tang poets, Wang Wei is perhaps most closely associated with the imagistic methods just described, a style that attempts to efface the overt and commenting presence of the poetic subject to yield the initiative to objects. This stance derives in large measure from the author's Taoist-Buddhist inclinations to deemphasize the human ego and suggest instead a union with and submergence in the natural world. Any number of his works might be summoned forth in illustration, although his regulated quatrains (*jueju* 絕句) are among the most striking. As Stephen Owen has noted in his history of high Tang poetry, Wang's quatrains in general probably represent his most significant contribution to generic development, particularly because of his substitution of enigmatic understatement for the witty epigrammatic closure more common at the time.[55] The Wang River Collection (*Wang chuan ji* 輞川集), a group of twenty pentasyllabic quatrains, each of which names a site on Wang's country estate outside Chang'an and was written in the company of a close friend, the minor official Pei Di 裴迪 (b. 716), offers several examples of Wang's achievement. The most famous among them is the fifth poem, "Deer Fence" (*Lu zhai* 鹿柴):

Empty mountain, no men seen,	空山不見人
Only hearing echoes of men's talk.	但聞人語響

[54] For a general discussion of these features, see Kao Yu-kung and Mei Tsu-lin, "Syntax, Diction and Imagery in T'ang Poetry," *Harvard Journal of Asiatic Studies*, 31 (1971), pp. 49–136. For somewhat different purposes, Stephen Owen suggests a very illuminating juxtaposition of two poems, one by Zhang Jiuling 張九齡 (673–740) and the other by Qiwu Qian 綦母潛 (692–749), that also illustrates the differences between the two types of imagery (*The Great Age*, pp. 24, 58–59).

[55] Owen, *The Great Age*, p. 38.

A backcast glow enters the deep forest   返景入深林
And shines again upon the green moss.[56]   復照青苔上

This poem exemplifies typical quatrain procedure in narrowing its focus from the massiveness of a mountain to a ray of the setting sun entering a mossy grove. From the virtual denial of the concreteness of human presence in the first couplet it moves to the lucidly concrete depiction of a natural event in the second, suggesting the priority of the image. The apparently flat or "bland" simplicity of the sequence of images is deceptive, for each line presents a perception that must be qualified or amplified by the next. The "emptiness" of the mountain seems difficult to accept until Wang Wei specifies the particular kind of absence: it is devoid of any visible human presence. And the "emptiness" (kong 空) could be even more fundamental than that. Kong is also the translation of the Sanskrit word śūnyatā, a key term in the Mahāyāna Buddhist traditions with which Wang was familiar, referring to the doctrine that no phenomenon possesses any permanent, unconditioned nature—not a mountain, much less a person, and, carrying the logic to its end, not even the doctrine itself. This emptiness as the ultimate reality is evoked frequently in Wang Wei's poetry though always retaining its non-philosophical sense as well, an example of the suggestive resonance of Wang's descriptions.

Whether or not the mountain actually is unpopulated, it turns out to reverberate with the echoes of human voices in the second line. Remaining unclarified, however, is the question as to whether these are echoes of people who are actually present on the mountain at some distance or are simply memories in the poet's mind of conversations from some altogether different place and time. The third line focuses on the perceptions of one person who is there, locating him temporally and spatially: toward sunset, when "returning" (fan 返) light sends a "backcast" or "reflected" (also fan) glow through an opening into a glade. And line 4 suggests that the poet's experience is not just of the moment, for although the word fu may function here solely as a conjunction and not a temporal adverb, it may also be that he has been in the grove that same morning, or even all day, and thus knows that the light is shining on the moss "again." Wang Wei tells us nothing directly about the duration of or reason for his presence— has he been lost in silent contemplation, with moments of illumination analogous to the flashes of sunlight entering the glade?—but the quatrain is all the more effective for what remains unsaid. The Ming critic Li

---

[56] Included in Zhao Diancheng 趙殿成 ed., *Wang Youcheng ji jian zhu* 王右丞集箋註 (1736; rpt. Taipei: Heluo, n.d.), 13/p.243, and Gao Buying, II,8/p.754. Cf. my *Poetry of Wang Wei* for an earlier translation (p. 202) and discussion (pp. 167–68).

Dongyang 李東陽 (1447–1516) describes its almost paradoxical qualities in the following passage:

> In poetry one values meaning, and in meaning one values what is distant and not what is accessible, what is bland and not what is dense. What is dense and accessible will be easy to recognize; what is bland and distant will be difficult to know.... Wang Mojie's 摩詰 [Wei] "A backcast glow enters the deep forest / And shines again upon the green moss" is utterly bland and yet more dense, accessible and yet more distant. It can be conveyed to those who know but is difficult to impart to the vulgar.[57]

In other words, the poem's apparently plain and simple imagery does carry a profound significance, unaided by discursive comment and hence all the more effective.

A similarly disarming and deceptive directness characterizes other quatrains in the Wang River Collection, and in particular the eighteenth poem, "Bamboo Lodge" (*Zhu li guan* 竹里館):

I sit alone within the dark bamboo,	獨坐幽篁裏
Pluck my zither and whistle long again.	彈琴復長嘯
In the deep wood men do not know	深林人不知
The bright moon comes to shine on me.[58]	明月來相照

As is true of many others in the group, this poem alludes to a passage in "The Mountain Spirit" of the *Nine Songs* in the *Songs of Chu*, in which the speaker laments that the spirit has not yet arrived as he waits alone in a dense grove of bamboo.[59] Here, however, Wang Wei rejects the grieving tone of the earlier poem, accepting his solitude with equanimity and perhaps true pleasure. He may lack human company, but not the harmonies of and with nature, which will reverberate to the quiet strains of his zither and the sound of his "whistle" (*xiao* 嘯), a special kind of Taoist breathing exercise. The ambiguous syntax of the third line is particularly suggestive: what is it that others "do not know"? The whereabouts of the grove? Its very existence? His presence there? The true nature of his experiences there? Are they simply unaware that the moon shines on him

---

[57]Li Dongyang, *Lutang shihua* 麓堂詩話, *Congshu jicheng* ed. (Shanghai: Shangwu, 1939), 1/p.1. Also cited in Peng Guodong 彭國棟, ed., *Tang shi sanbai shou shihua hui bian* 唐詩三百首詩話薈編 (Taipei: Zhonghua wenhua chubanshe, 1958; 2 vols. in 1), p. 361.

[58]Zhao Diancheng, *Wang Youcheng ji jian zhu*, 13/p.249; cf. Yu, trans., p. 204 and discussion, pp. 168–69.

[59]*Chu ci bu zhu*, 2/21a/p.137; trans. Hawkes, *Ch'u Tz'u*, p. 43.

there, and, if so, what does that mean? Wang Wei may be suggesting that they lack the special kind of selfless, intuitive cognition of and identification with nature that brings him the mutuality reflected in his peaceful solitude and perception of a special relationship with the moon. It may also be that, since the moon appears so frequently in Buddhist literature as a symbol of enlightenment, he is hinting at a religious experience of enlightenment as well. Yet the poem offers no overt indication of such possibilities; each image and utterance functions equally plausibly as a simple element of a literally depicted scene, and the reader is left to assess the likelihood and nature of any further significance.

Other high Tang poets exploited the opportunities for evocative understatement afforded by the regulated quatrain form as well. Li Bo, as scholars have frequently pointed out, was perhaps less likely than many to exemplify the distinctive imagistic practices of his age. He is much better known for his preference for older, less restrictive poetic forms (as in the "Ancient Airs") and for an unprecedented exuberance of direct self-expression and self-definition,[60] neither of which coincided with directions in which his contemporaries were moving. Yet, for all his cultivated eccentricity, a number of poems, and especially his quatrains, demonstrate the typical features of the developing style. The following is one of his best-known quatrains, "Jade Stairs Grievance" (*Yu jie yuan* 玉階怨):

On jade stairs arises white dew,　　　　　玉階生白露
In the long night soaking through gauze stockings.　夜久侵羅襪
Still she drops the crystalline screen—　　　卻下水精簾
Gleaming bright, a gaze at the autumn moon.[61]　玲瓏望秋月

Works of this title are included in a section of palace lady laments in Guo Maoqian's 郭茂倩 (ca. 1100) *Yuefu shiji* 樂府詩集.[62] Thus Li Bo's poem is classified as a Music Bureau song in both Wang Qi's Qing edition of his works and the *Three Hundred Poems of the Tang Dynasty*.[63] Despite its tonal irregularities, however, Gao Buying groups it with pentasyllabic regulated quatrains in his selection of Tang and Song poetry, noting that it differs from the others in the *yuefu* anthology. Indeed, the distinctiveness of Li Bo's poem can best be measured by comparing it with its two predecessors, the first by Xie Tiao and the second by Yu Yan 虞炎:

[60] For a discussion of his poetry, see Owen, *The Great Age*, esp. pp. 109–43.
[61] Wang Qi, *Li Taibo quanji*, 5/p.144, and Gao Buying, II,8/p.764.
[62] Guo Maoqian, *Yuefu shiji* (rpt. Peking: Zhonghua, 1979; 4 vols.), II,43/p.632.
[63] Wang Qi, *Li Taibo quanji*, 5/p.244; also Yu Shouzhen 喻守眞, ed., *Tang shi sanbai shou xiangxi* 唐詩三百首詳析 (Hong Kong: Zhonghua, 1977), p. 283.

At dusk in the hall she lowers the pearl screen.	夕殿下珠簾
Fireflies drift by in flight, then cease.	流螢飛復息
In the long night she stitches a gauze shirt.	長夜縫羅衣
Thoughts of her lord: when will this end?	思君此何極
Wisteria grazes the blossoming trees;	紫藤拂花樹
Yellow orioles cross their verdant limbs.	黃鳥度青枝
Thoughts of her lord: a single sigh.	思君一歎息
Bitter tears answering words course down.[64]	苦淚應言垂

Each of these poems presents the plight of a courtesan out of favor with her lord, a subgenre inspired by a well-known lament attributed to Ban Jieyu 班婕妤 (fl. 48 to 6 B.C.), concubine to the Han emperor Chengdi 成帝 (r. 32 to 7 B.C.).[65] The elements are similar: an autumn evening by a richly screened window, in the case of the versions by Li and Xie. Li Bo's poem, however, is markedly less explicit in its presentation of the woman's actions and emotions. We are not informed directly that she has been waiting unheeded on the steps for her lord—only the fact that the cold night dew has penetrated her light stockings tells us so. Nor does the poet follow precedent in referring to the object and nature of her thoughts: we simply see her gazing mutely at the autumn moon, whose gleam through the crystal screen completes the tableau of chilly, somber whiteness drawn by each line of the quatrain. Li Bo thus relies entirely on an integrated succession of scenic elements to suggest rather than state overtly the reason for the lament, a method recognized by traditional commentators like Xiao Shibin 蕭士斌 of the Yuan, who noted that "in this piece Taibo has not a single word expressing lament but conceals the meaning of her secret grievance, which appears beyond the words. Is this not what Huian 晦菴 [Zhu Xi] called being a sage of poetry?"[66]

Music Bureau poems, with their typical focus on stock personae of the literary lexicon, would naturally create the expectation of a certain measure of distance from the poetic self, though not necessarily of such extreme emotional reticence. Several other of Li Bo's regulated poems (*lü shi* 律詩), however, also work by means of a series of coherently juxtaposed images rather than direct statement, among them the following two farewell pieces:

[64] Both poems are in the *Yuefu shiji*, II,43/p.632.

[65] Ban Jieyu, *Yuan ge xing* 怨歌行, included in *Wen xuan*, 27/22a–b/p.510. For a translation see J. D. Frodsham and Ch'eng Hsi, *An Anthology of Chinese Verse: Han Wei Chin and the Northern and Southern Dynasties* (Oxford: Clarendon, 1967), p. 22.

[66] From his *Fenlei bu zhu Li Taibo shi* 分類補註李太白詩, cited in Wang Qi, 5/p.144, Gao Buying, II, 8/p.764, and Peng Guodong, p. 390.

Farewell to a Friend (*Song youren* 送友人)

Verdant mountains behind the northern ramparts,	青山橫北郭
White waters wind around the east city wall.	白水遶東城
From this place once parting has ended,	此地一爲別
The lone tumbleweed flies a myriad miles.	孤蓬萬里征
Floating clouds: a traveler's thoughts.	浮雲遊子意
Setting sun: an old friend's feelings.	落日故人情
Waving hands, you go from here—	揮手自茲去
Horses neigh gently as they leave.[67]	蕭蕭班馬鳴

Crossing at Jingmen Mountain: A Farewell (*Du Jingmen songbie* 渡荆門送別)

We've crossed from afar beyond Jingmen Mountain,	渡遠荆門外
Journeying here through the state of Chu.	來從楚國遊
The mountains follow the flat plains to their end,	山隨平野盡
The river enters the vast wastes, flowing.	江入大荒流
The moon descends, a flying heavenly mirror.	月下飛天鏡
Clouds arise to build ocean towers.	雲生結海樓
You still cherish your native province's waters—	仍憐故鄉水
For a myriad miles sending your traveling boat.[68]	萬里送行舟

Both of these poems treat a situation conventionally associated with sadness, yet Li Bo is remarkably laconic about his emotions, allowing the images to suggest them instead. Elements of a plausibly observed scene succeed one another with a minimum of discursive comment, rather than being interjected as non-empirical emblems inviting a political reading. In "Farewell to a Friend," Li Bo opens with an imagistic parallel couplet that evokes the vast stretches of mountains and river extending beyond the familiar boundaries of the city, which his friend presumably is leaving. The propositional couplet that traditionally opens a regulated verse then follows, with its stock image of the tumbleweed for traveler given almost literal reality by the backdrop of the scene just presented.

Li Bo employs another set of conventional images in the third couplet, but to even more unconventional effects. Commentators recall for us the lines in the first of the "Nineteen Ancient Poems" that run: "Floating clouds obscure the white sun; / The traveler thinks not of return," where the clouds were explained as images of schemers or slanderers at court; the setting sun similarly was usually regarded as an omen of a ruler's de-

---

[67] Wang Qi, 8/p.406; Gao Buying, II,4/p.458.
[68] Wang Qi, 5/p.358; Gao Buying, II,4/pp.457–58.

cline in earlier poetry. Here, however, the clouds and sun are not effaced from the scene in favor of another situation: not only do we read them as objects actually observed by the poet because of the scenic context in which they occur, but Li Bo also restricts the range of their associations to his concrete, personal concerns, rather than more general or political ones. Moreover, the juxtaposed images leave the reader to surmise the nature of their relationship, acknowledging the real presence of both elements—are they similar or dissimilar, and if so, how?—rather than inviting a stereotypical substitution. Wang Qi writes that "once floating clouds go off they lack any certain traces, thus they are used as comparisons to the traveler's thoughts; the setting sun is held by the mountains and does not leave hurriedly, hence it is used as a comparison to the old friend's feelings" (8/p.406), but this is only one of several possibilities. Finally, the last couplet remains on the level of evocative description, withholding the expected emotional utterance. As Wang Qi notes, "The host's and guest's horses are about to take separate paths and neigh *xiao xiao* for a long time, as if they were responding emotionally to leaving the others. If beasts feel this way, how can the humans bear it?" (*Ibid.*)

"Crossing at Jingmen Mountain" is less imagistically dense and perhaps for that reason somewhat less emotionally charged. Its middle two couplets have understandably elicited, however, a considerable amount of critical attention. Lines 5 and 6 might at first appear to provide us with examples of metaphors,[69] but on reconsideration such an identification becomes problematic. In line 5, as in "Farewell to a Friend," Li Bo rejects the possible substitution and simply juxtaposes the two elements being compared; the association of the moon with metal and specifically with mirrors was a cultural commonplace.[70] Similarly, his evocation of the elaborate mirages constructed by watery clouds draws upon earlier textual precedents recalled for us by commentators. Furthermore, Li Bo again retains both images, juxtaposed, rather than calling upon us to replace one with the other in a mode more familiar to Western metaphor. In other words, for all the insight these pairings may provide us into the poet's imaginative propensities, he preserves the primacy of the literal object as observed.

This conviction of the poem as a document of experience emerges in an exchange of critical comments on the couplet preceding this one that measure it against one appearing in the same position in Du Fu's renowned "Traveling at Night, Writing My Thoughts" (*Lü ye shu huai* 旅夜書懷):

[69] See Kao Yu-kung and Mei Tsu-lin, "Meaning, Metaphor, and Allusion in T'ang Poetry," *Harvard Journal of Asiatic Studies*, 38.2 (Dec. 1978), pp. 289, 302–03.

[70] On this see Edward H. Schafer, *Pacing the Void: T'ang Approaches to the Stars* (Berkeley and Los Angeles: University of California Press, 1977), pp. 171–210.

Slender grass, a faint wind on the shore.　　　　細草微風岸

Tall mast, a lonely night on the boat.　　　　　危檣獨夜舟

Stars hang down on the flat plain's expanse,　　星垂平野闊

The moon surges up in the great river, flowing.　月湧大江流

A name—how can writing make it known?　　　名豈文章著

An office—for age and sickness given up.　　　　官因老病休

Fluttering, floating, what is there for likeness?　飄飄何所似

On heaven and earth, one sandy gull.[71]　　　　天地一沙鷗

To some eyes Li Bo's couplet suffers from the comparison. Huang Boshan 黃白山 notes that "the syntax of both is approximately the same, but [Li Bo's] only mentions river and mountains, whereas [Du Fu's] has the plain's expanse, stars hanging down, river flowing, and moon surging—four situations in all."[72] Hu Yinglin agrees that "the bones and energy" of the latter couplet exceed the former.[73] Presumably on Li Bo's behalf, Weng Fanggang 翁方綱 (1733–1818) argues that the two couplets "were not intended to be placed side by side, and should certainly not be made to depend on one another, nor to be submitted to any distinction as to superior and inferior."[74] The defense of Ding Longyou 丁龍友, however, is most telling in the straightforward simplicity of its assumptions. Responding specifically to Hu Yinglin's judgment, he writes: "I say that Li's is a daytime scene and Du's a nighttime scene. Li's is from a moving boat, glimpsing things in passing; Du's is from a moored boat, observing things in detail. They cannot be discussed as of a piece."[75] In other words, we are reminded not only that images carry the heaviest load of meaning on their own in a Tang poem, but that they are also more than vehicles substituting in a one-ton-one relationship for some abstract concept: they give the impression that they have been selected not just for their possible connotations, but also because the poet actually happened to perceive them.

Whatever one's final judgment on the relative merits of these two couplets, Du Fu's mastery of the evocative powers and density of imagistic combination should be evident. Rather than employing the traditional tripartite form of regulated verse, which would enclose the middle scenic couplets with propositional statements, Du Fu opens his poem with four image-laden lines presenting two very different scenes. The first couplet's

---

[71] Included in Qiu Zhaoao 仇兆鰲, ed., *Du shi xiang zhu* 杜詩詳註 (1767; rpt. Taipei: Wenshizhe chubanshe, 1973; 2 vols.), II, 14/p.735. Cf. trans. by Cyril Birch in Birch, ed., *Anthology of Chinese Literature*, I, 238–39.

[72] Cited in Gao Buying, II,4/p.487, and Qiu Zhaoao, II,14/p.735.

[73] Hu Yinglin, *Shi sou, nei bian*, 4/p.69. Cited by Wang Qi, 5/p.359 and Gao Buying, II,4/p.457.

[74] Weng Fanggang, *Shizhou shihua* 石洲詩話, cited by Peng Guodong, p. 191.

[75] Cited by Wang Qi, 5/p.359, and Gao Buying, II,4/p.457.

effects of loneliness, isolation, diminution, and stasis are given particular emphasis by the absence of any verbs. In the second couplet, however, he shifts to a much larger vista of water, earth, and sky, elements of which move dramatically to join with and reflect one another. The next two lines offer a bleak assessment of his likelihood of fulfilling the Confucian mission which Du Fu embraced and provide as well a retrospective understanding of the impulse behind the contrast established in the first half of the poem: aspiration and reality in his personal life are, Du Fu suggests, as incommensurate as the images of individual powerlessness and isolation in line 1 are with the cosmic dynamism and merging of line 2. Yet he has made the effort, if unsuccessfully, maintaining the stark dignity suggested by the "tall mast." The final couplet encapsulates this contrast and also calls attention to the typical imagistic practice of Tang poetry. Du Fu tells us explicitly that he is giving us an image of himself—one that finds echoes in many other of his poems as well—but he does not spell out the nature of the comparison. Moreover, the gull soaring between sky and earth is not an isolated, arbitrary emblem of the self; it is drawn as likely from the scene as from the poet's personal vocabulary and, furthermore, reiterates the mood and context of the poem as a whole, one among many that "inevitably reduced him to the dignified but impotent individual."[76]

A similar vision is created by a slightly later regulated verse (Qiu Zhaoao gives autumn of 769 as the likely time of composition, four years after "Traveling at Night"), "Yangzi and Han" (*Jiang Han* 江漢):

At Yangzi and Han a traveler thinking of home—	江漢思歸客
Twixt *qian* and *kun* a lone, stale scholar.	乾坤一腐儒
A slip of cloud, the sky as distant, too.	片雲天共遠
A long night, the moon sharing its solitude.	永夜月同孤
Setting sun: a heart still strong.	落日心猶壯
Autumn wind: from sickness about to revive.	秋風病欲蘇
Since ancient times old horses have been kept	古來存老馬
And need not take to the long road.[77]	不必取長途

Even more than the previous poem, "Yangzi and Han" abounds in images corresponding to the poet, directly in the opening line and then successively more covertly. The soaring sandy gull becomes here a self-mocking, worn-out Confucian scholar, still, however, envisioned as alone between *qian* and *kun*, the hexagrams in the *Classic of Changes* linked respectively with heaven and earth. As in Xie Lingyun's poem on "Climbing the Pond-

---

[76] Owen, *The Great Age*, p. 212.

[77] Qiu Zhaoao, *Du shi xiang zhu*, II,23/p.1,158. Cf. trans. by Graham, *Poems of the Late T'ang*, p. 48, and Owen, *The Great Age*, pp. 215–16.

side Tower," discussed in Chapter Four, we can see the effortless identification of the apparently abstract concepts of the text and the concrete
scene, suggesting the lack of a dichotomy between the two that a Western
reader might take for granted. Unlike Xie, however, Du Fu continues to
build on these images, allowing them to carry the freight of the poem's
meaning.

The images in the second couplet are dense, ambiguous, and complex in
syntax and reference. It is unclear precisely with whom the sky and moon
share their respective distance and solitude—presumably not only with
the cloud and night but the poet as well—but, in any event, the mention
of heavenly counterparts serves to mitigate those very qualities. However
remote and lonely the poet may feel, he is not totally isolated. This subtle
shift in mood becomes more definite in the next two lines, whose juxtaposed images seek to reverse their conventional associations. More directly than Li Bo in "Farewell to a Friend," Du Fu refuses the connotations of
decline linked with the setting sun and asserts his continued strength in
old age. Similarly, whereas an autumn wind in earlier poetry would have
served as an omen of wintry death, here Du Fu gains from it an imminent
sense of renewal. Both images reject as well the structural signals for
emblematic function, incorporating both sun and wind into a scenic
tableau, rather than setting them apart. Zhao Fang 趙汸 (1319–1369)
comments on the remarkable integration of self and world in these two
couplets:

> In these middle four lines feeling and scene are fused together as if
> transformed. Cloud, sky, night, moon, setting sun, and autumn wind
> are all scene (*jing* 景). "The sky as distant, too," "the moon sharing
> its solitude," the heart seeing the setting sun yet still strong, and a
> sickness encountering autumn wind yet about to be overcome are all
> feeling (*qing* 情). Other poems usually match scene against scene and
> feeling against feeling. Here his matching feeling with scene is rare
> indeed. When what is empty and what has substance form one thread
> like this, they cannot be separated. Those who can imitate this are
> especially rare.[78]

Zhao gets to the heart here of the Tang poetic achievement, which was
to generate a host of similar critical observations and appreciations in
later centuries.

The last couplet of "Yangzi and Han" brings the increasingly hopeful
movement of the poem to its close. Here Du Fu suggests as likeness for
himself an aging horse still worth keeping instead of sending on its way to

[78] Cited by Qiu Zhaoao, *ibid.*

suggest his continued usefulness even in old age. Less lofty perhaps than the fluttering gull, the image nonetheless conveys a similar pathetic dignity. Once again we have gained much knowledge about the poet's sense of self, knowledge conveyed not through abstract statement, however, but in the coherently progressing images of a natural scene.

A much earlier poem (dated by Qiu to the third month of 757) anticipates the gentle self-mockery of these late works while focusing on a considerably larger situation, the country ravaged by the An Lushan 安祿山 rebellion of 755–757. This is the renowned pentasyllabic regulated verse, "Spring Gaze" (*Chun wang* 春望):

The country shattered, mountains and rivers remain.	國破山河在
Spring in the city—grasses and trees are dense.	城春草木深
Feeling the times, flowers draw forth tears.	感時花濺淚
Hating to part, birds alarm the heart.	恨別鳥驚心
Beacon fires for three months in a row;	鋒火連三月
A letter from home worth ten thousand in gold.	家書抵萬金
White hairs scratched grow even shorter—	白頭搔更短
Soon too few to hold a hairpin on.[79]	渾欲不勝簪

The structural tightness of this poem has impressed countless readers over the ages, who have remarked on how skillfully Du Fu has interwoven images of the world of men and world of nature, of human feelings and natural scene. The first half of the poem generally focuses on the latter and the second half on the former, yet lines 1–4 each link elements from both realms as well. The effects of a "country shattered" can be felt in the pain of separation and pricelessness of a letter from home; "spring"— normally an occasion for joy—must be defined ironically as the "times" that elicit tears, having been illuminated for the entirety of the season by beacon fires of war.

As Du Fu narrows his focus to detail his own reaction to the situation he has so powerfully sketched, one might expect a more explicitly emotional response than the one he provides in the final couplet. Instead, however, the almost pathetically comical reference to his balding pate resolutely continues the trust he has placed throughout the poem in evocative imagery rather than direct statement. And for all their stark simplicity, the images by their very juxtaposition have conveyed a complex cluster of emotions. What might otherwise serve as consoling testaments to the permanence of nature in the first couplet, for instance, become instead agonizing evidence of the enormity of human loss. The compressed syntax of lines 3–4 seems to suggest that it is the flowers and birds that are

---

[79] Qiu Zhaoao, I,4/p.263. Cf. trans. by Watson, *Chinese Lyricism*, p. 162.

responding sympathetically to the devastation, yet in fact they confirm a now almost perverse continuity of nature, which, oblivious to human affairs, persists in producing beautiful sights and sounds that can only wrench the poet's heart. Nowhere in the poem does Du Fu use a word expressly denoting grief, yet it comes through all the more powerfully for that very reason.

In a frequently cited passage on "Spring Gaze," Sima Guang 司馬光 (1019–1086) makes many of these same points in a way that demonstrates later critical conceptions of what imagery can do:

> When the ancients wrote poetry, they valued a meaning beyond words, which would make one think before getting it. Thus the speaker would be without blame and the hearer sufficiently advised. In recent ages only Du Zimei 子美 [Fu] has achieved in great measure this style of the poets. As in the poem "Spring Gaze": "The country shattered, mountains and rivers remain" makes clear that nothing else is left. "Spring in the city: grasses and trees are dense" makes clear that no human traces are left. Flowers and birds in normal times are objects that can give pleasure: the poet sees one and weeps, hears the other and grieves, thus one can understand the times.[80]

Although Sima Guang must credit the composers of the songs in the *Classic of Poetry* with the consummate mastery of this technique (a citation from that anthology introduces this passage), it is in fact only during the Tang that it reaches its peak in a poetry of concentrated vision whose condensed, coherently developed imagery evokes a "meaning beyond words."

The assumption that images were selected for the purposes of conveying this meaning, however implicitly, should argue against a view that the Chinese poet was simply aiming to present things "as they are." Wai-lim Yip, for example, has claimed that the objects in a Chinese poem do not refer to something other than themselves because the poet does not "force the perspective of the ego upon Phenomenon."[81] Instead, the writer gives "paramount importance to the acting-out of visual objects and events, letting them explain themselves by their coexisting, coextensive emergence from nature, letting the spatial tensions reflect conditions and situations rather than coercing these objects and events into some preconceived artificial orders by sheer human interpretive elaboration" (*ibid.,*

[80] Sima Guang, *Wen gong xu shihua* 溫公續詩話, in *Lidai shihua*, I, 277–78. Also cited, among others, by Qiu Zhaoao, I,4/p.263.

[81] Wai-lim Yip, *Chinese Poetry: Major Modes and Genres* (Berkeley and Los Angeles: University of California Press, 1976), p. 19.

pp. 22–23). Yip feels that objects are not metaphorical vehicles because in fact the ultimate substitutive act has occurred before the writing of the poem. As he writes of Wang Wei, for example, "The poet has become, even before the act of composition, Phenomenon itself and can allow the things in it to emerge *as they are* without being contaminated by intellectuality. The poet does not step in; he views things as things view themselves."[82] At the same time, however, it is even more difficult than was the case with the emblematic imagery discussed earlier to call the methods of the high Tang poems just analyzed "metaphorical" ones. The conventional emblems of pine or tumbleweed do formally resemble Western metaphor, for they are substituted for the poet's real topic, be it an object, concept, or individual, as vehicle for tenor. Yet their recognized status as pre-established elements in a shared cultural code by virtue of which such associations exist independently of any individual's intervention distinguishes them even more fundamentally from metaphor in the West, premised as it is on poetry as constructing an elaborate fictive artifice. The case is the same for the images in the poems we have just examined, which lack, moreover, the superficial resemblance of substitutive form, their empirical origins and reality unquestioned. Whatever intellectual or affective meaning they convey is something they embody or illustrate of themselves, exploited—not contrived—by the poet.[83]

This is not to say, of course, that Tang poetry does not employ rhetorical tropes similar to those generally classified under the amorphous heading of metaphor in Western literature. In addition to the many emblematic vehicles, one can also identify countless examples of simile, personification, and the like. Even sustained parallels that are not based on conventional and generally political or moral correspondences can be found. Li He's 李賀 (791–817) "Grave of Little Su" (*Su xiaoxiao mu* 蘇小小墓), for instance, reveals a clear fascination with such possibilities, as the poet moves from the cautious distance of simile (lines 2, 5–6) to the bold equivalence of a copula (lines 7–8) and kenning (line 11):

Secret orchid's dew	幽蘭露
Like weeping eyes.	如啼眼
Not a thing to bind hearts together.	無物結同心
Misty flowers one cannot bear to cut.	煙花不堪剪
Grass like a cushion,	草如茵
Pine like a canopy,	松如蓋

[82] Yip, *Hiding the Universe: Poems by Wang Wei* (New York: Grossman, 1972), p. vi.

[83] Qian Zhongshu suggests both "illustration" and "embodiment" as appropriate epithets for such imagery and links them with the concept from traditional poetics of *li qu* 理趣, "the interest of ideas." See his *Tan yi lu*, p. 275.

The wind is a skirt,	風爲裳
And water, pendants.	水爲珮
An oiled-wall carriage	油壁車
Awaits one at night.	夕相待
Cold kingfisher candles	冷翠燭
Toil for brilliance.	勞光彩
Beneath West Mound	西陵下
Wind blows the rain.[84]	風吹雨

This poem does, however, elaborate on a received text (included in the *Yuefu shiji*, IV,85/p.1,203) and legend that the songs of a fifth-century singing girl could be heard near her grave on stormy nights, but even those infrequent occurrences of analogies which are novel, not derivative of some tradition or text, and extend over the course of a poem are instructive by their very unorthodoxy. Jia Dao's "Written in Jest to a Friend" (*Xi zeng youren* 戲贈友人) is a good example.

If for a day I do not write a poem,	一日不作詩
My mind's source is dry as an empty well.	心源如廢井
Brush and inkstone are my pulleys,	筆硯爲轆轤
Humming and chanting serve as winding ropes.	吟詠作麋綆
Next morning I pull and draw again:	朝來重汲引
As before I get something clear and cool.	依舊得清冷
I write this for a like-minded man:	書贈同懷人
Our verses are full of bitter pain.[85]	詞中多苦辛

This poem is reminiscent of a Metaphysical conceit in the elaborateness of the parallel it draws between two basically unlike activities—writing poetry and drawing water from a well. Yet Jia Dao strains to make the two as similar in kind as possible, by referring primarily not to abstract processes and problems of composition but to the clearly physical objects and activities involved (brush, inkstone, humming, and chanting). He also undermines the seriousness with which we are to take such a contrived comparison through the title of the poem: it may be clever, but it is a joke. The final couplet suggests Jia Dao's self-consciousness in offering something so unusual, and, significantly, he, like Li He, belongs to the group of late-Tang poets singled out by later critics for their tendency to wander from the mainstream of the tradition.[86]

[84] *Quan Tang shi*, 390/p.4,396; cf. trans. by Graham, p. 113.

[85] *Quan Tang shi*, 571/pp.6,626–67. Cf. trans. of James J. Y. Liu in *The Art of Chinese Poetry* (Chicago: University of Chicago Press, 1962), p. 113.

[86] In connection with this see Qian Zhongshu's discussion of the poetry of Meng Jiao 孟郊 (751–814) in *Tan yi lu*, p. 287.

Thus, unlike Western metaphor, Chinese poetic imagery does not allude to a realm that is fundamentally other from the concrete world or establish correspondences de novo between the sensible and the supra-sensible. Those correlations already existed, to be discovered by the poet, not manufactured. Because he was affirming equivalences and not creating or asserting them, he was not "teaching" something new in the way his Western counterpart is presumed to be doing nor creating a purely fictional realm on the model of some divine creator. He was expected to offer the reader, rather, the pleasure of recognizing the unstated affinities which both took for granted and of reconstructing the circumstances that must have inspired his poem.

IV.

We should at this point perhaps consider some of the possible reasons behind the development of the imagistic practices just illustrated. The most obvious response would call attention to the form of the poems by the three high Tang poets discussed: all of them, though some less un-ambiguously than others, have been classified as regulated verse, whose formal rules would have required the devotion of at least half the poem to a concentrated vision of densely packed imagery. Regulated verse, in turn, as Stephen Owen has discussed in his history of early Tang poetry, was cultivated during the first century of the dynasty by poets at court, who were expected to produce self-effacing works that would reject the ex-pression of intensely moral or political sentiments and focus instead on the sensuous richness of the world around them.[87] Wang Wei occupies a pivotal position as not only the best-known inheritor and master of the conventions that evolved during that time but also their transformer—someone who endowed the object-laden world of court poetry with a greater philosophical and emotional significance. Less immediately apparent, perhaps, is the likely role of Buddhism in fostering the emer-gence of a poetry that devoted such attention to a depiction of the con-crete world.

Buddhism of course was implicated as well in the development of the prosodic rules of regulated verse, for there is evidence suggesting the links between an interest in exploiting the tonal properties of the language and the influence of both Sanskrit linguistic scholarship and the chanting of Buddhist hymns, with Shen Yue serving as the first great systematizer.[88]

---

[87] See Owen, *Early T'ang*, esp. pp. 234–55.
[88] For a discussion of these connections, see Bodman, pp. 99–160.

The Buddhist tradition was also to supply a host of conventional images like the moon and pearl symbolic of enlightenment to the already large indigenous poetic lexicon. And the Buddhist attitude to nature as the embodiment of ultimate reality has already been suggested as a key influence behind the genesis of landscape poetry at the hands of Xie Lingyun.

The otherworldly thrust traditionally associated with Buddhism might lead one to expect a denigration of sensory concerns that would be inhospitable to a poetry of the concrete. Such was not the case, however, with the Mahāyāna traditions that found congenial ground in China. In contrast to the older strain of the Theravādins, which emphasized the distinction between the enlightened and unenlightened state, and between beings destined for enlightenment and others not so favored, Mahāyāna Buddhism insisted on the fundamental emptiness (śūnyatā) of all beings and states, the constant rising and ceasing to which all phenomena were subject and which denied them any permanent essence or selfhood, a denial extending even to the very concept of emptiness itself. The sweeping holism of this doctrine posited true knowledge as similarly non-dualistic; prajñā or wisdom, the highest of the six "perfections" (pāramitās) discussed in key Mahāyāna scriptures, is thus formulated as an intuitive cognition that makes no distinction between the knower and the known, the self and others, the concrete world of suffering, contingency, and change (saṃsāra) and the transcendent realm of enlightened release (nirvāṇa). True knowledge understands that all of these entities are equally real because equally empty, and only the realization of their ontological equality and mutual dependence will approach ultimate reality. As T.R.V. Murti puts it, there is

> no difference whatever between Nirvāṇa and Saṃsāra; Noumenon and Phenomenon are not two separate sets of entities, nor are they two states of the same thing.... The absolute looked at through the thought-forms of constructive imagination is the empirical world; and conversely, the absolute is the world viewed *sub specie aeternitatis*, without these distorting media of thought.[89]

For those who might have difficulty achieving such a sweeping non-dualistic insight, some Mahāyāna thinkers developed a system of "double truth" as an expedient device (upāya) to help the mind resolve the tension—however delusory—between the mundane and the transcendental. The second-century A.D. Indian philosopher Nāgārjuna and then the Chinese monk Jizang 吉藏 (549–623) thus posited a temporary distinc-

[89]T. R. V. Murti, *The Central Philosophy of Buddhism: A Study of the Mādhyamika System* (London: Allen and Unwin, 1955), p. 274.

202

tion between a level of absolute truth (*paramārtha-satya*), the ultimate universal reality devoid of all dichotomies and predicates, inexpressible in words, and one of conventional truth (*saṁvṛti-satya*), the provisional phenomenal realm of particularity, language, and common distinctions. Nevertheless, true wisdom still consisted in being able to transcend this distinction and all others as well.

These notions were important in the development of all Mahāyāna traditions, among them Chan or Zen, the uniquely Chinese strain that flourished during the Tang and Song dynasties and exerted great influence on traditional Chinese poetics.[90] In terms of salvation, non-dualism for the Chan Buddhist meant obliterating the distinction between unenlightenment and enlightenment; an individual's fundamental task consisted in seeing into his "original nature" and coming to an awareness that he was always already enlightened, that Buddhahood was not merely a hope for the future but universally in existence, awaiting the realization of the individual. Thus the *Laṅkāvatāra Sūtra*, which became the key scripture for Chan,

> emphasizes the doctrine of inner realization, which is equivalent to enlightenment. In the case of one who has achieved this inner realization, he is no longer subject to any dualistic thinking. Dualism arises when the individual does not perceive the truth that all things are empty, uncreated, and do not possess any individual characteristics. When the individual realizes the *śūnya* nature of all things, he transcends mental discriminations and attains the absolute truth, the absolute truth that is beyond words and analytical reasoning.[91]

And in terms of one's attitude to everyday reality, non-dualism meant that

> for the Ch'an Buddhist nothing is transcendental apart from the concrete. In other words, the man of Ch'an engages in ordinary daily activities and simultaneously transcends them, so that the concrete and the transcendent in his life are one and the same. He lives, as do all men, in time and space, but he is not limited by either. For him the finite dwells within the infinite, the infinite within the finite. They are totally and inseparably identified as one.[92]

[90] For an examination of the relationship between Chan and Chinese poetry and poetics, see Du Songbo 杜松柏, *Chan xue yu Tang Song shi xue* 禪學與唐宋詩學 (Taipei: Li ming wenhua shiye gongsi, 1978).

[91] Kenneth Chen, *The Chinese Transformation of Buddhism* (Princeton: Princeton University Press, 1973), p. 195n36.

[92] Chang Chung-yuan, *Original Teachings of Ch'an Buddhism* (New York: Vintage, 1971), p. 92.

The Sixth Chan patriarch Huineng 慧能 (638–713) expressed this assumption of unity to his disciples in an apparently paradoxical excerpt from a verse affirming the immanence of the transcendental Buddhist law or Dharma (*fa* 法):

From the outset the Dharma has been in the world;	法元在世間
Being in the world, it transcends the world.	於世出世間
Hence do not seek the transcendental world outside,	勿離世間上
By discarding the present world itself.[93]	外求出世間

In other words, he suggests, true reality does not lie beyond the sensible world, which, conversely, deserves as much attention as the contemplation of the absolute. This notion is best captured by the well-known Chan saying that before enlightenment one sees a mountain as a mountain or a river as a river, i.e., in their pure physicality; in the process of realizing one's enlightenment, the mountain is no longer a mountain, the river no longer a river, i.e., one begins to discriminate between the finite and the infinite, the provisional and the ultimate; and after obtaining enlightenment the mountain is once more a mountain, the river once more a river—one realizes that concrete and transcendental reality are one and the same.[94]

It is this attitude in particular that in its early forms must have helped to inspire the Chinese poet to turn his attention to rendering details of the concrete world around him. J. D. Frodsham hints at such a motivation in his statement about Buddhism and Xie Lingyun cited in Chapter Four, but he does not go into the doctrinal background for it, and Xie's poetry at any rate represents but the beginnings of the trend. Indigenous Chinese ways of thinking like Confucianism and Taoism also stressed the immanence of the transcendent, the ubiquity of the cosmic Tao, but poetry embodying those traditions was dominated by moral or philosophical precepts and purposes. It remained for Buddhism's "ontological egalitarianism"[95] to inject a renewed dignity into sensory reality—especially the world of nature—and provide poets with the assurance that a poem focusing on the coherent presentation of images could appeal simul-

[93] Philip B. Yampolsky, tr., *The Platform Sutra of the Sixth Patriarch* (New York: Columbia University Press, 1967), p. 161. The original text is given on p. 18.

[94] Cited, *inter alia*, by Chang Chung-yuan, p. 93, and D. T. Suzuki, *Zen Buddhism*, ed. William Barrett (New York: Doubleday Anchor, 1956), p. 14.

[95] The phrase is William R. LaFleur's, from his *The Karma of Words: Buddhism and the Literary Arts in Medieval Japan* (Berkeley and Los Angeles: University of California Press, 1983). LaFleur discusses the relevance of many of the concepts I have touched on here and their influence in the development of new attitudes toward and modes of symbolism throughout his work, but see esp. Chapters 1 and 4.

taneously to both the senses and the intellect, that the concrete world could embody meaning on its own, without discursive explanation.

The high Tang poets, as we have seen, rejected the one-to-one correspondence of tenor and vehicle for images that would resonate in a less mechanical way with emotional and intellectual significance. Could we not view this, perhaps, as the poetic corollary to the Mahāyāna emphasis on a non-dualistic cognition just discussed? In support of this claim, we might consider the well-known gāthas recorded in the *Platform Sūtra* and attributed to the two contenders for the robe of the sixth Chan patriarch. The first is said to have been composed by Shenxiu 神秀 (d. 706), and the second by Huineng:

The body is the Bodhi tree,	身是菩提樹
The mind is like a clear mirror.	心如明鏡臺
At all times we must strive to polish it,	時時勤佛拭
And must not let the dust collect.	莫使有塵埃
Bodhi originally has no tree,	菩提本無樹
The mirror also has no stand.	明鏡亦無臺
Buddha nature is always clean and pure;	佛性常清淨
Where is there room for dust?[96]	何處有塵埃

The composer of the sūtra and Chan tradition give the victory to Huineng, primarily because his verse reflects the doctrine that enlightenment is always there as the instantaneous realization of one's original nature. This view was central to the southern school of Chan that made him its patriarch, as opposed to the northern school that adhered to Shenxiu's view of enlightenment as requiring a constant and gradual effort. In somewhat different terms, Shenxiu's lines could also be criticized because they "were devoid of logical contradiction and could be interpreted readily by resolving the two allegories; they were therefore not acceptable as an expression of true enlightenment."[97] Huineng's verse thus prevails because it rejects the distinctions implied by Shenxiu's equations, asserting instead the fundamental unity, the universal emptiness, of all things. A similarly monistic view, I would argue, lies behind the treatment of imagery in the Tang poetry we have considered.

Needless to say, very little evidence exists to document the connections I have suggested, and of the major Tang poets only Wang Wei demonstrates a clear commitment to the practice of Buddhism. The influence of Chan on post-Tang poetics can be much more easily argued, and has been by countless critics. Nevertheless, Buddhism's pervasiveness in late Six

[96] Trans. Yampolsky, pp. 130, 132; original texts on pp. 3, 4.
[97] Heinrich Dumoulin, *A History of Zen Buddhism* (Boston: Beacon, 1971), p. 82.

Dynasties and Tang culture is also not subject to question, and I remain convinced that the doctrines just sketched exerted a considerable influence in some form on achieving for imagery its central position in Tang poetry.

V.

Given the reliance on concrete imagery that seems to characterize poetry of the Tang dynasty, one might have expected a concomitant development of a poetics of description centering on the faithfully mimetic representation of the external world. Such a tradition, however, never took root. Various reasons behind this significant absence have already been suggested: the lack of the philosophical underpinnings essential to the Western concept of mimesis; a view of the image that focused primarily on its conceptual meaning; the literary division of labor between the lyric and the exposition; a stimulus/expression/affect conception of the literary process that emphasized the dynamic interaction between poet and reader as much as the specific qualities of the work itself. And, for all of its rehabilitation of the concrete, Chan Buddhism was never interested in the sensory world for its own sake, but as an embodiment of transcendent value. Similar attitudes seem to have lain behind discussions of the image in theoretical and critical texts of the Tang and afterward.

One could almost call this a literature of the "beyond" (*wai* 外), for that term appears almost ubiquitously—usually in the phrase X *wai zhi* 之 Y ("the something beyond something else")—in the texts that come to mind. Something is always incommensurate with that which exists to convey it, whether it be words or imagery, and the poet is advised, therefore, to take care that what is of primary importance manages to get through. Expressions of linguistic inadequacy were commonplaces in the Chinese philosophical tradition, going back, for example, to well-known sections of the *Dao de jing*, the *Zhuangzi*, and the passage from the Great Commentary to the *Classic of Changes* cited in Chapter One. Lu Ji worried about this insufficiency in his own text, writing at the beginning of his *Exposition on Literature* that "meaning will not correspond to objects and the text will not reach the meaning,"[98] but later critics transformed this potential inadequacy into a positive transcendence of the limitations of language. We have already seen Zhong Hong define the stimulus as a trope whose "words come to an end but meaning lingers on." Similarly, in

[98] Lu Ji, *Wen fu*, in the *Wen xuan*, 17/1b/p.307.

a chapter on "The Concealed and the Elegant" (*Yin xiu* 隱秀) of his *Literary Mind*, Liu Xie defines what is hidden as "the important meaning *beyond* the text." Furthermore, "when concealment is the form, then meaning lodges *beyond* the text, hidden echoes penetrate directly, and suppressed beauties emerge unobtrusively."[99] And he makes an analogous statement stressing that which exceeds the limits of physical description, writing in Chapter 46, as cited earlier, that "when the appearance of objects has been exhausted yet feeling lingers on, then one's understanding [of the art of writing] is complete."

The vocabulary of what is "beyond," "endless," and "inexhaustible" really begins to proliferate in Tang critical literature, all of whose authors were profoundly influenced by the Chan doctrines just discussed. Commentators on the "Nineteen Ancient Poems" and Ruan Ji, it will be recalled, had also praised their ability to "contain implicit meaning," but in the earlier cases had assumed a definite, if veiled, political critique. Now, however, such assumptions are difficult to discern. In his "Discussion of Literature and Meaning" (*Lun wen yi* 論文意), for example, Wang Changling states that "Only if the last line [of a poem] causes the thoughts to extend on endlessly will it be excellent."[100] The monk Jiaoran falls in step as well, not only defining the stimulus as "the significance *beneath* the image" but also praising the emotional "meaning *beyond* the text" successfully conveyed by the poetry of Xie Lingyun, of whom he happened to be a tenth-generation descendant.[101] Liu Yuxi 劉禹錫 (772–842), who in a preface to a poem presents one of the earliest explicit comparisons between poetry and Buddhism,[102] in a note to a collection of a friend's writings offers a praise of poetry that stresses these same attributes: "Is poetry not the treasure of letters? Once the meaning is attained then the words die away, thus it is subtle and difficult to accomplish. It

[99] *Wenxin diaolong zhu*, 8/p.632.

[100] In the *Wen jing mifu lun*, p. 139. Bodman discusses his affinities with Chan in "Poetics and Prosody," esp. pp. 80–86, 117–25.

[101] Jiaoran, *Shi shi*, in *Lidai shihua*, I, 31. Guo Shaoyu argues for the Buddhist inspiration behind the poetics of both Jiaoran and Sikong Tu 司空圖 (837–908) in his commentary on the *Shi shi*, *Zhongguo lidai wenlun xuan*, pp. 387–89. See also Yang Jialuo 楊家駱, *Zhongguo wenxue bai ke quan shu* 中國文學百科全書, *ce* 冊 3,2/79; cited by Thomas P. Nielson, *The T'ang Poet-Monk Chiao-jan*, Center for Asian Studies Occasional Paper No. 3 (Arizona State University: June 1972), p. 23n24.

[102] The poem is entitled "On an Autumn Day Visiting the Dharma Master Hongju's Monastery, then Bidding Farewell on His Return to Jiangling" 秋日過鴻舉法師寺院便送歸江陵, in *Quan Tang shi*, 357/4,015–16. Richard John Lynn translates the relevant passage in his review of my *Poetry of Wang Wei*, *Chinese Literature: Essays, Articles, Reviews*, 4.2 (July 1982), p. 261.

produces a scene *beyond* the image, thus it is exquisite and seldom matched."[103] But the best-known exponent of these notions is the late-Tang poet-critic, Sikong Tu 司空圖 (837–908).

His most extensive critical work, *The Twenty-four Types of Poetry* (*Ershisi shi pin* 二十四詩品), differs significantly from Zhong Hong's similarly titled *Shi pin* in failing to provide explicitly any real hierarchy of value among the various "classes" or "grades" he sets forth. Instead, as Du Songbo has noted, the series of poems presents and embodies what Wang Changling described as "worlds of ideas" (*yi jing* 意境), arranged in no particular order and without apparent distinctions in rank,[104] and indeed, with often barely perceptible differences among some of them. Although the poems are replete with natural imagery, one of Sikong Tu's major points seems to be that the best poetry, which arises out of the poet's intuitive identification with the cosmos, does not aim for precise mimetic description of external phenomena but rather employs those objects to suggest something ineffable and intangible.

References to this indirect and therefore evocative method of presentation occur throughout the series. In the first poem, for example, "Powerful and Grand" (*Xionghun* 雄渾), Sikong Tu urges the poet to "Leap *beyond* external appearance / To reach the center of the circle,"[105] and of the next mode presented, "Placid and Subtle" (*Chongdan* 沖淡), he writes that "If it has a formal likeness, / Grasped with the hand it escapes" (p. 38). There is a truer "likeness" to be achieved that does not correspond to merely external details, so that in the twentieth poem, "Presentation" (*Xingrong* 形容), he urges the poet to "Leave the form to reach the likeness" (p. 43). At times his advice verges on the paradoxical, as in the opening lines of the poem entitled "Concealed and Implied" (*Hanxu* 含蓄):

Without writing a single word,	不著一字
Completely attain the spirit of it.	盡得風流
One's language mentions no difficulty,	語不涉難
Yet the grief is already unbearable.	已不堪憂

(p. 40)

[103] Liu Yuxi, *Dong shi Wuling ji ji* 董氏武陵集紀, in *Liu Yuxi ji* 劉禹錫集 (Shanghai: Renmin, 1975), 19/p.173. Cited, among others, by Zhu Ziqing, *Shi yan zhi bian*, p. 90, and Mou Shijin 牟世金, "Shi xue zhi zheng yuan, fadu zhi zhunze: cong fu bi xing chuantong kan yishu gousi de minzu tese" 詩學之正源, 法度之准則: 從賦比興傳統看藝術構思的民族特色, in *Gudai wenxue lilun yanjiu congkan* 古代文學理論研究叢刊 ed. Zhongguo gudai wenxue lilun xuehui 中國古代文學理論學會, 1 (Shanghai: Guji chubanshe, 1979), pp. 51–52.
[104] *Chan xue yu Tang Song shi xue*, pp. 411–13.
[105] Included in *Lidai shihua*, I, 38; subsequent page references to be given in the text.

But the paradox is only apparent, for again Sikong Tu is simply advocating a subtle mode of presentation that is neither overly descriptive nor emotional, yet for those reasons all the more effective. As he writes at the beginning of "Real Worlds" (*Shi jing* 實境): "When the words selected are extremely direct, / The thoughts recorded will not be profound" (p. 40). And what should linger in the mind of the reader are not the words themselves but what they convey, as he suggests at the conclusion of "Leaping Beyond" (*Chao yi* 超詣): "Chant them, ponder them— / Their sounds gradually fade away" (p. 43).

Expressions of this poetics of transcendence also appear in Sikong Tu's correspondence that discusses poetry. In a frequently cited "Letter to Jipu" (*Wang Ji* 汪極, *jinshi* 891), for instance, he writes: 'Dai Rongzhou 戴容州 [Shulun 叔倫 (732–789)] said: 'The scenes of poets, such as "At Lantian when the sun is warm, smoke arises from fine jade," can be gazed at from afar but cannot be placed in front of one's eyebrows and lashes.' An image *beyond* the image, a scene *beyond* the scene—can these be easily discussed?"[106] Here the critic is alluding to the incommensurability of the poetic image to both concrete object and also any actualization in the mind of the reader. Another statement of how the poet should attempt to evoke what is "beyond" occurs in a "Letter to Master Li Discussing Poetry" (*Yu Li sheng lun shi shu* 與李生論詩書), which Sikong Tu opens with an extended comparison that suggests the influence of Zhong Hong's emphasis on "flavor":

> Prose is difficult, yet poetry is even more difficult. From antiquity to the present there have been many comparisons for this, but I believe that only when one distinguishes flavors can one talk about poetry. South of the Yangzi and the five mountain ranges [i.e., in southern, "barbarian" China], of all those condiments that enhance palatability, if they are pickled, it is not that they are not sour, but they stop at sourness and that is it. If they are salted, it is not that they are not salty, but they stop at saltiness and that is it. People of China [proper] will sate their hunger and stop eating, for they know that these lack what is *beyond* saltiness and sourness, an exquisite beauty.

[106] *Yu Jipu shu* 與極浦書, included in Zu Baoquan 祖保泉, *Sikong Tu shi pin zhu shi ji yiwen* 司空圖詩品注釋及譯文 (Hong Kong: Shangwu, 1966), p. 77. Li Shangyin 李商隱 (812?–58) may also have been alluding to Dai Shulun's example in his poem "The Ornamented Zither" (*Jin qin* 錦瑟 [*Quan Tang shi*, 539/p.6,144]), whose sixth line reads: "On Indigo Mountain, in the warm sun, jade engenders smoke." Trans. James J. Y. Liu, *The Poetry of Li Shang-yin: Ninth-Century Baroque Chinese Poet* (Chicago: University of Chicago Press, 1968), p. 51.

A more "civilized" population, then, will recognize the need for something more than the simply sour or salty and, similarly, the poet should go beyond merely adequate description; only when one's writing is "accessible but not superficial, far-reaching but inexhaustible, can one then speak of having gone *beyond* rhyme." And Sikong Tu concludes the letter by praising his friend's poetry for exemplifying "a meaning *beyond* flavor" (Zu, pp. 68–69; emphasis added).

One could summon up countless utterances in later critical literature echoing and expanding upon the ideas touched on only briefly by these Tang writers, most notably in the works of Yan Yu, Jiang Kui 姜夔 (ca. 1155–1221), Xie Zhen 謝榛 (1495–1575), Wang Fuzhi, and the Qing dynasty Wang Shizhen. All of these critics emphasized the desirability of a poetry that would employ concrete imagery in such a way as to create a scene resonant with rich and unstated emotional and/or intellectual implications. Their statements about the unstated and thus inexhaustible "meaning beyond words" or "fusion of emotion and scene" have been frequently cited, and I shall not recapitulate them all here but simply offer one representative statement encapsulating all of those notions, from the hand of Ye Xie 葉燮 (1627–1703):

Where poetry reaches the utmost, its marvelousness lies in an endless concealed implication that conveys thoughts with a subtle vastness. It lodges [meaning] between the sayable and the unsayable; what it points to rests where the explicable and the inexplicable meet. The words are here and the meaning there. It obliterates demarcations and leaves the formal image, cuts off discussion and exhausts all things, leading a person to a deep, boundless, vague realm—this is what is called the utmost.[107]

Two other points are even more germane to my concerns. The first is that these critics find their prime examples of these qualities in the kind of poetry by the high Tang poets that we have just considered. And, second, these same qualities figure significantly in the markedly different set of

[107] Ye Xie, *Yuan shi* 原詩, *nei pian xia* 內篇下, in *Qing shihua* 清詩話, ed. Ding Fubao 丁福保 (rpt. Shanghai: Guji chubanshe, 1978; 2 vols.), II, 584. Cited in Zhu Rensheng 朱任生, ed., *Shi lun fenlei zuanyao* 詩論分類纂要 (Taipei: Shangwu, 1971), p. 357. For summaries of various other utterances in this tradition, see Richard John Lynn, "Orthodoxy and Enlightenment: Wang Shih-chen's Theory of Poetry and Its Antecedents," in William Theodore deBary, ed., *The Unfolding of Neo-Confucianism*, Studies in Oriental Culture, 10 (New York: Columbia University Press, 1975), pp. 217–69; James J. Y. Liu, *Chinese Theories of Literature*, pp. 16–62; Wong Siu-kit, "*Ch'ing* and *Ching* in the Critical Writings of Wang Fu-chih," in Rickett, ed., *Chinese Approaches to Literature*, pp. 121–50; and the "Critical Introduction" to my *Poetry of Wang Wei*, pp. 2–22.

definitions of the classical rhetorical tropes we have been following that appear in critical literature from the Song dynasty and onward.

We have already seen how confused the terminology of *fu*, *bi*, and *xing* was from its very inception, no doubt primarily because it represented a vocabulary developed several centuries post hoc to describe the disparate methods of a large and venerated anthology. Canonical commentators and early literary critics stressed different aspects of the nature and function of these tropes imputed to the authors of songs in the *Classic of Poetry*, although modern scholars do not agree on how precisely to distinguish the major emphases in these definitions.[108] Whatever the case, we have also seen how Tang poets like Chen Ziang and Bo Juyi implicitly or explicitly collapsed the terms *bi* and *xing* into one simply denoting political critique, not only finessing thereby the problem of how to distinguish two exasperatingly similar devices, but also eliminating their original roots in imagery altogether. Later scholars generally share Bo Juyi's inclination to group *bi* and *xing* together—to the clear detriment of *fu*—but reject his emphasis on a political function for a focus on the effects of subtlety and evocative openendedness arising out of the indirectness of their presentation, with a consideration of their resulting effects on the reader.[109] And even the commentators on the *Classic of Poetry*, while retaining an interest in distinguishing the three types from each other, begin to offer definitions of the terms that focus on their formal and affective properties instead of any didactic intent and purpose.

Already during the Tang we can find a scholar employing, like Bo Juyi, *bi* and *xing* together as a compound term but to very different effect. This occurs in a brief discussion by Liu Zongyuan 柳宗元 (773–869) regarding what he calls the two paths of literature, one based on narration (*zhu shu* 著述) and the other on comparison and stimulus (*bi xing*):

> The tradition of narration derives from the maxims of the *Classic of History*, the "Images" and "Appended Words" of the *Classic of Changes*, and the corrections of the *Spring and Autumn Annals*. It

[108] François Cheng, for example, prefers to divide the literature on the subject into two tendencies, one defining *bi xing* on formal grounds, the other according to content. See his "*Bi* 比 et *xing* 興," *Cahiers de linguistique Asie orientale*, 6 (Sept. 1979), pp. 63–74. Wang Yunxi in "Tan Zhongguo gudai," *passim*, however, concurs with my distinction between those definitions stressing didactic function and those focusing on aesthetic effect.

[109] This is not to say, of course, that several critics would not continue to try to keep the tropes separate and identify examples of their usage in noncanonical poetry as well. Luo Dajing, for example, applies this method of analysis to Du Fu's poems in a passage in his *He lin yu lu* (10/p.104), an effort repeated recently and at much greater length by Xiao Difei, in "Shi lun Du Fu shi ge zhong de bi xing" 試論杜甫詩歌中的比興, in *Wenyi luncong*, 4 (Shanghai: Wenyi chubanshe, 1978), pp. 22–41.

demands loftiness, strength, breadth, and sincerity; the language must be proper and the reasoning complete, what is best preserved in records and documents. The tradition of comparison and stimulus derives from the songs of Shun and Yu and the Airs and Elegances of the Shang and Zhou dynasties. It demands beauty, pattern, clarity, and transcendence, lucidity of word and excellence of meaning, best handed down in songs. When one examines the principles behind these two types, they are not the same at all, so that scholars who wield the brush can generally master one only, and rarely both.[110]

We should note at least two important points about this passage. First, while in keeping with his advocacy of the resurgence of Confucian values during the Tang, Liu Zongyuan prefaces this discussion with a statement that both paths share a purpose basic to all writing, namely criticism and remonstrance, the actual characterization he provides here of the comparison and stimulus emphasizes aesthetic qualities almost exclusively. And, second, he is making an implicit distinction between prose and poetry, alluding to the different types of talent required for each and identifying *bi xing* as the methods distinctive of and most appropriate to the latter, much as Western critics would define metaphor as the distinctive feature of poetry.

The Song critic Li Zhongmeng 李仲蒙 similarly emphasizes the varying techniques of the three tropes and consequently different emotional effects, although unlike Liu Zongyuan he keeps them separate:

Describing objects in order to state emotions is called exposition; both emotions and objects are therein exhausted. Searching for objects in order to invest them with emotion is called comparison; the emotion adheres to the object. Contacting objects such that emotions arise is called a stimulus; the objects stir the emotions.[111]

Zhong Hong, it will be remembered, presented a very similar series of definitions, but he also cautioned against an overuse of any one of the three: the best poetry would employ them all. Notable in Li Zhongmeng's discussion, however, is an implicit hierarchy among them, with exposition

[110] From his *Dali pingshi Yang jun wenji houxu* 大理評事楊君文集後序, in *Quan Tang wen* 全唐文 (1814; rpt. Taipei: Huiwen, 1961; 20 vols.), XII, 577/5b–6a/p.7,407. Also cited by Luo Genze, *Zhongguo wenxue piping shi*, p. 427.

[111] Cited by Hu Yin 胡寅 (1098–1156), *Yu Li Shuyi shu* 與李叔易書, *Peiran ji* 裴然集, 18, and Yang Shen, *Sheng an shihua*, in *Xu lidai shihua*, II, 12/pp.1,037–38. Also cited by Guo Shaoyu and Wang Wensheng 王文生, in "Lun bi xing" 論比興, *Wenxue pinglun*, 4 (1978), p. 51. Qian Zhongshu points out the importance of apparent spontaneity as the distinctive feature of the stimulus in his brief discussion of this passage in *Guan zhui bian*, I, 63.

the most directly descriptive, limited, and thus inferior, and the stimulus the most spontaneous and evocative. Concrete images are essential to a poem, but what is important about them is not descriptive detail but what they provoke.

Later remarks in various *shihua* 詩話 ("talks on poetry") develop Li Zhongmeng's valorization of the obliquity of the comparison and stimulus and implicit denigration of direct exposition as downright "unpoetic." The Ming scholar Li Dongyang, for example, clearly elevates the latter two over the former:

> There are three principles of poetry, and exposition is only one of them; the other two are comparison and stimulus. What are called comparison and stimulus consist of relying on objects in order to lodge one's feelings. For if one speaks properly and narrates directly, then one's [language] will be easily exhausted and one's responses will come out with difficulty. Only when feeling has something to lodge in, described and copied, can it be chanted and savored over and over again, until the reader gets it on his own. When words come to an end but meaning is endless, then the spirit will be refreshed and move as if in flight, hands will dance and feet will stomp without one's being aware of it. This is the reason why poetry values emotional thought and disesteems real events.[112]

Although Li Dongyang's mention of dancing hands and stomping feet recalls the orthodox Confucian Great Preface to the *Classic of Poetry*, the rest of this passage explicitly denies the main premise of the Preface as well as the shorter prefaces to individual poems in the anthology: that the songs allude to concrete historical events or situations during the Zhou dynasty. That was, of course, the same assumption of specific referentiality underlying the writings of Chen Ziang, Bo Juyi, and Jia Dao. Li Dongyang rejects both the direct mode of presentation of exposition and the possibility of topical allusion as limiting the emotionally evocative powers of poetry. The extent to which the definition of these terms has been transformed should be clear.

A similar conviction is shared by the later critic Li Mengyang 李夢陽 (1472–1592), who writes that when the ancients wanted to move men, they would begin with the stimulus of a resemblance, rather than with a direct statement; they relied on objects, and not language.[113] He does not dismiss the critical function of poetry but pays greatest attention to its

[112] From his *Lutang shihua*, 1/p.6.
[113] From *Qin jun jian song shi xu* 秦君餞送詩序, in *Kongtong xiansheng ji* 空同先生集, *Mingdai lunzhu congkan* 明代論諸叢刊 ed. (rpt. Taipei: Weiwen tushu chubanshe, 1976), 51/4a/p.1,461.

emotional sources and effects, in connection with which the comparison
and stimulus are essential for distinguishing the good from the bad, sincere feeling from mere craft. In the preface to his own collection of poetry,
for example, he cites with approval the following assertions of his friend
Wang Shuwu 王叔武:

> There are six principles of poetry, of which comparison and stimulus
> are necessities. Yet among the works of literati and scholars, com-
> parison and stimulus are lacking and direct straightforwardness pre-
> dominates. Why is this so? Because they are short on feelings and
> long on verbal skill. Now simple villagers are, of course, uncultured.
> Yet of their ballads, their drumbeats, their hums and their chants—
> whether whispered while walking or sung while sitting, cried out
> at meals or sighed in bed, with one person singing and another
> harmonizing—not one lacks comparison and stimulus, and none is
> without feeling.[114]

The Qing critic Wu Qiao 吳喬 or Wu Shu 殳 (ca. 1660) returns to the
emphasis on the indirectness and suggestiveness of the comparison and
stimulus in praising Tang poetry over that of the Song: "Tang poetry has
meaning, yet relies on comparison and stimulus to manifest it in various
ways. Its language is indirect and subtle, like a person wearing clothes and
cap. Song poetry also has meaning, but uses exposition and rarely comparison and stimulus. Its language is direct and straightforward, like a
person completely naked."[115] The directness of exposition is "substan-
tial" (*shi* 實) and therefore limited and "dead," whereas the indirectness
of comparison and stimulus—exemplified by Tang poetry and forgotten
by the Song—is "empty" (*xu* 虛) and thus evocative, alive, and "marvelous" (*miao* 妙) (1/p.10 and 5/p.107). Evoking the tradition which
goes back to Zhong Hong's definition of the stimulus through various
critics' esteem of the "meaning beyond flavor" or beyond words, Wu Qiao
explicitly links the use of the comparison and stimulus with these ideas:

> A man may have feeling that is endless and he cannot set it forth
> directly with brush or tongue, nor can it be exhausted with language.
> He responds to an object and is moved; this is a stimulus. If he relies
> on an object to set forth [his emotion], this is a comparison. This is
> certainly how the writer brews to completion. Therefore when you

[114] From his *Shi ji zi xu* 詩集自序, *Kongtong xiansheng ji*, 50/3a/p.1,437. Also cited by
Guo Shaoyu and Wang Wensheng, "Lun bi xing," p. 52.
[115] Wu Qiao, *Weilu shihua* 圍爐詩話, *Congshu jicheng* ed. (Shanghai: Shangwu, 1939),
1/p.2. Later he notes that these techniques distinguish one type of language from another,
for "in poetry the meaning generally emerges from the side," whereas "in prose it emerges
from the front" (3/p.72).

read the poem, it is also as if you have just drunk some wine: one who is sad will be happy, and one who is solemn will become uninhibited, all without their knowing how this came about. (1/p.8)

Recurrent throughout his *Weilu shihua* is this insistence on comparison and stimulus as techniques for indirectly suggesting an endless meaning or emotion in the reader. Rather than being attached to any categorical concept or didactic function, they are essential, he writes, to the achievement of the "marvelous awakening" (*miao wu* 妙悟) which Yan Yu had viewed as the way of poetry. Wu Qiao declares, in fact, that "if one does not know the comparison and stimulus and discusses poetry, as soon as he opens his mouth he will be in error."[116]

In his *Weilu shihua* Wu Qiao links himself with a poetic tradition not generally characterized by a stress on overtly Confucian ideals. What is noteworthy, however, is the fact that even commentators on the *Classic of Poetry* after the Tang often define the comparison, and especially the stimulus, in ways which deny their analogical properties and by implication their morally illustrative functions. Several such statements were given in Chapter Two; here I shall limit myself to one example, the Qing scholar Chen Qiyuan 陳啓源 (d. 1689), whose definition and valuation of the stimulus are clearly rooted in the poetics of evocation and transcendence I have discussed. While acknowledging their similarities, he tries to make their differences even more crucial:

> Although the comparison and stimulus both rely on comparison, the stimulus is concealed and the comparison overt; the stimulus is roundabout and the comparison direct; the stimulus is broad and the comparison narrow. A comparison uses that to compare with this, just like a simile in prose: it is absolutely unlike the stimulus.

Thus, he explains, when Zhu Xi was commenting on the *Classic of Poetry*, whenever he came upon an image originally annotated as a stimulus by Mao but whose meaning was clear, he labeled it a comparison instead. Chen gives several instances of such changes and then continues:

> Stimulus and comparison both compare, but their forms are dissimilar. What is stimulated has come through inspired apprehension (*xing hui* 興會): it only arrives spontaneously. The words are here and the meaning there; the language is subtle and the significance far-reaching. A comparison involves a proper meaning and what it is compared to, and both are mutually comparable. Its language is defi-

---

[116] *Weilu shihua*, 5/p.107. For Yan Yu's discussion, see, for example, *Canglang shihua jiao shi*, p. 10.

nite and significance apparent. Moreover, it can be interwoven with straight exposition to form a text, unlike the stimulus, whose words are used to start off and are usually at the beginning.[117]

Not only does Chen Qiyuan resume some of the arguments of earlier exegetes of the *Classic of Poetry*, who had advanced many of the strictly formal distinctions he embraces here, but he also harks back to statements and concepts from texts less directly connected with the anthology, if at all. The opposition of concealment in the stimulus and directness of the comparison goes back to Liu Xie, and the term "inspired apprehension" is associated more closely with advocates of the poetics of intuitive cognition, infinite meaning, and transcendence discussed earlier[118] than with the embracing of a resolutely didactic view of poetry.

What this discussion should make clear is that, *pace* the laments of Liu Xie and claims of modern critics like Zhu Ziqing, the key method of the stimulus first ascribed to the *Classic of Poetry* did not, in fact, die out. Rather, it experienced a significant transformation, whether coupled with the comparison or on its own, in the hands of the major poets of the Tang dynasty and went on to form the nucleus of later critical views of the nature and function of poetry. From being identified by Confucian exegetes as an opening natural image whose provenance was continually subject to dispute—was it empirical or was it conventional, or both?—but whose purpose was always seen as merely facilitating—introducing or illuminating (however obscurely) the "real" subject matter of a work—it evolved into a poem's very center, no longer arbitrary or forced. For some critics this older notion of the stimulus remained the only one. Thus Wang Changling, for example, criticized the stimulus and comparison as artificial conventions,[119] and in recent years Qian Zhongshu has argued that, for similar reasons, they had nothing to do with the later critical concepts of the fusion of emotion and scene.[120] Such views, however, do not take into account shifts both in the poetic use of imagery and in the consequent reformulations of the ancient tropes.

By the Tang dynasty poets had perfected the skill of integrating images together to present coherent scenes functioning on different yet equally important levels. On the one hand, the vividness and perceptual accuracy

---

[117] Chen Qiyuan, *Mao shi ji gu pian* 毛詩稽古篇, 23; cited in Hu Puan, *Shi jing xue*, pp. 41–42, and Li Jinxi 黎錦熙, *Xiuci xue bi xing pian* 修辭學比興篇 (Shanghai: Shangwu, 1936), pp. 81–82.

[118] See, for example, James J. Y. Liu, *Chinese Theories of Literature*, pp. 43–44, and Richard John Lynn, "Orthodoxy and Enlightenment," pp. 243, 249.

[119] As noted by Bodman, p. 58.

[120] See *Tan yi lu*, pp. 274–75.

216

of the imagery seemed to attest to their powers of observation and description and to the putative empirical origins of the poem. This impression of an apparently direct transcription of experience is what has led some critics to describe the main method of classical poetry as in fact that of straightforward exposition. Yet, on the other hand, it seems clear—and certainly was to traditional critics—that the imagery was not ultimately important for what it presented directly but for what it concealed and evoked in the reader. This unstated emotional and/or intellectual meaning was ideally to be embodied in the images and their concatenation, so that poets could rely more heavily on them than on abstract propositional discourse. Such a method then came to be defined as in fact the method of *bi xing* and the quintessentially "poetic" one, a position remarkably similar to ideas about metaphor in the West.

Some things did not change in this conception of the stimulus or evocative image. For one thing, the original preference for juxtaposition that left connections implicit rather than spelled out persisted, although the links among images became much tighter. The absence of any overt explanation of the exemplary significance of the image fueled the conviction that natural imagery could and did evoke some "meaning beyond words" which was shared by exegete, poet, and critic alike. They only parted ways in their views of the nature of that meaning. For commentators on the Classic and their heirs, it was something pre-established, conventional and generally moral, allowing the poet to speak critically of his world and the scholar to reconstruct that context. For later critics, however, that meaning was much more subtle and indeterminate, no longer defined as strictly political but equally accessible to the appropriately sensitive reader.

Second, no traditional conception of imagery would have assumed that objects—and natural phenomena in particular—were to be used solely as "pure phenomenon," "things as they are," for no one would have denied the validity of cosmic correspondences presumed to link all things in a network of associations to be elicited by the poet, however elusively. No matter what their orientation, scholars and critics would have agreed with Fang Hui 方回 (1227–1296) that "the profound meaning of the comparison and stimulus is to establish the secret links that hold together all things in the universe."[121] Canonical exegetes may have focused on the moral implications of an object and non-canonical critics on the way an object could embody a feeling or a scene be fused with emotion, but their premises of the existence of such links were identical.[122]

---

[121] Fang Hui, *Wang Zhifang shihua* 王直方詩話, cited by François Cheng, p. 68.
[122] See Mou Shijin, "Shi xue zhi zheng yuan," pp. 47–49.

Finally, constant throughout was a belief that the meaning elicited was anchored firmly in the lived world of the poet. Although opinions about the degree to which images themselves were literal varied, there was little question as to their ultimate reference to the poet's historical world and not some fictional construct. As I have tried to demonstrate, not only were images felt to belong to a culturally shared lexicon within which correspondences of meaning were pre-established, but the poem as a whole was viewed as a record of the poet's actual experience. Subgenres involving fictional situations and the use of personae did exist, to be sure, but they did not comprise a significant portion of all poetic forms taken together and, moreover, came to be read as topically referential, too. For all of these reasons, then, Chinese poetic imagery should be distinguished from the metaphors and allegories of Western literature, whose fundamental premises are so very different.

Selected Bibliography

A. CLASSICAL CHINESE RESOURCES

Ban Gu 班固 (39–92). *Li sao xu* 離騷序, in Hong Xingzu, ed., *Chu ci bu zhu*, pp. 88–89.

———. *Li sao zan xu* 贊序, in Hong Xingzu, ed., *Chu ci bu zhu*, pp. 91–92.

Bo Juyi 白居易 (772–846). *Yu Yuan Jiu shu* 與元九書, in *Bo Juyi xuan ji* 白居易選集, ed. Wang Rubi 王如弼. Shanghai: Guji chubanshe, 1980, pp. 344–64.

Chen Hang 陳沆 (1785–1826). *Shi bi xing jian* 詩比興箋. Rpt. Peking: Zhonghua, 1965.

Chen Huan 陳奐 (1786–1863). *Shi Mao shi zhuan shu* 詩毛氏傳疏 [Shanghai]: Shangwu [1936].

Chen Kui 陳騤 (1128–1203). *Wen ze* 文則. *Congshu jicheng* 叢書集成 ed. Shanghai: Shangwu, 1939.

Chun qiu Zuo zhuan zheng yi 春秋左傳正義, in Ruan Yuan, ed., *Shisan jing zhushu*, II, 1,697–2,188.

Ding Fubao 丁福保, ed. *Xu lidai shihua* 續歷代詩話. Rpt. Taipei: Yiwen yinshuguan, 1974; 2 vols.

Du shi yinde 杜詩引得. Harvard-Yenching Institute Sinological Index Series, Supp. No. 14. Rpt. Taipei: Chinese Materials and Research Aids, 1966.

Fang Dongshu 方東樹 (1772–1851). *Zhaomei zhanyan* 昭昧詹言, ed. Wang Shaoying 汪紹楹. Peking: Renmin, 1961.

Gao Buying 高步瀛, ed. *Xin jiao Tang Song shi juyao* 新校唐宋詩舉要. Rpt. Taipei: Shijie, 1968; 2 vols.

Gu Longzhen 顧龍振, ed. *Shi xue zhi nan* 詩學指南. 1759; rpt. Taipei: Guangwen, 1970.

Guo Maoqian 郭茂倩 (ca. 1100), ed. *Yuefu shiji* 樂府詩集. Rpt. Peking: Zhonghua; 1979; 4 vols.

Guo Shaoyu 郭紹虞, ed. *Zhongguo lidai wenlun xuan* 中國歷代文論選. Hong Kong: Dawen she, 1978.

Han shu 漢書. Rpt. Hong Kong: Zhonghua, 1970.

He Wenhuan 何文煥, ed. *Lidai shihua* 歷代詩話. 1740; rpt. Peking; Zhonghua, 1982; 2 vols.

Hong Xingzu 洪興祖 (1070–1135), ed. *Chu ci bu zhu* 楚辭補註. Rpt. Taipei: Yiwen, 1973.

Hu Yinglin 胡應麟 (1551–1602). *Shi sou* 詩藪. Rpt. Taipei: Wenxing chubanshe, 1973.

Huang Jie 黃節, ed. *Ruan Bubing yong huai shi zhu* 阮步兵詠懷詩註. Peking: Renmin, 1957.

———, ed. *Xie Kangle shi zhu* 謝康樂詩註. Peking: Renmin, 1958.

Jia Dao 賈島 (779–834). *Er nan mi zhi* 二南密旨. *Xue hai lei bian* 學海類編 ed., compiled by Cao Rong 曹溶 (1613–1685). 1831; *Congshu jicheng* ed. Changsha: Shangwu, 1939.

Jiang Ji 蔣驥. *Shandaige zhu Chu ci* 山帶閣注楚辭, preface dated 1713. Rpt. Shanghai: Zhonghua, 1962.

Jiaoran 皎然 (734–?799). *Shi shi* 詩式, in He Wenhuan, ed., *Lidai shihua*, I, 25–36.

Kong Yingda 孔穎達 (574–678), ed. *Mao shi zheng yi* 毛詩正義. Hong Kong: Zhonghua, 1964; 6 vols.

Kūkai 空海 (Henzō Kinkō 遍照金剛 [774–835]), ed. *Wen jing mifu lun* 文鏡秘府論. Ed. Zhou Weide 周維德. Peking: Renmin, 1975.

Li Dongyang 李東陽 (1447–1516). *Lutang shihua* 麓堂詩話. *Congshu jicheng* ed. Shanghai: Shangwu, 1939.

Li Mengyang 李夢陽 (1472–1529). *Kongtong xiansheng ji* 空同先生集. *Mingdai lunzhu congkan* 明代論諸叢刊 ed. Rpt. Taipei: Weiwen tushu chubanshe, 1976.

Liang Han wenxue shi cankao ziliao 兩漢文學史參考資料. Ed. Beijing Daxue Zhongguo wenxue shi jiaoyan shi 北京大學中國文學史教研室. Rpt. Hong Kong: Hongzhi, n.d.

Liu Xie 劉勰 (ca. 465–523). *Wenxin diaolong zhu* 文心彫龍注, ed. Fan Wenlan 范文瀾. Rpt. Taipei: Daming, 1965.

Liu Yuxi ji 劉禹錫集 (772–842). Shanghai: Renmin, 1975.

Lu Ji 陸機 (261–303). *Wen fu* 文賦, in *Zeng bu liu chen zhu Wen xuan*, 17/pp.307–22.

Lu Shiyong 陸時雍 (fl. 1633). *Chu ci shu* 楚辭疏. 1705 woodblock ed.

Luo Dajing 羅大經 (Song dyn.) *He lin yu lu* 鶴林玉露. *Congshu jicheng* ed. Shanghai: Shangwu, 1939.

Ma Ruichen 馬瑞辰 (1782–1853). *Mao shi zhuan jian tong shi* 毛詩傳箋通釋. Rpt. Taipei: Zhonghua, 1968.

Meng Qi 孟棨. *Ben shi shi* 本事詩, preface dated 886, in Ding Fubao, ed., *Xu lidai shihua*, I, 11–34.

Peng Guodong 彭國棟, ed. *Tang shi sanbai shou shihua hui bian* 唐詩三百首詩話薈編. Taipei: Zhonghua wenhua chubanshe, 1958; 2 vols.

Qiu Zhaoao 仇兆鰲, ed. *Du shi xiang zhu* 杜詩詳註. 1767; rpt. Taipei:

Wenshizhe chubanshe, 1973; 2 vols.

Quan Tang shi 全唐詩. Rpt. Taipei: Minglun, 1971; 12 vols.

Quan Tang wen 全唐文. 1814; rpt. Taipei: Huiwen, 1961; 20 vols.

Ruan Yuan 阮元 (1764–1849), ed. *Shisan jing zhushu* 十三經注疏. Rpt. Peking: Zhonghua, 1979; 2 vols.

Shen Deqian 沈德潛 (1673–1769). *Gu shi yuan jian zhu* 古詩源箋註 Rpt. Taipei: Guting, 1970.

Sikong Tu 司空圖 (837–908). *Ershisi shi pin* 二十四詩品, in He Wenhuan, ed., *Lidai shihua*, I, 37–44.

Sima Guang 司馬光 (1019–1086). *Wen gong xu shihua* 溫公續詩話, in He Wenhuan, ed., *Lidai shihua*, I, 273–82.

Sima Qian 司馬遷 (ca. 145–90 B.C.). *Shi ji hui zhu kaozheng* 史記會注考證. Taipei: Hongye shuju, 1973.

Sui Shusen 隋樹森, ed. *Gu shi shijiu shou ji shi* 古詩十九首集釋. Rpt. Hong Kong: Zhonghua, 1975.

Tao Zhu 陶澍 (1778–1839), ed. *Tao Jingjie ji* 陶靖節集. Rpt. Taipei: Shangwu. 1967.

Wang Bi 王弼 (226–249). *Ming xiang* 明象, *Zhou yi lue li* 周易略例, in *Zhou yi zhushu* 周易注疏, ed. Han Kangbo 韓康伯, Lu Deming 陸德明, and Kong Yingda. 1871 woodblock ed., V, 12a–14a.

Wang Fuzhi 王夫之 (1619–1692). *Chu ci tong shi* 楚辭通釋, preface dated autumn 1685. Rpt. Shanghai: Zhonghua, 1965.

Wang Guowei 王國維 (1877–1927). *Ren jian cihua* 人間詞話. Rpt. Taipei: Kaiming, 1975.

Wang Hongxu 王鴻緒, ed. *Shi jing zhuan shuo hui zuan* 詩經傳說彙纂. 1727; rpt. Taipei: Dingwenhua chubanshe, 1967.

Wang Qi 王琦 (1696–1774), ed. *Li Taibo quan ji* 李太白全集. 1758; rpt. Taipei: Heluo, n.d.

Wang Shimou 王世懋 (1536–1588). *Yi pu xie yu* 藝圃擷餘, in He Wenhuan, ed., *Lidai shihua*, II, 774–84.

Wang Shizhen 王世貞 (1526–1590). *Yi yuan zhi yan* 藝苑卮言, in Ding Fubao, ed., *Xu lidai shihua*, II, 1095–1282.

Wang Shizhen 王士禎 (1634–1711). *Daijingtang shihua* 帶經堂詩話. Rpt. Peking: Renmin, 1982; 2 vols.

Wang Yi 王逸 (fl. 110–120). *Li sao jing zhang ju* 離騷經章句, in Hong Xingzu, ed., *Chu ci bu zhu*, pp. 10–84.

Wei Jin nan bei chao wenxue shi cankao ziliao 魏晉南北朝文學史參考資料. Ed. Beijing Daxue Zhongguo wenxue shi jiaoyan shi. Peking, 1961; rpt. Hong Kong: Hongzhi, n.d.

Wu Qiao 吳喬 (ca. 1660). *Weilu shihua* 圍爐詩話. *Congshu jicheng* ed. Shanghai: Shangwu, 1939.

Yan Can 嚴粲 (fl. 1248). *Shi qi* 詩緝. Rpt. Taipei: Guangwen: [1960].

Yan Yu 嚴羽 (fl. 1180–1235). *Canglang shihua jiao shi* 滄浪詩話校釋, ed. Guo Shaoyu 郭紹虞. Peking: Renmin, 1961.

Yang Shen 楊愼 (1488–1559). *Sheng an shihua* 升庵詩話, in Ding Fubao, ed., *Xu lidai shihua*, I, 773–864, and II, 865–1094.

Yang Yong 楊勇, ed. *Tao Yuanming ji jiao jian* 陶淵明集校箋. Hong Kong: Wuxingji shuju, 1971.

Yao Jiheng 姚際恆 (b. 1647). *Shi jing tong lun* 詩經通論. Rpt. Hong Kong: Zhonghua, 1963.

Ye Mengde 葉夢得 (1077–1148). *Shi lin shihua* 石林詩話, in He Wenhuan, ed., *Lidai shihua*, I, 403–40.

Ye Xiaoxue 葉笑雪, ed. *Xie Lingyun shixuan* 謝靈運詩選. Hong Kong: Hanwen chubanshe, n.d.

Ye Xie 葉燮 (1627–1703). *Yuan shi* 原詩, in Ding Fubao, ed., *Qing shihua* 清詩話. Rpt. Shanghai: Guji chubanshe, 1975 (2 vols.), II, 561–612.

Yin Fan 殷璠, ed. *He yue yingling ji xu* 河嶽英靈集序 (753), included in Guo Shaoyu, ed., *Zhongguo lidai wenlun xuan*, pp. 393–4.

Yu Shouzhen 喩守眞, ed. *Tang shi sanbai shou xiangxi* 唐詩三百首詳析. Hong Kong: Zhonghua, 1977.

Zeng bu liu chen zhu Wen xuan 增補六臣註文選. Rpt. Taipei: Huazheng, 1974.

Zhang Jie 張戒 (Song dyn.). *Suihantang shihua* 歲寒堂詩話, in Ding Fubao, ed., *Xu lidai shihua*, I, 541–76.

Zhao Diancheng 趙殿成, ed. *Wang Youcheng ji jian zhu* 王右丞集箋註. 1736; rpt. Taipei: Heluo, n.d.

Zhi Yu 摯虞 (d. 311). *Wenzhang liubie lun* 文章流別論, in Guo Shaoyu, ed., *Zhongguo lidai wenlun xuan*, pp. 156–8.

Zhong Hong 鍾嶸 (469–518). *Shi pin* 詩品, in He Wenhuan, ed., *Lidai shihua*, I, 1–24.

Zhou li Zheng zhu 周禮鄭注. *Si bu beiyao* 四部備要 ed.

Zhou li zhushu 周禮注疏, in Ruan Yuan, ed., *Shisan jing zhushu*, I, 631–939.

Zhou yi zheng yi 周易正義, in Ruan Yuan, ed., *Shisan jing zhushu*, I, 5–108.

Zhu Xi 朱熹 (1130–1200). *Chu ci ji zhu* 楚辭集注. Rpt. Taipei: Huazheng, 1974.

———. *Zhuzi yu lei* 朱子語類, ed. Li Jingde 黎靖德. Taipei: Zhengzhong, 1962; 8 vols.

Zhuangzi yinde 莊子引得. Harvard-Yenching Institute Sinological Index Series, Supp. No. 20. Cambridge, Ma.: Harvard University Press, 1956.

Zu Baoquan 祖保泉, ed. *Sikong Tu shi pin zhu shi ji yiwen* 司空圖詩品注釋及譯文. Hong Kong: Shangwu, 1966.

B. Modern Chinese and Western Resources on Chinese Literature

Allen, Joseph Roe III. "Chih Yü's *Discussions of Different Types of Literature*: A Translation and Brief Comment," in *Parerga*, 3: *Two Studies in Chinese Literary Criticism*. Seattle: Institute for Comparative and Foreign Area Studies, 1976, pp. 1–36.

Beijing Daxue Beijing Shifan Daxue Zhongwen xi jiaoshi tongxue 北京大學北京師範大學中文系教師同學, ed. *Tao Yuanming yanjiu ziliao hui bian* 陶淵明研究資料彙編. Peking: Zhonghua, 1961; 2 vols. in one.

Birch, Cyril, ed. *Anthology of Chinese Literature*, Vol. I. New York: Grove, 1965.

Bischoff, Friedrich. *Interpreting the Fu: A Study in Chinese Literary Rhetoric*. Münchener Ostasiatische Studien, Vol. 13. Wiesbaden: Franz Steiner Verlag, 1976.

Bodman, Richard W. "Poetics and Prosody in Early Mediaeval China: A Study and Translation of Kūkai's *Bunkyō Hifuron*." Ph.D. Diss. Cornell University, 1978.

Brooks, E. Bruce. "A Geometry of the *Shr Pin*," in Chow Tse-tsung, ed., *Wen-lin: Studies in the Chinese Humanities*, pp. 121–50.

Bush, Susan and Christian Murck, eds. *Theories of the Arts in China*. Princeton: Princeton University Press, 1983.

Chan, Ping-leung. "Ch'u Tz'u and Shamanism in Ancient China." Ph.D. Diss. Ohio State University, 1972.

Chang, Chung-yuan. *Original Teachings of Ch'an Buddhism*. New York: Vintage, 1971.

Chao, Chia-ying Yeh. "The Ch'ang-chou School of *Tz'u* Criticism," in Rickett, ed., *Chinese Approaches to Literature*, pp. 151–88.

—— and Jan W. Walls. "Theory, Standards, and Practice of Criticizing Poetry in Chung Hung's *Shih-p'in*," in Ronald C. Miao, ed., *Studies in Chinese Poetry and Poetics*, Vol. I. San Francisco: Chinese Materials Center, 1978, pp. 43–80.

Chaves, Jonathan. *Mei Yao-ch'en and the Development of Early Sung Poetry*. New York: Columbia University Press, 1976.

Chen, Kenneth. *The Chinese Transformation of Buddhism*. Princeton: Princeton University Press, 1973.

Chen, Shih-hsiang, tr. "Essay on Literature," in Cyril Birch, ed., *Anthology of Chinese Literature*, I, 204–14.

——. "The Genesis of Poetic Time: The Greatness of Ch'ü Yüan, Studied with a New Critical Approach" (published posthumously), *Tsing Hua Journal of Chinese Studies*, N.S. X.1 (June 1973), 1–44.

—— "The *Shih-ching*: Its Generic Significance in Chinese Literary

History and Poetics," in Cyril Birch, ed., *Studies in Chinese Literary Genres*. Berkeley and Los Angeles: University of California Press, 1974, pp. 8–41.

Cheng, François. "*Bi* 比 et *xing* 興," *Cahiers de linguistique Asie orientale*, 6 (Sept. 1979), 63–74.

Chou, Ying-hsiung. "The Linguistic and Mythical Structure of *Hsing* as a Combinational Model," in John J. Deeney, ed., *Chinese and Western Comparative Literature Theory and Strategy*. Hong Kong: Chinese University Press, 1980, pp. 51–78.

Chow, Tse-tsung. "The Early History of the Chinese Word *Shih* (Poetry), in Chow, ed., *Wen-lin: Studies in the Chinese Humanities*, pp. 151–209.

——, ed. *Wen-lin: Studies in the Chinese Humanities*. Madison: University of Wisconsin Press, 1968.

Demiéville, Paul. "La Montagne dans l'art littéraire chinois," *France-Asie*, CLXXXIII (Paris, 1965), 7–32; included in *Choix d'études sinologiques*, ed. Yves Hervouet et al. Leiden: E. J. Brill, 1973, pp. 364–89.

——. "Présentation d'un poète" (review of Frodsham, *The Murmuring Stream*), *T'oung Pao*, LXV. 4–5 (1970), 241–61.

Diény, Jean-Pierre. *Les Dix-neuf poèmes anciens. Bulletin de la Maison Franco-Japonaise*, N.S. VII.4. Paris: Presses universitaires de France, 1963.

Dumoulin, Heinrich. *A History of Zen Buddhism*. Boston: Beacon, 1971.

Du Songbo 杜松柏. *Chan xue yu Tang Song shi xue* 禪學與唐宋詩學. Taipei: Li ming wenhua shiye gongsi, 1978.

Fang, Achilles. "Rhymeprose on Literature," *Harvard Journal of Asiatic Studies*, 14 (1951), 527–66; rpt. in John L. Bishop, ed., *Studies in Chinese Literature*. Cambridge, Ma.: Harvard University Press, 1965, pp. 3–42.

Frodsham, J. D. and Ch'eng Hsi. *An Anthology of Chinese Verse: Han Wei Chin and the Northern and Southern Dynasties*. Oxford: Clarendon, 1967.

——. *The Murmuring Stream: The Life and Works of the Chinese Nature Poet Hsieh Ling-yün (385–433), Duke of K'ang-lo*. Kuala Lumpur: University of Malaya Press, 1967; 2 vols.

——. "The Origins of Chinese Nature Poetry," *Asia Major*, 8 (1960), 68–104.

Graham, A. C. *Poems of the Late T'ang*. Harmondsworth: Penguin, 1965.

Granet, Marcel. *Festivals and Songs of Ancient China*. Tr. E. D. Edwards. London: George Routledge, 1932.

Gu Jiegang 顧頡剛, ed. *Gu shi bian* 古史辨. Rpt. Taipei: Minglun, 1970.

Guo Shaoyu 郭紹虞. "Liu yi shuo kaobian" 六義說考辨, in Zhu Dongrun 朱東潤, ed., *Zhonghua wenshi luncong* 中華文史論叢, 7. Shanghai: Guji chubanshe, 1978, pp. 207–38.

Guo Shaoyu and Wang Wensheng 王文生. "Lun bi xing" 論比興, *Wenxue pinglun* 文學評論, 4 (1978), 47–54.

Hartman, Charles. *The Profound Sense of the "Two Souths": A T'ang Primer of Metaphor*. Unpub. ms.

Hawkes, David, tr. *Ch'u Tz'u: The Songs of the South*. Boston: Beacon, 1959.

———. "The Quest of the Goddess," *Asia Major*, N.S. XIII.1–2 (1967), 71–94.

Hightower, James Robert. "Ch'ü Yüan Studies," *Silver Jubilee Volume of Jinbun-Kagaku Kenkyūsyo*. Kyoto: 1954, pp. 192–223.

———. "The *Han-shih wai-chuan* and the *San-chia shih*." *Harvard Journal of Asiatic Studies*, 11 (1948), 241–310.

———, tr. Sima Qian, "Letter to Jen An," in Birch, *Anthology of Chinese Literature*, I, 95–102.

———. *The Poetry of T'ao Ch'ien*. Oxford: Clarendon, 1970.

Holzman, Donald. *Poetry and Politics: The Life and Works of Juan Chi (A.D. 210–263)*. Cambridge: Cambridge University Press, 1976.

———. "Confucius and Ancient Chinese Literary Criticism," in Rickett, ed., *Chinese Approaches to Literature*, pp. 21–42.

Hu Nianyi 胡念貽, "Shi jing zhong de fu bi xing" 詩經中的賦比興, *Wenxue yichan zengkan* 文學遺產增刊, 1 (1957), 1–21.

Hu Puan 胡樸安. *Shi jing xue* 詩經學. Shanghai: Shangwu, 1928.

Huang Jiusheng 黃究生. "Liushi nian lai de Chu ci xue" 六十年來的楚辭學. Ph.D. Diss., National Taiwan Normal University, 1977.

Huters, Theodore D. *Qian Zhongshu*. Boston: G. K. Hall, 1982.

Jao Tsung-i 饒宗頤. *Bibliography of Chü Tzu* 楚辭書錄. Hong Kong: Tong Nam, 1956.

Jiang Liangfu 姜亮夫. *Chu ci shumu wu zhong* 楚辭書目五種. Shanghai: Zhonghua, 1961.

Jiang Shanguo 蔣善國. *Sanbai pian yanlun* 三百篇演論. Taipei: Shangwu, 1976.

Jiang Zuyi 蔣祖怡. "'Wenxin diaolong: Wu se pian' shi shi" 文心雕龍物色篇試釋, *Wenxue yichan* 文學遺產, 2 (1982), 29–38.

Kao Yu-kung and Mei Tsu-lin. "Meaning, Metaphor, and Allusion in T'ang Poetry," *Harvard Journal of Asiatic Studies*, 38.2 (Dec. 1978), 281–356.

———. "Syntax, Diction and Imagery in T'ang Poetry," *Harvard Journal of Asiatic Studies*, 31 (1971), 49–136.

Karlgren, Bernhard. *The Book of Odes*. 1950; Stockholm: Museum of Far Eastern Antiquities, 1974.

———. *Glosses on the Book of Odes*. Stockholm: Museum of Far Eastern Antiquities, 1964.

Knechtges, David R. "Two Han Dynasty *Fu* on Ch'ü Yüan: Chia I's *Tiao Ch'ü Yüan* and Yang Hsiung's *Fan Sao*," in *Parerga*, 1: *Two Studies on the Han Fu* (Seattle: Far Eastern and Russian Institute, 1968), pp. 5–43.

LaFleur, William. *The Karma of Words: Buddhism and the Literary Arts in Medieval Japan*. Berkeley and Los Angeles: University of California Press, 1983.

Lau, D. C., tr. *The Analects*. Harmondsworth: Penguin, 1979.

———, tr. *Tao Te Ching*. Harmondsworth: Penguin, 1963.

Legge, James. *The Chinese Classics*, Vol. 4: *The She King*. Oxford: Clarendon, 1871.

———. "The Li Sao Poem and Its Author," *Journal of the Royal Asiatic Society* (1895), I: "The Author," 77–92; II: "The Poem," 571–99; III: "The Chinese Text and Translation," 839–64.

Li Chi (Qi) 李祁. "*Yin-yü* and *Tai-yü* in Chinese Poetry," *Tsing Hua Journal of Chinese Studies*, N.S. II.2 (June 1961), pp. 343–60.

Li Jiayan 李嘉言. "Qu Yuan 'Li sao' de sixiang he yishu" 屈原離騷的思想和藝術, in *Chu ci yanjiu lunwen ji* 楚辭研究論文集, Vol. II; *Zhongguo gudian wenxue yanjiu lunwen ji huibian* 中國古典文學研究論文集滙編, Vol. II. Ed. Zhongguo yuwenxue she 中國語文學社 (1969), pp. 50–63.

Li Jinxi 黎錦熙. *Xiuci xue bi xing pian* 修辭學比興篇. Shanghai: Shangwu, 1936.

Li Zhifang 李直方. "Ruan Ji yong huai shi lun" 阮籍詠懷詩論, in *Han Wei liu chao shi lun gao* 漢魏六朝詩論稿. Hong Kong: Longmen shudian, 1978, pp. 69–102.

Lin Geng 林庚. *Shi ren Qu Yuan ji qi zuopin yanjiu* 詩人屈原及其作品研究. Shanghai: Gudian wenxue chubanshe, 1957.

Liu Guangyi 劉光義, "Shi Shi fu bi xing zhi xing" 釋詩賦比興之興, *Dalu zazhi* 大陸雜志, 34.2 (Jan. 31, 1967), 14–17.

Liu Zhengwu 柳正午. "*Guan ju* zhang yiduan" 關雎章臆斷, *Wenxue pinglun* 文學評論, 2 (1980), 77–81.

Liu, James J. Y. *The Art of Chinese Poetry*. Chicago: University of Chicago Press, 1962.

———. *Chinese Theories of Literature*. Chicago: University of Chicago Press, 1975.

———. *The Poetry of Li Shang-yin: Ninth-Century Baroque Chinese Poet*. Chicago: University of Chicago Press, 1968.

Lo, Irving Yu-cheng and Wu-chi Liu, eds. *Sunflower Spendor: Three Thousand Years of Chinese Poetry*. New York: Doubleday, 1975.

Luo Genze 羅根澤. *Zhongguo wenxue pipingshi* 中國文學批評史. Rpt. Hong Kong: Dianwen, n.d.; 3 vols.

Lynn, Richard John. "Orthodoxy and Enlightenment: Wang Shih-chen's Theory of Poetry and Its Antecedents," in William Theodore deBary, ed., *The Unfolding of Neo-Confucianism*. Studies in Oriental Culture, 10. New York: Columbia University Press, 1975, pp. 217–69.

———. Review of Pauline Yu, *The Poetry of Wang Wei*, in *Chinese Literature: Essays, Articles, Reviews*, 4.2 (July 1982), 259–69.

Mather, Richard B. "The Landscape Buddhism of the Fifth-Century Poet Hsieh Ling-yün," *Journal of Asian Studies*, XVIII.1 (Nov. 1958), 67–79.

Mei Yunsheng 梅運生. "Shi lun Bo Juyi de 'mei ci xing bi' shuo" 試論白居易的美刺興比說, in *Gudai wenxue lilun yanjiu* 古代文學理論研究, 1. Ed. Zhongguo gudai wenxue lilun xuehui 中國古代文學理論學會 Shanghai: Guji chubanshe, 1979, pp. 248–63.

Mote, Frederick R. "The Cosmological Gulf Between China and the West," in David Buxbaum and Fritz Mote, eds., *Transition and Permanence: Chinese History and Culture*. Hong Kong: Cathay Press, 1971, pp. 3–21.

———. *Intellectual Foundations of China*. New York: Alfred A. Knopf, 1971.

Mou Shijin 牟世金. "Shi xue zhi zheng yuan, fa du zhi zhunze: cong fu bi xing chuantong kan yishu gousi de minzu tese" 詩學之正源, 法度之准則:從賦比興傳統看藝術構思的民族特色, in *Gudai wenxue lilun yanjiu congkan* 古代文學理論研究叢刊, 1. Ed. Zhongguo gudai wenxue lilun xuehui 中國古代文學理論學會. Shanghai: Guji chubanshe, 1979, pp. 38–61.

Munakata, Kiyohiko. "Concepts of *Lei* and *Kan-lei* in Early Chinese Art Theory," in Bush and Murck, eds., *Theories of the Arts in China*, pp. 105–31.

Murti, T. R. V. *The Central Philosophy of Buddhism: A Study of the Mādhyamika System*. London: Allen and Unwin, 1955.

Needham, Joseph and Wang Ling. *Science and Civilization in China*, Vol. II: *History of Scientific Thought*. Cambridge: Cambridge University Press, 1951.

Nielson, Thomas P. *The T'ang Poet-Monk Chiao-jan*. Center for Asian Studies Occasional Paper No. 3. Arizona State University, June 1972.

Owen, Stephen. *The Great Age of Chinese Poetry: The High T'ang*. New Haven: Yale University Press, 1981.

———. *The Poetry of the Early T'ang*. New Haven: Yale University

Press, 1977.

———. "Transparencies: Reading the T'ang Lyric," *Harvard Journal of Asiatic Studies*, 34.2 (Dec. 1979), 231–51.

Peterson, Willard J. "Making Connections: 'Commentary on the Attached Verbalizations' of the *Book of Change*," *Harvard Journal of Asiatic Studies*, 42.1 (June 1982), 67–116.

Plaks, Andrew. *Archetype and Allegory in the Dream of the Red Chamber*. Princeton: Princeton University Press, 1976.

Qian Zhongshu 錢鍾書. *Guan zhui bian* 管錐編. Peking: Zhonghua, 1979; 4 vols.

———. *Tan yi lu* 談藝錄. Shanghai: Kaiming, 1948.

Rickett, Adele Austin, ed. *Chinese Approaches to Literature from Confucius to Liang Ch'i-ch'ao*. Princeton: Princeton University Press, 1978.

Schafer, Edward. *Pacing the Void: T'ang Approaches to the Stars*. Berkeley and Los Angeles: University of California Press, 1977.

Schneider, Laurence A. *A Madman of Ch'u: The Chinese Myth of Loyalty and Dissent*. Berkeley and Los Angeles: University of California Press, 1980.

Shchutskii, Iulian K. *Researches on the I Ching*. Tr. William L. MacDonald and Tsuyoshi Hasegawa, with Hellmut Wilhelm. Bollingen Series LXII.2. Princeton: Princeton University Press, 1979.

Shih, Vincent Y., tr. *The Literary Mind and the Carving of Dragons*. Bilingual ed. Taipei: Chung Hwa, 1975.

Shu, Chin-Ten. "Allegorical Structure in Literary Discourse: Western and Chinese." Ph.D. Diss. University of Wisconsin-Madison, 1981.

Som, Tjan Tjoe. *Po Hu T'ung: The Comprehensive Discussions in the White Tiger Hall*. Leiden: Brill, 1949; rpt. Westport: Hyperion Press, 1973; 2 vols.

Suzuki, D. T. *Zen Buddhism*. Ed. William Barrett. New York: Doubleday, 1956.

Tökei, Ferenc. *Naissance de l'élégie chinoise: K'iu Yuan et son époque*. Paris: Gallimard, 1967.

Waley, Arthur, tr. *The Book of Songs*. New York: Grove, 1960.

———. *The Life and Times of Po Chü-i*. London: Allen and Unwin, 1949.

———. *The Nine Songs: A Study of Shamanism in Ancient China*. San Francisco: City Lights Books, 1973.

———. *Translations from the Chinese*. New York: Vintage, 1971.

Wang Yuanhua 王元化. "Shi 'Bi xing pian' 'Ni rong qu xin' shuo" 釋比興篇擬容取心說, *Wenxue pinglun*, 1 (1978), 69–74.

Wang Yunxi 王運熙. "Tan Zhongguo gudai wenlun zhong de bi xing

shuo" 談中國古代文論中的比興說, *Wenyi luncong* 文藝論叢, 4. Shanghai: Wenyi chubanshe, 1978, pp. 42–58.

Wang, C. H. *The Bell and the Drum*: Shih Ching *as Formulaic Poetry in an Oral Tradition*. Berkeley and Los Angeles: University of California Press, 1974.

Waters, Geoffrey R. "Three Elegies of Ch'u: An Introduction to the Traditional Interpretation of the *Ch'u Tz'u*." Ph.D. Diss. Indiana University, 1980.

Watson, Burton. *Chinese Lyricism: Shih Poetry from the Second to the Twelfth Century, with Translations*. New York: Columbia University Press, 1971.

———, tr. *The Complete Works of Chuang Tzu*. New York: Columbia University Press, 1970.

Westbrook, Francis A. "Landscape Description in the Lyric Poetry and 'Fuh on Dwelling in the Mountains' of Shieh Ling-yunn." Ph.D. Diss. Yale University, 1972.

———. "Landscape Transformation in the Poetry of Hsieh Ling-yün," *Journal of the American Oriental Society*, 100.3 (July–Oct. 1980), 237–54.

Wilhelm, Hellmut. "The Interplay of Image and Concept," in *Heaven, Earth, and Man in the Book of Changes*. Seattle: University of Washington Press, 1977, pp. 190–221.

Wilhelm, Richard and Cary F. Baynes, tr. *The I Ching or Book of Changes*. Bollingen Series XIX, 3d ed. in new format. Princeton: Princeton University Press, 1969.

Wixted, John Timothy. "The Nature of Evaluation in the *Shih-p'in* (*Gradings of Poets*) by Chung Hung (A.D. 469–518)," in Bush and Murck, eds., *Theories of the Arts in China*, pp. 225–64.

Wong, Siu-kit. "*Ch'ing* and *Ching* in the Critical Writings of Wang Fu-chih," in Rickett, ed., *Chinese Approaches to Literature*, pp. 121–50.

———. *Early Chinese Literary Criticism*. Hong Kong: Joint Publishing Co., 1983.

Xia Zhuancai 夏傳才. "Lun Song xue Shi jing yanjiu de jige wenti" 論宋學詩經研究的幾個問題, *Wenxue yichan* 文學遺產, 2 (1982), 97–104.

Xiao Difei 蕭滌非. "Shi lun Du Fu shige zhong de bi xing" 釋論杜甫詩歌中的比興, *Wenyi luncong*, 4. Shanghai: Wenyi chubanshe, 1978, pp. 22–41.

Yampolsky, Philip. *The Platform Sutra of the Sixth Patriarch*. New York: Columbia University Press, 1967.

Ye Shan 葉珊 (C. H. Wang). "Shi jing Guo feng de cao mu he shi de biaoxian jiqiao" 詩經國風的草木和詩的表現技巧, *Xiandai wenxue* 現代文學, 33 (1967), 124–43.

Yip, Wai-lim. *Chinese Poetry: Major Modes and Genres.* Berkeley and Los Angeles: University of California Press, 1976.

———. *Hiding the Universe: Poems by Wang Wei.* New York: Grossman, 1972.

You Guoen 游國恩. *Chu ci lunwen ji* 楚辭論文集. Peking, 1965; rpt. Hong Kong: Wenxing, n.d.

———, ed. *Li sao zuan yi* 離騷纂義. Peking: Zhonghua, 1980.

Yu, Pauline. "Allegory, Allegoresis, and the *Classic of Poetry*," *Harvard Journal of Asiatic Studies*, 43.2 (Dec. 1983), 377–412.

———. "Metaphor and Chinese Poetry," *Chinese Literature: Essays, Articles, Reviews*, 3.2 (July 1981), 205–24.

———. *The Poetry of Wang Wei: New Translations and Commentary.* Bloomington: Indiana University Press, 1980.

Zhang Zhiyue 張志岳. "Lue lun Ruan Ji ji qi yong huai shi" 略論阮籍及其詠懷詩, in *Wei Jin liu chao shi yanjiu lunwen ji* 魏晉六朝詩研究論文集, Zhongguo wenxue yanjiu lun zhi ji huibian 中國文學研究論之集滙編, 2. N.p.: 1969, pp. 59–79.

Zheng Yuqing 鄭郁卿. *Shi ji zhuan zhi fu bi xing yanjiu* 詩集傳之賦比興研究. Taipei: Wenjin chubanshe, 1976.

Zhu Rensheng 朱任生, ed. *Shi lun fenlei zuanyao* 詩論分類纂要. Taipei: Shangwu, 1971.

Zhu Ziqing 朱自清. *Shi yan zhi bian* 詩言志辨. Rpt. Taipei: Kaiming, 1975.

C. OTHER WESTERN RESOURCES

Abrams, M. H. *The Mirror and the Lamp: Romantic Theory and the Tradition.* New York: Oxford University Press, 1953.

Aristotle. *Poetics*, tr. Ingram Bywater, and *Rhetoric*, tr. W. Rhys Roberts. New York: Modern Library, 1954.

Auerbach, Erich. "Figura," in *Scenes from the Drama of European Literature*. Tr. Ralph Manheim. Rpt. Gloucester, Ma.: Peter Smith, 1973, pp. 11–78.

Bakhtin, Mikhail. "Forms of Time and of the Chronotope in the Novel: Notes toward a Historical Poetics," in *The Dialogic Imagination: Four Essays*. Ed. Michael Holquist, tr. Caryl Emerson and Michael Holquist. Austin: University of Texas Press, 1981, pp. 84–258.

Bate, Walter Jackson, ed. *Criticism: The Major Texts.* Enlarged ed. New York: Harcourt Brace Jovanovich, 1970.

Beardsley, Monroe. *Aesthetics: Problems in the Philosophy of Criticism.* New York: Harcourt, Brace and World, 1958.

Benjamin, Walter. *The Origin of German Tragic Drama.* Tr. John Osborne. London: New Left Books, 1977.

Black, Max. *Models and Metaphors: Studies in Language and Philosophy.* Ithaca: Cornell University Press, 1962.

Bloomfield, Morton W., ed. *Allegory, Myth, and Symbol.* Harvard English Studies, 9. Cambridge, Ma.: Harvard University Press, 1981.

Boucher, Holly Wallace. "Metonymy in Typology and Allegory, with a Consideration of Dante's *Comedy*," in Bloomfield, ed., *Allegory, Myth and Symbol,* pp. 129–46.

Brooke-Rose, Christine. *A Grammar of Metaphor.* London: Secker and Warburg, 1958.

Brooks, Cleanth. "The Heresy of Paraphrase," in *The Well Wrought Urn.* New York: Harcourt, Brace and World, 1947, pp. 192–214.

———. "Metaphor and the Tradition," in *Modern Poetry and the Tradition.* Chapel Hill: University of North Carolina Press, 1967, pp. 1–17.

Christensen, Jerome C. "The Symbol's Errant Allegory: Coleridge and His Critics," *ELH,* 45.4 (1978), 640–59.

Clifford, Gay. *The Transformation of Allegory.* London: Routledge and Kegan Paul, 1974.

Coleridge, Samuel Taylor. *Biographia Literaria, or Biographical Sketches of my literary life and opinions.* Ed. George Watson. London: E. M. Dent and Sons, 1975.

———. *The Statesman's Manual.* Burlington: Chauncey Goodrich, 1882.

Croll, Morris. "Attic Poetry: Lipsius, Montaigne, Bacon," and "The Baroque Style in Prose," in Stanley E. Fish, ed., *Seventeenth Century Prose: Modern Essays in Criticism.* New York: Oxford University Press, 1971, pp. 3–25, 26–52.

Culler, Jonathan. "Commentary," *New Literary History,* 6.1 (Autumn 1974), 219–29.

———. "Literary History, Allegory, and Semiology," *New Literary History,* 7.2 (Winter 1976), 259–70.

Derrida, Jacques. "White Mythology: Metaphor in the Text of Philosophy," tr. F. C. T. Moore, *New Literary History,* 6.1 (Autumn 1974), 5–74.

de Man, Paul. "Pascal's Allegory of Persuasion," in Greenblatt, ed., *Allegory and Representation,* pp. 1–25.

———. "The Rhetoric of Temporality," rpt. in *Blindness and Insight: Essays in the Rhetoric of Contemporary Criticism.* 2d rev. ed. Theory and History of Literature, 7. Minneapolis: University of Minnesota

Press, 1983, pp. 187–228.

Fineman, Joel. "The Structure of Allegorical Desire," in Greenblatt, ed., *Allegory and Representation*, pp. 26–60.

Fletcher, Angus. *Allegory: The Theory of a Symbolic Mode*. Ithaca: Cornell University Press, 1964.

Frazer, Ray. "The Origin of the Term 'Image,'" *ELH*, 27 (1960), 149–61.

Frazer, Sir James George. *The Golden Bough*. Part IV, Vol. I: *Adonis, Attis, Osiris; Studies in the History of Oriental Religion*. London: Macmillan, 1913; rpt. 1980.

Friedman, Norman. "Imagery," in *Princeton Encyclopedia of Poetry and Poetics*, ed. Alex Preminger et al. Princeton: Princeton University Press, 1974, pp. 363–70.

Frye, Northrop. "Allegory," in *Princeton Encyclopedia of Poetry and Poetics*, ed. Alex Preminger et al. Princeton: Princeton University Press, 1974, pp. 12–15.

———. *Anatomy of Criticism: Four Essays*. Princeton: Princeton University Press, 1951.

Genette, Gérard. "Frontiers of Narrative," in *Figures of Literary Discourse*. Tr. Alan Sheridan. New York: Columbia University Press, 1982, pp. 127–44.

Gombrich, E. H. *Art and Illusion: A Study in the Psychology of Pictorial Representation*. Bollingen Series XXXV.5. Princeton: Princeton University Press, 1960.

Greenblatt, Stephen J., ed. *Allegory and Representation*. Selected Papers from the English Institute, 1979–80. N.S. 5. Baltimore: Johns Hopkins University Press, 1981.

Hamburger, Käte. *Die Logik der Dichtung*. 2d rev. ed. Stuttgart: Ernst Klett, 1968.

Hodgson, John A. "Transcendental Tropes: Coleridge's Rhetoric of Allegory and Symbol," in Bloomfield, ed., *Allegory, Myth, and Symbol*, pp. 273–92.

Hulme, T. E. "Romanticism and Classicism," in *Speculations*. New York: Harcourt, Brace and Co., 1924, pp. 113–40.

Jauss, Hans Robert. "Entstehung und Strukturwandel der allegorischen Dichtung," in *Grundriss der romanischen Litteratur des Mittelalters*, Vol. VI: *La littérature didactique, allégorique, et satirique*; Vol. I: *Partie historique*. Ed. Jürgen Beyer. Heidelberg: Carl Winter Universitätsverlag, 1968, pp. 146–244.

Johnson, Samuel. *Life of Cowley*. 1779–81; excerpted in Bate, ed., *Criticism: The Major Texts*, pp. 217–19.

Langer, Susanne. *Feeling and Form*. New York: Charles Scribner's Sons,

1953.

Levin, Samuel R. *The Semantics of Metaphor*. Baltimore: Johns Hopkins University Press, 1977.

Lewis, C. Day. *The Poetic Image*. New York: Oxford University Press, 1947.

Lewis, C. S. *The Allegory of Love*. London: Oxford University Press, 1936.

Lodge, David. *The Modes of Modern Writing: Metaphor, Metonymy, and the Typology of Modern Literature*. Ithaca: Cornell University Press, 1977.

Maclean, Norman. "From Action to Image: Theories of the Lyric in the Eighteenth Century," in R. S. Crane, ed., *Critics and Criticism: Ancient and Modern*. Chicago: University of Chicago Press, 1952, pp. 408–60.

MacQueen, John. *Allegory*. London: Methuen, 1970.

Miner, Earl. "On the Genesis and Development of Literary Systems," Parts I and II, *Critical Inquiry*, 5.2 (Winter 1978), 339–53, and 5.3 (Spring 1979), 553–68.

Mitchell, W. J. T. "What Is an Image?" *New Literary History*, 15.3 (Spring 1984), 503–37.

Murrin, Michael. *The Allegorical Epic*. Chicago: University of Chicago Press, 1980.

––––––. *The Veil of Allegory: Some Notes Toward a Theory of Allegorical Rhetoric in the English Renaissance*. Chicago: University of Chicago Press, 1969.

The Oxford Classical Dictionary. London: Oxford University Press, 1970.

Pépin, Jean. *Mythe et allégorie: les origines grecques et les contestations judéo-chrétiennes*. New rev. and enl. ed. Paris: Etudes augustiniennes, 1976.

Pitcher, Samuel M. "Epic," in *Princeton Encyclopedia of Poetry and Poetics*, ed. Alex Preminger et al. Princeton: Princeton University Press, 1974, pp. 242–47.

Plato. *The Republic*. Tr. H. D. P. Lee. Baltimore: Penguin, 1955.

Quilligan, Maureen. *The Language of Allegory: Defining the Genre*. Ithaca: Cornell University Press, 1979.

Quintilian. *The Institutio Oratoria*. Tr. H. E. Butler. Cambridge, Ma.: Harvard University Press, 1959; 4 vols.

Richards, I. A. *Philosophy of Rhetoric*. New York: Oxford University Press, 1936.

Ricoeur, Paul. "The Model of the Text: Meaningful Action Considered as a Text," *New Literary History*, 5.1 (Autumn 1973), 91–117.

––––––. *The Rule of Metaphor: Multi-disciplinary Studies of the Creation of Meaning in Language.* Tr. Robert Czerny et al. Toronto: University of Toronto Press, 1977.

Shelley, Percy Bysshe. *A Defence of Poetry.* 1821; rpt. in Bate, ed., *Criticism: The Major Texts,* pp. 429–35.

Shibles, Warren. *Essays on Metaphor.* Whitewater, Wi.: The Language Press, 1972.

Sidney, Sir Philip. *An Apology for Poetry.* 1595; rpt. in Bate, ed., *Criticism: The Major Texts,* pp. 82–106.

Smith, Barbara Hernnstein. *On the Margins of Discourse: The Relation of Literature to Language.* Chicago: University of Chicago Press, 1978.

———. *Poetic Closure: A Study of How Poems End.* Chicago: University of Chicago Press, 1968.

Stevens, Wallace. "Adagia," in *Opus Posthumous.* Ed. Samuel French Morse. New York: Alfred A. Knopf, 1966, pp. 157–80.

———. *Poems.* Ed. Samuel French Morse. New York: Vintage, 1959.

Tindall, William York. *The Literary Symbol.* Bloomington: Indiana University Press, 1967.

Todorov, Tzvetan. "On Linguistic Symbolism," *New Literary History,* 6.1 (Autumn 1974), 111–34.

Tuve, Rosamond. *Elizabethan and Metaphysical Imagery: Renaissance Poetic and Twentieth-Century Critics.* Chicago: University of Chicago Press, 1947.

Wellek, René. *A History of Modern Criticism.* New Haven: Yale University Press, 1955.

——— and Austin Warren. *Theory of Literature.* New rev. ed. New York: Harcourt, Brace and World, 1956.

Wheelwright, Philip. *Metaphor and Reality.* Bloomington: Indiana University Press, 1962.

Wordsworth, William. *The Prelude: A Parallel Text.* Ed. J. L. Maxwell. Middlesex: Penguin, 1971.

Index

235

LIBRARY OF CONGRESS CATALOGING-IN-PUBLICATION DATA

Yu, Pauline, 1949–   .
  The reading of imagery in the Chinese Poetic tradition.

  Bibliography: p.   Includes index.
  1. Chinese poetry—History and criticism.
2. Nature in literature.   I. Title.
PL2308.5.N3Y8   1986   895.1′1′009   86-42857
ISBN 0-691-06682-5 (alk. paper)

PAULINE YU is Professor of East Asian Languages and Cultures
at Columbia University in the City of New York